PRAISE FOR *JUS*

"... Margolin's best arguments draw on her courtroom experience to reveal how harsh and convoluted drug laws can be, even in states like California, where recreational cannabis sales are permitted."

—*PUBLISHERS WEEKLY*

"Allison's book could become a call to action for many.... As someone who has often been called the godfather of the Progressive Prosecutors' Movement in this country, I am excited for [it] to be published. *Just Dope* has the potential to become one of those once-in-a-generation books, shaking up popular beliefs about the role of drugs in American culture and tipping the scales toward a more humane and thoughtful approach in the future."

—GEORGE GASCÓN, district attorney of LA, former two-term district attorney of San Francisco, and former chief of police of San Francisco

"Allison is a true marijuana lover from the heart—it's in her bloodline. She knows nothing else and is always trying to help. If you really wanna know about marijuana laws, you must read this book."

—"FREEWAY" RICK ROSS

"With *Just Dope*, Allison Margolin uses a fluid writing style that seamlessly weaves together disparate threads of her own life and sense of justice with courtroom drama, history, science, and a blistering critique of the Drug War. She chronicles her very personal odyssey from hippie child to D.A.R.E. student to drug user to Dopest Defense Attorney and offers frank appraisals of political and prosecutorial policies along the way.... Masterful and well written—I highly recommend this book."

—CHRIS CONRAD, cannabis author, activist, and court-qualified expert witness

"Allison Margolin has addressed America's drug abuse crisis in a uniquely honest and compelling autobiography."

—EUGENE SCHOENFELD, MD, author of the 1960s–70s newspaper column "Dr. Hip" and *Dr. Hip's Natural Food and Unnatural Acts*

"With *Just Dope*, Margolin uses a fluid writing style that seamlessly weaves together disparate threads of her own life and sense of justice with courtroom drama, history, science and a blistering critique of the Drug War."

—*THE LEAF*

"Masterful, expansive, well-written and fun to read, we highly recommend this book."

—*L.A. CANNABIS NEWS*

JUST DOPE

JUST DOPE

A LEADING ATTORNEY'S
PERSONAL
JOURNEY
INSIDE THE WAR
ON DRUGS

ALLISON MARGOLIN

North Atlantic Books
Huichin, unceded Ohlone land
aka Berkeley, California

Published by
North Atlantic Books
Huichin, unceded Ohlone land
aka Berkeley, California

Cover design by Jasmine Hromjak
Book design by Happenstance Type-O-Rama

Printed in Canada

Just Dope: A Leading Attorney's Personal Journey Inside the War on Drugs is sponsored and published by North Atlantic Books, an educational nonprofit based in the unceded Ohlone land Huichin (*aka* Berkeley, CA) that collaborates with partners to develop cross-cultural perspectives, nurture holistic views of art, science, the humanities, and healing, and seed personal and global transformation by publishing work on the relationship of body, spirit, and nature.

North Atlantic Books' publications are distributed to the US trade and internationally by Penguin Random House Publisher Services. For further information, visit our website at www.northatlanticbooks.com.

MEDICAL DISCLAIMER: The following information is intended for general information purposes only. Individuals should always see their health care provider before administering any suggestions made in this book. Any application of the material set forth in the following pages is at the reader's discretion and is their sole responsibility.

Library of Congress Cataloging-in-Publication Data
Names: Margolin, Allison, author.
Title: Just dope : a leading attorney's personal journey inside the war on drugs / Allison Margolin.
Description: Huichin, unceded Ohlone land aka Berkeley, California : North Atlantic Books, [2022] | Includes bibliographical references and index. | Summary: "Leading attorney Allison Margolin's insider account of the War on Drugs and how to end it for good. Integrating pop culture and personal stories into social analysis, she puts drug criminalization on trial to advocate for an evidence-based, commonsense approach to drug use and legalization"— Provided by publisher.
Identifiers: LCCN 2021059010 (print) | LCCN 2021059011 (ebook) | ISBN 9781623176860 (trade paperback) | ISBN 9781623176877 (ebook)
Subjects: LCSH: Drug legalization—United States. | Drug control—United States. | Drug abuse—Government policy—United States.
Classification: LCC HV5825 .M25358 2022 (print) | LCC HV5825 (ebook) | DDC 364.1/770973—dc23/eng/20220228
LC record available at https://lccn.loc.gov/2021059010
LC ebook record available at https://lccn.loc.gov/2021059011

1 2 3 4 5 6 7 8 9 MARQUIS 27 26 25 24 23 22

TO MY LOVING AND SUPPORTIVE
HUSBAND, JON. THANK YOU FOR SHARING
YOUR LIFE AND SOUL WITH ME.

TO DR. JEFF CRAUSMAN, IN LOVING
MEMORY. I WOULD NEVER HAVE GOTTEN
THROUGH MY DARK DAYS WITHOUT YOU OR
BE HERE TO WRITE THIS WITHOUT YOU.

CONTENTS

PART 3: CLOSING ARGUMENTS

PREFACE

I'VE WANTED TO WRITE THIS BOOK since I was eight years old, sitting at the warm, yellowing Formica of my grandmother's kitchen table. For those who know anything about my background—two lawyers for parents, a stoner dad, growing up in Beverly Hills in the '70s and '80s—my writing this book will not come as a surprise. Somewhere in my brain, I kept the image of this book, even though I didn't know the shape it would take.

I grew up in the middle of the marijuana legalization movement. My dad, Bruce, counted people like Ram Dass and Timothy Leary as his friends. His career as a criminal attorney inspired me to follow the same path; at least, I'm sure that's the most obvious story to people on the outside looking in. But my grandmother Guta Peck was my greatest champion. If anyone encouraged me to write, it was she. Similarly, my career in the law, my even applying to Harvard Law School and taking the California Bar Exam, is owed to my mother, Elyse. Oddly enough, these two straitlaced women—who as far as I can tell rarely touched any drug stronger than aspirin—have been the biggest influence on my long-gestating book on drugs and the law. They showed me that drugs, the law, and society are connected.

Since becoming an attorney in December 2002, I have represented dealers and addicts, cartel bosses and alleged Russian crime lords. I've faced down corrupt prosecutors, crooked cops, and prejudiced, power-mad judges. All the while I kept this book in mind and told myself I was collecting material. I jotted notes on the reverse sides of transcripts and case briefs. I went in and out of practice with my dad. I started my own firm. Over fifteen years later, I had the stories, but my practice was failing.

When California legalized recreational marijuana in 2016, I was thrilled. Then the criminal cases dwindled, and my firm suffered. I had a terrible revelation: I had made a name for myself as a pro-legalization figure, and I vocally opposed drug prohibition every chance I got; yet I was still profiting off the very system I hated. My clients were the ones who had been caught in this system—and they were the lucky ones! Anyone who could afford me was in a far preferable position to that of the vast majority of defendants.

Then I thought back to my dad's career. He paid for my education, first at Columbia University, then Harvard Law, with money he earned by representing clients with drug possession charges. My life, my career, just about everything I had—it had all been funded by the spoils of antidrug legislation. I was humbled, to put it mildly.

My firm added cannabis business licensing to our list of services. In fact, as I write this preface, I'm arranging the license for a client I represented in a criminal case over ten years ago. The licensing services have not only offered me psychic relief; they've also given me the time and resources to finally sit down and make this book a reality. And my vision for the book has expanded from a straightforward autobiography—in which I was the scrappy young lawyer battling an unjust system—to a memoir with an argument.

The war on drugs is bullshit. No matter how many antidrug laws policy makers enact, people will always find some way to alter their consciousness. In my application to Harvard Law I argued that the drug war is a war on people's personal liberties. That lofty ideal aside, prohibition also simply does not work. My hope is that everyone who reads this book will understand that we all have something to lose in this fight.

My memories are the source of much of this material, although I have sought corroboration from family and friends when possible. Where accounts conflict, I make sure to note that the story is my perspective, not historical record. For stories like trials, I used court transcripts and media reports for reference. In addition, I'm lucky to have grown up with key figures in the movement. Where beneficial, I spoke to them about protests they held, activist meetings where everything went wrong, and events from before my time.

If you're approaching this book as a complete novice to this conflict, I hope you will understand that the prohibition system was never made to protect you. If you or someone you know has been caught in the crossfire of this war, I hope these pages will be illuminating. More than anything, I hope to deliver a strong message in a fun package. Prohibition doesn't work. It is time to legalize everything.

INTRODUCTION:
JURY SELECTION

THIS BOOK IS ABOUT how the law can be a bludgeon, a weapon, a curse, but also how one person can use nothing more than metaphysics to defeat those powers one by one, kind of like the Hindu goddess Kali, after whom my security dog, a Belgian Malinois, is named.

In the writing of this book, I have read various memoirs, stories of addiction, histories of the drug war and its combatants, and the journals that have quietly collected dust in the corner of my grandmother's kitchen. I set out to write a memoir, or more accurately, a story of my life and the role that drugs have played in my life. But over the course of my reading, and through conversations with family, friends, colleagues, and experts in these fields, I realized my story could not possibly contain all there is to say about drugs, the legalization movement, or addiction. The task ahead unfolded into a many-headed Hydra: I could not conclude one chapter without multitudes more sprouting up, begging for their place in the narrative.

Daunted by the size of this beast, I found myself retreating to what my original hopes for this book had been, to the reasons I had wanted to tell my story and write this book. I read more memoirs. They were sometimes lush, and at other times painful. In my favorite ones, I found a truth revealed, but I noted that this truth was inevitably limited by the perspective of the narrator. I questioned my own reliability and whether I was worthy of meeting the challenge that this work posed. Memoir often requires distance, and I couldn't be closer to the subject matter I was taking on. This wasn't just a story about me; it was about my family and the work I'd been called to pursue. I couldn't step far enough away to make sense of my story, partially because I have never been able to detach. The removal with which some are able to tell the stories of their lives is a skill that continues to elude me.

Then I turned to general nonfiction, believing there I would find the answer for what this book could become. I read works like *Dreamland, Chasing the Scream,* and *Smoke Signals.* I made sense out of decades I had never seen with books on the '50s, '60s, and most of the '70s. These histories were thorough, well-crafted, and often inspirational. Yet the prospect of removing myself from the book and approaching it from a purely journalistic standpoint seemed impossible. I was seized by what has been a lifelong yearning, if not a compulsion, to share my story—all parts of my story.

But where does that story begin? Does it begin with me? Does it begin with my parents? With their parents? With the very creation of the universe? Again, there was too much to consider. Paralysis took hold. Years passed.

The first revelation: I was afraid. Even now, as I write these words, I am still afraid. There are parts of my story, specifically a problematic cocaine habit in my twenties, that I am afraid to share for fear of professional and personal retaliation. I am not just an attorney or the daughter of attorney; I am also a mother. I am a mother who is in an ongoing dispute with my daughter's father. My paranoia—that he will use parts of this book to wrestle our daughter into his sole custody—is founded on our shared history. And as for professional concerns, is it any surprise that criminal attorneys can be a ruthless bunch? I cannot pretend to know how this work will be received and what effects it will have on my practice and my life.

The yearning lingered. I could not continue to ignore the increasingly urgent voice within, telling me to write this book. The voice was so loud, I wondered if I had any choice in the matter. So, I faced old notes jotted down in my phone, inside the covers and pages of other people's books, in my email inbox, and I found the same beast as before, expansive and complex. The difference this time, however, was that I did not see the beast's hostility; I saw its inevitability. My meeting with this book was fated. Like the tragic heroes in the ancient plays of Euripides and

Aeschylus, I could not have escaped the writing of this book no matter what I tried.

I surrendered myself to the process. Each day, the beast grew in size—with a stray thought in the bath, an idea for a new chapter over coffee—but I learned to tend to it, to accept the complexities and the challenges for what they were, and to incorporate them into the work as best as possible.

It is important to me to explain the story behind the creation of this work, because it is not simply a memoir or a work of nonfiction. It is the story that I had to tell. It is the story of the drug war, the Holocaust, my grandparents and parents, the city of Los Angeles, and myself. There are parts of this story that may not seem to fit together. Still, the universal thread is an argument for legalization—not just the legalization of marijuana, but of all drugs, with no distinction drawn between medical and recreational use. To many, complete drug legalization will seem unorthodox at best and dangerous at worst. My hope is that after people read this book, it will become clear that legalization is the more complicated but saner option than the current system in the United States.

For over thirty years, I have wanted to write a book about my life, my family, and the legalization movement. I knew I wanted to free people, to pursue justice, as my parents had done through their practice of law. But I believed my tool for the revolution would be the written word. I even chose the pen name Athena, inspired by the story of the goddess's birth, emerging fully armored from the skull of her father, Zeus. I was also inspired by the Victorian author Mary Ann Evans, who went by the pen name George Eliot. She created the pseudonym to conceal her gender and social status so she could write with freedom. I wanted my independence; I did not want to live in my dad's shadow, and I thought a pen name would give me more power. But since then I've realized that my own identity has its worth, and I don't use Athena anymore.

However, even though I wanted to be a professional writer, I could not fully resist the temptation of the law. When I was deciding whether to go to law school, my mom asked me two questions, the answers to which led me on my way: "Do you like nice things? Do you want to free people?" I then knew what I wanted to do—and that I could do it.

Before moving forward, let me take a step back to acknowledge an accusation I have heard my whole life. Given that I am a criminal defense attorney with a specialty in cannabis, and my father is a criminal defense attorney with a specialty in cannabis, I have heard cries of nepotism. Many people—even members of the hippies' section of the criminal defense bar—have had issues with me following in my dad's footsteps. For example, upon learning of my acceptance to Harvard Law School, Tony Serra, a Bay Area attorney known for representing the Black Panthers and the Hells Angels, told me I was "riding my father's coattails to success." All the "LA's Dopest Attorney" billboards I'd had put up around town probably didn't help, either.

So let me set the record straight: my father's ideas and beliefs were his biggest gift to me. The fact is that he was very diligent about never giving me preferential treatment. He thought that new lawyers like myself should know more about the law than the older, more established attorneys, because that had been his experience. Any of my academic and professional success can be credited to my own hard work and my mother's encouragement.

The history of the world could probably be told through the history of one family. I intend to provide context for current US drug policy through a history of my family and a history of the United States. Like many Angelenos before me and many who will come after, my backstory takes place in a foreign land, and the main story begins and ends a few miles from Hollywood.

PART 1
OPENING STATEMENT

1

WHEN THE BIRDS CHIRP

ON A DECEMBER MORNING IN 2002, I climbed into the passenger seat of my dad's BMW with bloodshot eyes and half a gram of cocaine burning a white-hot hole in my pocket. He was patiently waiting for me, parked outside my mother's house on a quiet street, as he had done so many times before. It felt like the first day of school, except that I was twenty-five and exhausted. Instead of dropping me off at kindergarten, my father was driving me to my first court appearance as a freshly admitted lawyer. I had been working toward this day since I was eight.

The day before, I, along with the hundreds of other bright-eyed and bushy-tailed lawyers who had passed the notoriously difficult California Bar Exam, had gathered in the federal courthouse in downtown Los Angeles. A judge whose face I don't remember swore us in. I was still dazed from my flight from Michigan, and the ceremony was about as romantic as a cattle call, with throngs of neophytes all snapping pictures and making plans for lunch. It wasn't a big deal to me.

But it should have been. After years of all-night study sessions in the dim libraries of Columbia and Harvard Law, after weeks of listening to tapes in preparation for the bar exam, after a lifetime of following my dad—another criminal defense attorney—to courtrooms across the state and watching him defend his clients like a pothead Atticus Finch, I was about to join that exclusive club. I was going to cross the bar and join the real lawyers on the other side. And the man who was ushering me into this elite group was my father, whose politics had inspired me to devote my career to freeing people.

Yet here I was, about to fuck it all up before I started.

Let me explain. At the age of twenty-five, I only owned one suit—the same one my mother had bought for me to wear to my mock trial competitions in high school—and two dressy shirts. I don't remember if I wore the lavender silk button-down or the black-and-white shirt with the abstract geometric print. I do know that, whichever one I had on, I wore my beloved vest over it: a sleek, black thing lined with gray leopard print and, most importantly, discreet pockets.

Although it was probably a typical overcast December morning, all I can remember is how bright and harsh the sky seemed that day, how oppressive. I saw my father before I got into his car. He had a short, silver beard and a long-receded hairline. Our eyes are similar, a hazel color that straddles brown and green. I would be willing to bet money that he was listening to chimes and chants on one of his Hare Krishna tapes. If he noticed how exhausted I looked, he didn't say anything. He likely didn't notice.

My mother's house sits on the edge of a misshapen cul-de-sac carved into the hills of Coldwater Canyon. In that area, one of the many unincorporated sections of Los Angeles County, the towering pine trees, serpentine roads, and nightly chorus of howling coyotes make you feel like you aren't in the city at all. I never saw police in my mother's neighborhood, but I did see neighborhood dogs roaming the streets in a wild pack. In fact, when I was little, two of my dogs were part of that pack. Rodeo Drive and Beverly Hills are only a fifteen-minute drive away, but they might as well be another world.

It always seemed fitting to me that the drive from Coldwater Canyon into Beverly Hills is a literal descent.[1] If you aren't used to the altitude, your ears will begin to pop around the Franklin Canyon Reservoir. As you wind your way downhill, the landscape narrows, from sweeping views of the sprawling city and white and red stucco homes that dot the hills to the street before you with towering pine trees bracketing each side. You lose sight of the city. You feel claustrophobic. Or, at least, I felt claustrophobic, locked into the car with my dad and his tapes and the war going on in my head: *Why did I bring the blow?*

I had just passed the bar; I knew the stakes if I were caught. If, while going through the metal detector screening, the baggie of coke fell out of my pocket, I would incur a felony charge and lose my bar card—which allowed me to appear in court—less than twenty-four hours after receiving it. In 2003, possession of a Schedule II drug was still a felony in California.

Why did I bring the blow? Here is how fucked up I must have been that morning: I knew there was coke in my vest when I put it on. It would have been so easy to place the baggie in the drawer of my nightstand. It would have been so much smarter. *So why didn't I?*

I might have been too tired and fucked up to think about it. I couldn't sleep at all the night before and did a modest couple of lines out of boredom. Then I really couldn't sleep. I was staying at my mother's house for about a week, just for the swearing-in and this first appearance. But I hadn't lived at home since I was seventeen, and my childhood bedroom no longer felt familiar. I was surrounded by the same purple flower wallpaper and the books I'd read in grade school. But now I felt so far removed from that childhood self.

Truthfully, I missed Steve, my boyfriend at the time. Steve had dark hair and dark eyes that disappeared into bright slits when he laughed. I met him after I graduated from Columbia, in the summer of 1999. My mother brought me to a party at her friend's house. She told me to look nice. It turned out she knew Steve's mother was also at this party along with her son.

The first thing I noticed about Steve was the red, angry scar blazing along the length of his left arm. I thought it made him seem exciting, gave him the edge of danger I was looking for. I must have asked him, "How'd that happen?" He might have sighed and said, "Car accident," not wanting to talk about the accident that had snapped his head back so far it caused permanent damage to his neck and spine.

That was the first time I noticed his face. *He's cute,* I realized.

We had our first date a week later. It was the same day that Steve had plastic surgery on his arm. We had tickets to see Al Green at the Hollywood Bowl. When he picked me up, his arm was bandaged, and I could see pale pink blood seeping through the gauze. For some reason I thought this was sexy. I took it as a sign that he must really like me if he was willing to see a show while his arm oozed.

The Hollywood Bowl is a grand old outdoor amphitheater at the base of the Hollywood Hills. It was June, the days were long, and the sun was just starting to set, turning the sky into that magical shade of pink and coral fading into cool lavender. Steve described the surgery to me while I tried not to stare at the bandages. When Al Green came on, the sky had turned dark, and the lights of the stage blinded us from the sight of the silhouetted hills in the background. Al Green strode on and sang, "I'm so tired of being alone," and I looked at Steve and saw his eyes close as he listened to the rhythm of the Reverend of Soul.

When we hooked up later that night, his bandage started to peel off. I got a glimpse at the raw wound underneath. This peek at his inner darkness, the physical wound representing the psychic demons I sensed within him, made me want to know more. I was like Alice peering into the inky blackness of the rabbit hole, nanoseconds from falling into Wonderland.

That was the summer I started dabbling in "hard" drugs, the summer before I started at Harvard Law School. Steve introduced me to X, which made our nights blaze into Technicolor and our sex turn electric. I started to dabble in cocaine with Steve as my guide. We went out to clubs around LA: the Roxbury, an Italian restaurant Steve's friend's parents owned in Hollywood, and on rare occasions, the Whiskey A Go Go on Sunset Boulevard. I did bumps in dark corners tucked under his arm. Steve made me develop an appreciation for Los Angeles, the city where I was born and raised. I'd never experienced the club scene before. My nightlife consisted of staying inside and reading salacious passages in Philip Roth novels or the latest Judith Krantz. With Steve, I ordered drinks at the same bars I'd read about. We stayed up all night in the clubs, and at around 5:00 a.m. we swallowed Valium or Xanax or Vicodin or whatever we'd bought off our "pharmacist" in Benedict Canyon to try to snatch a few hours of sleep.

Lest you think Steve corrupted me, I should say that I knew what I was doing. I didn't so much fall into the rabbit hole as I cannonballed into it. I'd spent my senior year at Columbia writing a thesis on the medical marijuana movement in my home state. In New York City in the '90s, heroin was as common as bagels—and you could get both delivered if you knew the right person. When my girlfriend and I walked down Amsterdam Avenue at night, we'd hear people whisper, "Crack? Want crack?" On the walk from the corner of 116th and Broadway to Ruggles Hall, just a few blocks away, I am certain we could have purchased anything our hearts desired.

Still, I avoided it all: Drugs. Alcohol. Parties. My ideal night involved me reading odd Beatles trivia and the psychedelic-fueled manifestoes of people like Timothy Leary and Ram Dass. I had long been fascinated by drugs and the people who used them—in sixth grade, I even wrote my year-end research paper on the Medellín drug cartel for Mr. Brown's social studies class—but I never touched drugs in high school. My only concession to experimentation in college was smoking pot.

I was paranoid that any drug use would mean sacrificing precious brain cells. Since a pivotal moment in the second grade when my teacher asked me why tourism was good for the economy and I responded with, "Terrorism is bad," I've been insecure about my intelligence. My anxiety, my insatiable need to succeed, my secret fear that I would never be as smart as my classmates who seemed to grasp concepts with ease, drove me to sit my butt in hard, wooden library chairs until the wee hours of the morning throughout my adolescence and college years.

In the summer of 1999, with college behind me and my acceptance into law school in hand, I finally had time to test the subject that had intrigued me since I was a young girl. A week into my summer vacation I met Steve. *Kismet,* I thought. *Fate.*

We hooked up, partied, tripped, danced, laughed, went to shows, and gazed deeply into each other's dilated pupils. We watched sunsets turn into sunrises. I smoked, ate, snorted, or swallowed whatever he acquired for us. All summer, my feet never touched the ground.

I left him that fall to hop on a plane to Cambridge, Massachusetts, and Harvard Law. The leaves turned golden and fell, and the air turned crisp and cold, feeling good against my face. But I rarely noticed much of anything outside my classes. I lived in the library again. Occasionally, my classmates would convince me to join them for a drink, but I always felt guilty. *I should be studying,* I thought. Near the end of the semester, the sun would set at 3:00 p.m. and I would trudge through the snow and sniffle, from cold instead of coke, as the harsh winter air rubbed my face raw.

I went home for Christmas, met up with Steve, partied a little. Steve was also in school, getting his MD, but as far as I could tell his partying never stopped. I didn't understand how he could refrain from worrying about his grades, how he could say "whatever" about a B or a C.

In January, I returned to law school and my self-imposed seclusion. Between my marathon study sessions and occasional debaucheries with Steve, by the time I graduated in the spring of 2002, I felt as if I'd survived a war I had waged against myself.

Steve had finished medical school the year before, and his middling grades meant the only internship he could get was in Flint, Michigan. I joined him there, moving into the stoic, gothic apartments near Hurley Medical Center. I started haunting a sketchy pizza parlor where I bought drugs off Chris, the restaurant manager. Chris was nice. He had a cute face and a girlfriend. She had long acrylic nails and dark Rapunzel hair. Both of them reeked of cigarettes. I hung out with them right around the time the movie *8 Mile* came out, and our scene in Flint reminded me of Eminem's adventures in Detroit.

Soon enough Steve had me involved in a weird swinging situation between the two of us, Chris, and Chris's girlfriend. I spent my nights partying with Steve, snorting coke like a fiend, and trying to dull any weird feelings I had about seeing my boyfriend have sex with another woman, or about myself having sex with another man. I would wake up with the afternoon sun cutting through the blinds, drag myself out of bed, and go to the Hurley Center gym. I saw the hours I spent in the gym as a test. If my heart didn't burst while I was on the treadmill, my cocaine consumption was not as bad as I thought. Then I'd go back to the apartment, wait for Steve to return, and start the process over again.

My mom wanted me to take the bar exam immediately. She must have sensed that if I didn't take it that year, I might go completely off the rails. She had no idea how far off the deep end I was from the moment I arrived in Flint. I told her I'd take the bar next year.

"Why not this year?" she demanded. "What else are you going to do?"

"Sleep!"

"Sleep?"

"Oh my god," I moaned. "Everyone else took a gap year after college." She scoffed. I ignored her and said, "Why can't I get a break?"

"To do what?"

"I just want to sleep and party for a year."

She inhaled. I waited.

"Don't be a fucking idiot," she snapped.

This was neither the first nor the last time she would call me an idiot. Usually I would back down at this point, but now I felt righteous anger pumping through me. I told her she didn't know what it had been like for me at Harvard. She had no idea how hard I'd worked. I went quiet, sulking.

After a few tense moments, she relented. "How about this," she said. "Why don't you just try to study for the bar and take it in July and we'll see what happens? If you pass, great. If you don't, you take it next year." She waited. "What do you think?"

This, as it happened, was the perfect thing to say. My mom was telling me to approach the bar exam—which I dreaded with every atom of my being—like it was a practice test. Just a trial run. Unimportant, really. "Okay," I told her. "I'll take it."

Ideally, you are supposed to study for the California Bar Exam eight hours a day for six to eight weeks, according to BARBRI, the company offering the leading review course for the California bar. I studied no more than four hours a day for about a month. I listened to the BARBRI study tapes while pumping my arms and legs on the elliptical. (Another thing Steve introduced me to was the concept of exercise, which I characteristically took to an unhealthy level.) I stopped all the partying, stopped using drugs entirely. I listened to those tapes and exercised in Hurley Medical Center's gym until my whole body ached. A quiet voice within me hoped this would be enough and I'd pass in one try.

A few weeks later, I was zooming down the 110 North toward Pasadena, where the exam would take place. The 110 is one of the city's major highways, connecting Long Beach to Pasadena. Three years later, Nicole Richie would get pulled over for driving the wrong way on this same highway. She would admit to the cops that she was high on pot and Vicodin, and get slapped with a DUI charge. I followed all the news related to celebrity DUIs and stints in rehab, privately congratulating myself on never getting *that* fucked up.

At the convention center we were herded into a room the size of a football field. There were tables set up throughout, and I quickly claimed one so I could spread out my books and keep studying until the last minute, doing my best to ignore the slow crescendo of small talk around me as more and more people arrived at the site.

At that time, the California Bar Exam happened over three eight-hour days. The exam was all multiple-choice questions. During the exam, at the end of each section, I would scribble down any subjects that I didn't know well so I could read up on them during the lunch break. When the break came, I would walk around the corner from the convention center to a nearby Italian restaurant with my prep book in hand. I would study while I ate, gather my stuff together when I was done, and return for the second half of the test.

On the second day of the exam, I used my lunch break to wander into a Betsey Johnson store. There I found a long, witchy velvet coat with a collar made of jet-black feathers. I put the coat on hold, telling myself it would be my reward when I finished the exam the next day. I told my mom about the coat when I called her from the hotel that night. "Well," she said smugly, "you must be doing all right."

A few days later I returned to Flint and Steve. I completely devolved into a nocturnal animal, partying just about every night or as often as Steve's schedule would allow. For the first time in a long time, I had nothing to do in the months between taking the bar and finding out my results, and I began using cocaine more and more, along with anything else Pizza Chris had for us. In the back of my mind, I knew I was anxious about the results. I kept thinking about the 97 percent of Harvard Law grads who passed the bar on the first try. I thought about my dad, who graduated from community college, went to a no-name law school, and still managed to pass the bar on the first try.

The bar results came out at 5:00 p.m. on a random Friday in November. I checked the official website, scanning for my last name with the other Ms. I saw my name listed among the blessed and felt a deluge of relief. I immediately called my mom with the good news. "How about that!" she screamed. Later she told me she thought my passing was a miracle, given all of my recent extracurricular activities.

I expected comparable excitement from my dad, the man who had carted me along to court appearances as often as he could, who flew across the country time and again to sit in on my classes at Columbia and later at Harvard Law.

"That's great," he said flatly.

That was odd. I had spent the past few months telling him I didn't think I was going to pass. I told him I hadn't studied as much as I should have and I would likely have to retake the exam. And this was his response?

"Just great?"

"Yeah, great," he said. We chatted for a few more minutes and hung up.

I found his reaction confusing. Over the next couple of weeks, confusion turned to disappointment. It wasn't that I expected him to cheer or to make a big deal out of my passing. Still, I'd hoped he'd say he was proud.

I blinked, and a month passed. On December 8, 2002, I was sworn into the State Bar of California in a large courtroom in Pasadena. We smiled and took pictures. Afterward, we made our way to a nice restaurant for lunch, where my dad told me he would be taking me to my first court appearance as a bar-certified lawyer in the morning. We had already agreed that I would be going to work for him in his law firm when I moved back from

Michigan. I turned down a six-figure offer from a law firm where I had interned to accept a position with him.

Finally, that long but exciting day came to an end. Between the flight from Michigan and my fatigue from weeks of partying, I had crashed the night before the swearing-in. But now, on the eve of my first day as a real lawyer, I was back home, alone in my childhood bedroom, wide awake and bored.

My bedroom in my mother's house faced the backyard, overlooking the pool. Behind the pool, a steep ridge with steps carved into it towers over the roof of our house. This is what happens when you build homes in the mountains. When I was a kid, I used to be afraid of serial killers hiding in those hills, which were dark shadows in the night. I would only breathe easy when the sun rose from behind the ridge, casting an amber glow over the backyard.

But the night before my first court appearance, I wasn't looking out the window. I was hacking at my stash of blow with the sharp edge of my credit card on an issue of *Cosmopolitan* magazine. I rolled a dollar bill, leaned over, and inhaled. *Just this line and I'll go to sleep,* I thought. But another line followed. And another.

To this day, I don't know why I did coke all night. I had never before done it by myself, and I've never used it alone since. Hours passed without my noticing. And then I heard the first birds begin to chirp. Their song would become familiar to me over the next eight years, my notice that time was up, the day was starting, and I was pinned—that awful purgatory of intoxication without euphoria. The sky outside lightened to a pale, dove gray that matched the bags under my eyes.

I got dressed, sliding a shirt over my head. I looked at the coke on the nightstand. I knew I was going to a courthouse. I knew I couldn't have a controlled substance on me when I finally crossed the bar. But at that moment, I didn't care about being a lawyer or what my dad would think. I didn't want to get pinned. That was my only concern. So, I swept the remainder into a bag and tucked it into one of my vest pockets.

I'd taken many road trips with my dad up and down the state of California. We had been partners, more like figures in a buddy comedy than father and daughter. We played ding-dong-ditch in the Four Seasons. Once I helped him ditch about six ounces of herb in the Muir Woods before one of his court appearances. Another time, I rode shotgun with him while he picked up $25,000 in cash from a warehouse near the loading docks of San Francisco's Fisherman's Wharf. He still points to that day as the day I decided I wanted to join the legal profession.

I watched him with his clients and I watched him with his friends. I saw how kind he was to the underprivileged, the empathy coming from his own troubled upbringing in the San Fernando Valley. I saw how he approached his criminal clients as human beings worthy of grace. Every Christmas break, from high school through college, I'd watch my dad work simple magic before judges and juries. Nothing had ever stopped me from walking through the courtroom with him. Now half a gram of cocaine anchored me to my seat.

Dad found a spot on the street and switched off the engine. I tried to avoid his gaze.

"Okay, let's do it," he said.

"I can't go in," I told him.

"Why not?" He sounded irritated. He hates to be late.

"I've got blow on me," I muttered to the dashboard.

I don't remember what he said, or if he responded at all to what I'd confessed. But as I sat stuck in the passenger seat and watched his small, lean frame stride up the path leading into the courthouse, I knew something in our relationship had shifted.

That day I stayed in the car. My dad drove me back to my mother's house hours later. It would be another six months before I made my first court appearance as a licensed attorney. It was in Chino, thirty miles outside of LA city limits. I went alone.

2

WHAT ABOUT ADDICTS?

YOU DON'T HAVE TO BE supremely fucked up or have super-traumatic experiences in your past to be a drug addict. It can arise from being in love, being in love with life, or being sick of being afraid. It can happen after the intimacy that comes from doing drugs and not caring too much about tomorrow, even if you haven't been extremely wounded or abused. Also, the trauma every human experiences can be passed down.

For example, in 2013 researchers Kerry Ressler and Brian Dias conducted a study of epigenetic inheritance, which the Centers for Disease Control and Prevention defines as "how your behaviors and environment can cause changes that affect the way your genes work. Unlike genetic changes, epigenetic changes are reversible and do not change your DNA sequence, but they can change how your body reads a DNA sequence."[1] In their study, Ressler and Dias studied mice that had been trained to fear the odor of acetophenone, a chemical that smells like cherries and almonds. An article about the study, published in *Scientific American*, described the study:

> [The researchers] wafted the scent around a small chamber, while giving small electric shocks to male mice. The animals eventually learned to associate the scent with pain, shuddering in the presence of acetophenone even without a shock. This reaction was passed on to their pups. . . . Despite never

having encountered acetophenone in their lives, the offspring exhibited increased sensitivity when introduced to its smell, shuddering more markedly in its presence compared with the descendants of mice that had been conditioned to be startled by a different smell or that had gone through no such conditioning. A third generation of mice—the "grandchildren"—also inherited this reaction, as did mice conceived through in vitro *fertilization with sperm from males sensitized to acetophenone. Similar experiments showed that the response can also be transmitted down from the mother.*[2]

Something I have found common to all humans is that everyone has their vice, their thing that makes them human and is somewhat contrary to life and at the same time celebratory of it. Also, anything can be addictive. Some say that when kids play a game for more than thirty minutes, it gives them a boost of adrenaline similar to shooting heroin that has even been known to cause heart problems in children.[3]

"Addiction broadly defined is the continued and compulsive consumption of a substance or behavior (gambling, gaming, sex) despite its harm to self and/or others," says Dr. Anna Lembke, author of *Dopamine Nation.* Describing her own experience of being addicted to romance novels, she shares the following: "What happened to me is trivial compared to the lives of those with overpowering addiction, but it speaks to the growing problem of compulsive overconsumption that we all face today, even when our lives are good. I have a kind and loving husband, great kids, meaningful work, freedom, autonomy, and relative wealth—no trauma, social dislocation, poverty, unemployment, or other risk factors for addiction. Yet I was compulsively retreating further and further into a fantasy world."[4]

Most people mark President Nixon's signing of the Controlled Substances Act in 1970 as the official start of the War on Drugs. Nixon's aide John Ehrlichman would later tell journalist Dan Baum:

The Nixon campaign in 1968, and the Nixon White House after that, had two enemies: the antiwar left and black people. You understand what I'm saying? We knew we couldn't make it illegal to be either against the war or black, but by getting the public to associate the hippies with marijuana and

*blacks with heroin, and then criminalizing both heavily, we could disrupt
those communities. We could arrest their leaders, raid their homes, break
up their meetings, and vilify them night after night on the evening news. Did
we know we were lying about the drugs? Of course we did.[5]*

What most people do not realize is that this was only the latest in a
series of prohibition movements in the United States that started nearly a
century earlier. America's first drug war began in 1875 in San Francisco,
and it was motivated by the same anxieties that drove the Prohibition
amendment in the 1920s, which are the same fears that later fueled Nixon's
Controlled Substances Act. President Nixon also saw his War on Drugs as
a vigorous, and cheap, alternative to the War on Poverty that President
Lyndon B. Johnson had declared in 1964.

We have President Johnson to thank for programs like food stamps,
Medicare, and Medicaid, social infrastructure that would improve the
living standards of America's impoverished people and hopefully enable
them to climb out of their class. While Nixon did not cut these programs,
he did shift their focus from poverty to drug addiction. His answer to the
seemingly endless stream of heroin addicts was a methadone maintenance program. Nixon was convinced that the methadone program would
decrease crime rates; he thought heroin addicts looking for their next hit
were responsible for the spike in crime. Under the guidance of psychiatrist
Jerome Jaffe—a portly, bespectacled man you can see standing behind
President Nixon in pictures of him announcing his War on Drugs—the
methadone program spread nationwide. Heroin and opiate "addicts"
could go to clinics for their cup of orange juice with dissolved methadone
in it and make it through the rest of the day. As should be clear to anyone
paying attention to the current opiate epidemic, the methadone program
did not work. It was just the latest in a series of reactionary events—the
middle- and upper-class backlash to any perceived rise in addiction rates
and loss of power to people of color.

These attempts at prohibition have never succeeded and never will
succeed, but politicians throughout the years have found it easier to
blame drugs for a society's ills than to fix the root problems of that society.

Blaming the drug and not the system was also a convenient way to foster public support from relatives and friends who were seeing loved ones incarcerated for long terms.[6]

When I propose the decriminalization of all drugs, the first question I usually get is: "What about addicts?" This question arises from the mistaken sense that the only barrier between an uncontrollable population of addicts and the rest of the public is the drug laws currently in place. It's an understandable question, sometimes asked by well-intentioned people. I have realized that people love to bring up addicts as an issue because they have never learned about the history of drugs in America—a topic that used to not be taught in school, and even now you have to wait until you get to college for a real education on the subject. People also don't know the story behind the rise of the image of the strung-out addict we are so used to seeing in popular culture, and how it is connected with America's first and second Wars on Drugs.

In his book *White Market Drugs,* David Herzberg explains how a lack of historical knowledge affects the way people see today's opioid crisis in the United States:

> *To see the opioid crisis as new and unprecedented in this way required a radical act of forgetting. During the last 150 years, small town and suburban white communities have suffered repeated crises of addiction to pharmaceuticals. Indeed, they have been home to far more drug use and addiction than poorer communities with less access to the medical system. . . . White markets, I show, have been home to three major addiction crises in the modern era, far larger than any crises associated with illegal drugs. The first, at the turn of the twentieth century, began with sharp increases in medical sales of opioids and cocaine. The second, from the 1930s to the 1970s, came during a historic boom in sales of pharmaceutical sedatives and stimulants. The third, at the turn of the twenty-first century, grew from dramatic increases in medical use of all three classes of white market drugs—sedatives, stimulants, and opioids. These crises, I argue, all happened for the same reason: a presumption of therapeutic intent that left white markets with insufficient consumer protections. . . . The great*

majority of white market drug use, after all, did not lead to addiction or death. To desire and to use drugs under such circumstances was not foolish or aberrant; it did not require having been tricked by an evil industry or misled by physicians. White markets thrived, in part, because of the perfectly understandable, human decisions of countless consumers.[7]

Herzberg also explains how the concept of addiction had stigma built into it from the beginning:

Beyond its policy implications, the disorganized white market experiment with morphine maintenance also invites us to rethink our conceptions of addiction itself. Early twentieth-century experts built a highly stigmatized concept of addiction by studying consumers in informal urban markets— people whose experiences were shaped by poverty and anti-vice policing, and whose daily lives were further distorted by the perception and moral judgments of experts and authorities. They provided the clinical material for a "junkie" paradigm that incorporated poverty and criminality as elements of addiction itself. . . . Our ideas of addiction should include their experiences too. Remembering their stories can help us disentangle the realities of addiction from a century of inherited stigma.[8]

There was a time when all drugs were legal in the United States, although there is nobody alive today who would remember it. In fact, I might not have learned about this history as early as I did if not for my Grandma Guta. When Guta lived in Poland in the 1930s, both drugs and prostitution were legal.

She would tell me about this time, while I sat in her kitchen in Beverly Hills. Guta had seen addict maintenance since she was a young girl, and she was far more progressive than anyone would have expected an older Eastern European Jewish woman to be. Because of Guta's stories, I always knew that drugs had once been completely legal and therefore could be made legal again. It is easy to forget that the state of drug prohibition is an unnatural one; for the majority of human history there has not been a civic law governing what people put into their bodies. That authority was typically left to religious authorities, if it was not considered a sovereign right.

The United States was no different. Hemp has always been a cash crop for the states, although that is kept quiet. The founding fathers wrote the original draft of the Declaration of Independence on hemp paper imported from the Netherlands. President George Washington and other colonial farmers grew hemp for its fiber, enabling the colonies to manufacture their own fabric and rope instead of relying on England's hemp product. Hemp, not tea, was the first source of discord between the colonies and the Crown.[9]

Over a century later, the US government would once more promote hemp production. *Hemp for Victory* was a 1942 American propaganda film released at the start of World War II that urged farmers to serve their country by growing as much hemp as possible for ropes, parachutes, naval towlines, and even boot laces. Japan's alliance with Germany had blocked the US supply of imported hemp from the Philippines, and *Hemp for Victory* was an attempt by the US Department of Agriculture (USDA) to meet the war shortages of its fiber. Once the war ended and trade opened again, the USDA buried the film and banned domestic production of hemp once more. Importing hemp was more profitable than growing it domestically, so its production in the United States became obsolete.

America has had an equally tumultuous relationship with opium and its derivatives, such as morphine, heroin, and Vicodin. After serving his two terms as president, Thomas Jefferson grew hemp and poppies on the grounds of Monticello, his five-thousand-acre estate in Charlottesville, Virginia. It is not known if the poppies were merely ornamental or practical (their seeds are the source of opium), but the hemp crops were certainly intended to be harvested. In fact, Jefferson encouraged its cultivation even outside his walls. It is even known that Jefferson took laudanum, a tincture made of opium and alcohol, as prescribed by his personal doctor, Robley Dunglison. If you visited Monticello before 1991, you probably saw the vibrant red poppy flowers dotting the estate's lawn. The US Drug Enforcement Agency (DEA) pulled up the plants that June, to prevent any would-be opiate chemists from profiting from the supply.

The first War on Drugs actually targeted the by-products of the opium poppy, specifically the trade in the opium dens that flourished in San Francisco's Chinatown in the late nineteenth century. After the completion of the Central Pacific Railroad in 1869, Chinese immigrants moved to San Francisco in such large numbers that they made up over 10 percent of the city's population by 1880. With the flood of Chinese immigrants came reactionary hate groups who protested the foreigners allegedly taking their jobs. In 1877, a group of laborers led by the Irish-born Denis Kearney formed the Workingmen's Party of California (WPC), whose primary goal was to run the Chinese out of town through a series of targeted attacks in the fifteen blocks of Chinatown throughout the 1870s and 1880s. Their infamous slogan was "The Chinese Must Go!" Although San Francisco was the epicenter of these riots, anti-Chinese sentiment occurred throughout California. In 1878, the WPC won control of the state legislature and altered the state constitution to deny voting rights to Chinese citizens. This is how California passed the nation's first immigration legislation, the Chinese Exclusion Act of 1882.

Before the Chinese Exclusion Act, San Francisco's white majority was living with the fear that the Chinese immigrants were bringing opium with them, despite the fact that opium had been in the United States for at least one hundred years at that point, and that about three hundred thousand pounds of opium were already arriving in the country every year in 1857, according to a report in *Harper's Weekly*. White Americans were seen lounging in opium dens next to the Chinese laborers—in fact, white people seemed to be keeping these dens in business—but most whites considered opium use a despicable habit that they could not separate from their racist feelings toward the Chinese. In 1875, six years after the completion of the railroad, San Francisco passed the nation's first ordinance banning the keeping or visiting of opium dens. This ordinance was the first in the United States to regulate drug use. As a similar scenario played out in cities across the nation, it became the setting for America's first drug war.

The 1875 ordinance in San Francisco was not born out of a concern for the well-being of addicts, but out of anti-Chinese sentiment. Never mind that opium pods had long been used in folk remedies. Never mind that in the late 1860s, doctors invented morphine—the highly effective painkiller made from a distillate of opium—and the hypodermic syringe, which combined to create the popular injectable form of morphine. Injectable morphine blunted pain much faster than the home remedies of midwives and homeopaths. At first, injectable morphine was considered harmless, and doctors prescribed it for everything from headaches to menstrual cramps. These physicians would soon realize their overeager prescriptions had created an opiate epidemic. This was when the word *addict* was first used in the sense in which we understand it today—the state of being "enslaved" to a substance or behavior—to describe mostly middle- and upper-class white women who became physically dependent on the morphine their doctors prescribed.

One man made an appearance in all three US prohibition movements: media mogul William Randolph Hearst. Hearst got his start in publishing when he bought the *San Francisco Examiner* in 1887. With this acquisition, Hearst published salacious tabloids throughout the 1890s, peddling stories of white women under the influence of opium smoke being seduced by Chinese men. Hearst used his tabloids and their cartoons to play on the public fear of the "Yellow Peril," a tactic he would use over and over again to wield political influence. His campaign found success in the 1909 passage of the Smoking Opium Exclusion Act, a federal measure that banned the import of opium for smoking.

We can blame this first opiate epidemic and drug war for our modern conception of the addict. The word *addict* is derived from the Latin conjunctive verb *addicere,* which means "to assign to." The verb *addicere* is also the origin for the Latin noun *addictus,* which means "slave." However, until the panic of the 1860s, the word *addict* was not used to denote habitual substance abuse. To be addicted to something was considered a harmless or even positive status, similar to what we might call "a strong inclination." You might addict yourself to gardening or the study of Japanese calligraphy. Although there were certainly drug addicts in the modern sense before 1860, nobody called them that.

In the seventeenth century, William Shakespeare coined the term *addiction* by inventing a noun based on the verb phrase "to addict oneself to." The opening scene of *Henry V* shows the archbishop of Canterbury illustrating the character of the king when he was a young prince:

> So that the art and practice part of life
> Must be the mistress to this theoric;
> Which is a wonder how his Grace should glean it,
> Since his addiction was to courses vain,
> His companies unlettered, rude, and shallow . . .

In this line, the archbishop is saying he's surprised at the competence of Henry V, given how he devoted himself to useless pursuits in his aimless youth. When the United States encountered its first drug crisis with the nineteenth-century opiate epidemic, the noun *addict* came into popular use. Once the noun supplanted the verb, the behavior wasn't kept separate from the individual—it *was* the individual. Now the term *addict* is weighted.

Over the years, the medical definition of the term *addict* has changed. The fifth edition of the *Diagnostic and Statistical Manual of Mental Disorders,* the most recent edition of the manual, made the switch from the term *addiction* to the less stigmatized *substance use disorder.* The characteristics are the same: generally, an addiction is defined as a repeating behavior that has a negative impact on the individual. This could mean that the person is taking the substance in excess, finding themselves incapable of stopping their pursuit of the substance due to physical withdrawal, losing control of their personal life, or putting themselves in harm's way for the sake of obtaining that substance.

In the 1860s, the addicted people who caused the most worry were the women receiving morphine prescriptions from their doctors. The first sanatoriums were opened in order to get these women to kick their habits. Public fear over the susceptibility of white women—to morphine, opium, and the sexual advances of Chinese men—combined with prejudices against the Chinese minority to spur the first drug war. As we will see, similar sentiments contributed to the 1920 passage of the Eighteenth Amendment, which inaugurated the era of Prohibition.

The temperance movement began in earnest nearly a century before the Eighteenth Amendment, in the 1830s and 1840s. Alcohol abuse and its physical effects were being felt by just about every American; an 1830 estimate showed that the average American over the age of fifteen consumed about seven gallons of pure alcohol a year. The temperance movement, born in the country's Protestant churches, began as a way to suggest more moderate alcohol consumption. Abolitionists started to join the cause too, arguing that drinking was as evil as slavery. The movement ramped up in the 1870s, when European immigrants brought with them the drinking habits of their home countries. Clergymen from the Methodist and Baptist denominations began to protest the increasing alcohol consumption.

The preachers were joined by thousands of Christian women. Women then did not possess the right to vote or own land; nor did they have a host of other rights they enjoy today. The foremothers of the suffragist movement, like Susan B. Anthony and Elizabeth Cady Stanton, allied themselves with the temperance movement as a way to decrease domestic abuse and the wayward spending habits of alcoholic husbands. In the summer of 1874, the Women's Christian Temperance Union (WCTU) was formed, led by a formidable schoolteacher named Frances Willard. The WCTU established chapters around the nation and won smaller battles like local laws limiting access to alcohol.

But it wasn't until the formation of the Anti-Saloon League (ASL) that the Prohibition movement gained nationwide political momentum. The ASL managed to unite people from opposing sides—something that seems all the more incredible in today's political climate—including Republicans and Democrats, Progressives and Populists, members of the Ku Klux Klan and the NAACP, and the International Workers of the World and monopolists like Henry Ford, John Rockefeller Jr., and Andrew Carnegie. The ASL had one goal: to pass a constitutional amendment banning the manufacture, sale, and transportation of alcohol.

Under its savvy political leadership, the ASL also capitalized on rising anti-German sentiment in the 1910s. They successfully associated the German enemy with the beer and brewers that had taken root in the United States. And since the 1913 passage of the income tax amendment, the federal government no longer needed liquor taxes to fund its operations. In 1917, the Eighteenth Amendment passed the House and the Senate, and it was ratified by the states just after midnight on January 17, 1920. As the most successful lobbyist group of the time—and perhaps in all of US history—the ASL did not have a single political opponent. The only person who made a stand was President Woodrow Wilson, who unsuccessfully attempted a veto.

Liquor prohibition was a miserable failure, by all accounts. It lasted for thirteen years, until thirty-six of the forty-eight states ratified the Twenty-First Amendment in 1933. The Eighteenth Amendment became the first, and only, US constitutional amendment to be overturned. Under Prohibition, Al Capone and the mob flourished, and crime skyrocketed. Tens of thousands of people died either from drinking unregulated alcohol or from Prohibition-related violence. The violence was enough to convince the states to repeal the Eighteenth Amendment.

Of all the arguments against the use of psychoactive substances, moral arguments are perhaps the most long-standing and the most difficult to oppose. I think the most provocative moral argument is "enslavement theory": the notion that using drugs can lead to addiction (whether physical, psychological, or both) and that addiction deprives the addict of free will. Therefore, people must be prevented from using psychoactive substances, especially those that can create physical addiction, in order to preserve their freedom.

As James A. Inciardi explains in *The Drug Legalization Debate*, "For the better part of this century there has been a concerted belief that addicts commit crimes because they are 'enslaved' to drugs, that because of the high prices of heroin, cocaine, and other illicit chemicals on the drug black market, users are forced to commit crimes in order to support their drug habits."[10] The notion underlying this belief is that becoming addicted to drugs deprives the addict of the right to make free choices, and in doing so, deprives the individual of the capacity to exercise her rights. It is as though the drug were controlling the person's actions, so the government must prohibit people from using substances that can wrest so much control from them as to deprive the users of their ability to make choices about their lives. The government is, in essence, saving people from themselves, ensuring the individual's ability to continue to have freedom of choice.

But modern addiction theory and science support the idea that drugs are not necessarily any more enslaving than any other thing to which you can become addicted. Though addiction is used to generally describe one's relationship to a drug he or she uses over and over, recent research suggests that no pharmacological property alone—nor any combination of them—can enslave a person or animal.

In the 1960s, researchers defined addiction strictly on the basis of physical dependence, meaning that anyone who experienced withdrawal symptoms qualified as an addict. The problem with this definition, however, is that it is too broad. For example, the average habitual coffee drinker knows the dull headache that accompanies a day when coffee is denied for some reason. But outside of joking conversation, most of these coffee drinkers would not consider themselves addicted to caffeine.

In his 2002 book *The Heart of Addiction*, Lance Dodes, MD, discusses the conception of addiction to which most of the lay public subscribes:

> *Many people take for granted that addiction is a physical problem. The very words used to describe addictions—that one is "hooked on" drugs, or even the less colloquial version of this, that one is "addicted to" drugs—suggest that drugs somehow physically capture people. Adding to this impression are movies and television shows that almost everyone has seen in which people are shown in physical agony withdrawing from narcotics, or feeling desperate to get a "fix" of their drug to prevent withdrawal effects. This desperate search looks as though it must be an important factor at the very core of addiction.*[11]

Many consider addictions to fall into two types: physical and psychological. However, Dodes suggests that calling both of these an addiction is somewhat of a misnomer. He ultimately concludes that "an addiction, then, is truly present only when there is a psychological drive to perform the addictive behavior—that is, only when there is a psychological addiction."[12] According to Dodes, "physical addiction" is "a state in which both tolerance and withdrawal are present. The drugs to which the body reacts by developing tolerance, and subsequently withdrawal, are said to be 'physically addictive' drugs."[13]

There are many addictions with no physical addiction present at all. Dodes contends that "there is no sharp distinction between drug and nondrug addictions." His most persuasive argument for this controversial statement is the "fact that many people with addictions routinely switch back and forth between drug and nondrug addictions, or perform both addictions at the same time." He additionally points out the prevalence of people switching from a drug of one pharmacological type to one of another type. "This switching would be impossible if physical addiction to one drug were essential to the nature of their problem," he says. "If physical addiction were the major problem, they could only switch between drugs when they were capable of physically substituting for each other." It is the switching phenomenon that provides Dodes with the linchpin of his theory: "The drive behind addiction is a psychological compulsion to perform a particular action, such as using a drug, regardless of type."[14]

Anecdotal evidence discussed in other works on addiction support Dodes's theories. The evidence marshaled by psychiatrist Nils Bejerot in his book *Addiction and Society* also shows that the insight Dodes has gleaned from his experience with addiction in the United States mirrors the experiences of those involved in drug-using communities in other parts of the world, such as Sweden, where Bejerot practiced. For example, in an account titled "A Girl Related Her Boyfriend's Story," Bejerot quotes the girl as saying "it is quite easy to take enough [drugs] to get physical withdrawal symptoms without becoming an addict."[15]

As Michael Weil, MD, and Winifred Rosen explain in *Chocolate to Morphine: Understanding Mind-Active Drugs,* "Dependence on anything is not easy to break. More often than not, people simply switch dependencies, substituting one for another without achieving greater freedom."[16] As the authors indicate, dependence on drugs may not be the worst way in which a person can manifest her need to be dependent upon an object or activity.

The truth is that the majority of drug users never develop addictions. Only an estimated 10–15 percent of drug users develop addictions to even the most addictive substances, like heroin and cocaine. Every administration's antidrug campaigns portray all drugs as equally dangerous to everyone, but the situation is not as simple as Nancy Reagan's "Just Say No" campaign suggested.

It is an unusual individual who has never drunk alcohol or tried a drug recreationally. If you were to review your past twenty-four hours, you too might find that you'd used a few drugs, be they caffeine or cocaine. The desire to alter one's consciousness is as natural as the desire for lunch. Professor Ronald K. Siegel at UCLA called this instinct the fourth drive, after hunger, thirst, and sex. In his fascinating book *Intoxication,* Siegel detailed his experiments wherein he explored how animals responded to different drugs. He gave psychedelics to mongooses and opium to water buffalo. What he found is that every class of animal possesses the instinct to use drugs, drink alcohol, or otherwise experiment with altering their perspectives.

Humans are no different. From the ambitious twentysomething throwing back drinks in between handing out business cards, to the doctor filling his own Vicodin prescriptions, to the meth-addicted woman struggling to make ends meet in her rural town, drug use is universal. It has not been eradicated by strict drug laws and mandatory minimum prison sentences.

Spinning in circles is how most people first experiment with altering their consciousness. Watching my son Jax spin on the swing while making starfish arms reminds me of the childhood games I watched my peers indulge in as a child—specifically the one where you stand a baseball bat on the ground, place your forehead on top, and spin around the bat until you fall over and get to enjoy your first "trip," with the clouds in the sky roiling about topsy-turvy above you. According to Professor Siegel, this fourth drive arises from the interaction between the body's internal chemistry and the chemistry of the drug, like the opiate receptors and endocannabinoids every mammal has in their bodies.

The disease model of addiction has become popular because it allows people around the addicted person to separate the drug problem from the individual. It has also allowed for the problem of addiction to be handled as a health crisis, therefore freeing up the vital research grants that fund studies of this behavior. However, the disease model also promotes the false idea that the person is a slave to their habit and that they do not have control over their plight. This perspective might make the people around the addicted person feel better, but it strips agency from the individual in question.

Recent research into addiction, covered in the books *The Botany of Desire* and *Unbroken Brain,* has shown that it is more accurate to characterize addiction not as a disease, but as a learning disorder or the formation of a habit. To put it simply, nobody starts using a drug in an addictive manner— meaning compulsively and to the detriment of their health and safety—right away. At first they take the drug every so often, maybe as a way to relax at the end of a long day, to stay up for a long night, or just to participate in a group activity. Over time, the individual may begin using the drug to cope with stress, and every time they do that, they are forming a feedback loop in their brain. Feeling anxious? Take the drug. Feeling sad? Take the drug. Angry? Take the drug. That feedback loop will sometimes develop into a habit that becomes very difficult, but not impossible, to break.

Again, addictions only develop in a minority of drug users. The overwhelming majority of drug users who never develop addictions will likely continue to use recreationally, no matter the state of the law. As Professor Siegel said, the drive to alter consciousness is an adaptive evolutionary trait. Using drugs allows people to experience pleasure or think about the world in a new way. Nearly fifty years after Nixon's War on Drugs began, people continue to use them, and that seems unlikely to change.

There was one man in particular who devoted much of his life to forming extremely negative perceptions of addiction and its victims. Decades before Ronald and Nancy Reagan declared war on drugs and urged America's youth to "Just Say No," and before Richard Nixon branded drugs as "public enemy number one," Harry Anslinger stalked the country.

Harry Anslinger was already an old man by 1970. He was the son of German immigrants, a railroad wunderkind turned government employee, and the head of the US Federal Bureau of Narcotics (FBN) for over thirty years. When he took office, it was the beginning of the end of America's Prohibition on alcohol. The FBN was about to shutter its doors because of an existential crisis. What was its purpose if there wasn't an illegal substance to go after?

Anslinger knew how to create enemies out of ideas. He was the same person who solved a railroad issue at thirteen. He identified a run of organized crime called the Black Hand, or the modern mafia. And now he was going to create a problem for the FBN to solve so his bureau could stay in business. To spread his message, Anslinger partnered with the experienced propagandist William Randolph Hearst.

Hearst and Anslinger had a few things in common: they were old, very racist, white, and male. Anslinger had his motivation for demonizing drugs, specifically marijuana: if marijuana was illegal, there was a reason for the FBN to exist. It was also convenient to target marijuana, which could easily be associated with pesky Mexican immigrants and flagrant Black jazz musicians. And Hearst was staunchly antidrug because of economic interests. In addition to his publishing empire, Hearst owned acres of wooded land. If marijuana and hemp were legal, people would buy paper products made from hemp—a cheaper, more sustainable alternative—rather than products made from trees. Together these men created a campaign against marijuana use and other drugs that continues to affect American drug policy.

Perhaps their most infamous collaboration was the 1936 US government propaganda film *Reefer Madness,* a bombastic story of a young couple's lives ruined by the marijuana they smoked and sold to other unsuspecting young people.[17] The film depicts an innocent white girl who tries smoking pot and thus begins her descent into the seedy world of druggies and dealers. It ends with her life tragically cut short, presumably by her "reefer madness." The film was financed by a church group and was intended to be a cautionary tale for parents about their teens' drug use. Critical reception at the time was bleak, to put it mildly, and over the decades, *Reefer Madness* became a cult classic, something for people to laugh at while they light up.

Still, Anslinger and Hearst formed an effective partnership and ran a strong campaign. In 1937, Congress approved the Marihuana Tax Act, which placed a tax on the sales of cannabis. Anslinger's FBN had its new mission, and Hearst sold many, many newspapers. Anslinger's reign continued throughout the 1940s and '50s, and the villains changed from joint-smoking jazz players to commie scum. President Kennedy replaced Anslinger in 1962, but the damage was already done.

However, it would be a mistake to say that the only reason for Anslinger's campaign against drugs was professional self-interest. Johann Hari's moving account of the drug war, *Chasing the Scream*, derives its title from a story about a prepubescent Harry Anslinger in the small farming community of Altoona, Pennsylvania. Apparently, young Harry heard a woman screaming in agony one day, her cries carrying over the landscape. The woman was addicted to morphine, and her withdrawal was intense enough to cause her screams. He was sent to the druggist to purchase morphine to soothe the poor woman. Hari writes that the woman's plight followed Anslinger throughout the rest of his life, giving him a moral as well as a professional imperative to eradicate drug abuse in the United States.[18]

Anslinger's antidrug morality endured throughout his time as head of the FBN and persisted until the end of his life. In one of his last public appearances before he died, Anslinger participated in a 1970 roundtable about the "drug problem" that was moderated by *Playboy*. The other panelists included novelist William Burroughs, psychedelic expert Ram Dass, and pro-drug reform professors Joel Fort and Leslie Fiedler.[19]

Anslinger was not the only prohibitionist on the panel, but he was certainly the most extreme, as demonstrated by his responses to the other panelists. When Ram Dass suggested creating brick-and-mortar "centers for the LSD experience in the same way that universities are settings for the rational mind," Anslinger declared, "only a disordered mind would entertain such a proposal. It is utterly monstrous and ridiculous."

It is not surprising that Anslinger would regard the long-bearded Ram Dass with apprehension. His words, however, are heightened and biting, imbuing every suggestion with the stain of moral failure. A center for LSD—which Ram Dass had already been a part of, as a graduate student at Harvard University—may seem a little unusual; but "utterly monstrous"? Later in the conversation, when Burroughs—author of the semiautobiographical novel *Junkie: Confessions of an Unredeemed Drug Addict*—suggested legalizing heroin for medical purposes, Anslinger blew up again. "Do you want to make [heroin] legal?" he raged. "Do you realize that if it weren't for the efforts of the Federal Bureau of Narcotics, we'd have as many addicts as there were back in 1914, when one in four hundred Americans was hooked?"

The veracity of Anslinger's statistic is questionable. As Dr. Fort points out, "There was no medical definition of addiction at that time and no survey research, so we don't know how many addicts there were." And we don't know how Anslinger sounded when he made his retort, although his tone shouts even from the page.

But we do know that in 1904, the year he heard the scream of the addicted woman, Anslinger was twelve years old. And we know that Anslinger saw himself and his Federal Bureau of Narcotics as the protectors who were keeping drugs out of the hands of pitiful addicts like the woman from his childhood. Anslinger certainly had political reasons for creating drug prohibition, but he also had his personal motivations: *it's immoral to just let people remain addicts.* If there was a way to prevent people from ending up like that screaming, morphine-addicted woman, it was Anslinger's moral obligation to pursue that.

To be clear, Anslinger was not someone most people would consider a "good" person. He was racist—even by the lax standards of the midtwentieth century—and he willfully ignored any reports showing that drug prohibition did not actually reduce the number of addicts. But somewhere in his mind, Anslinger thought of himself as a hero, the only person keeping more people from screaming for substances. *You think drug addiction is a problem now? Imagine if the drugs were legal!*

Most well-intentioned people have their own inner Anslinger; they believe both that addicted persons deserve help and that it would be dangerous to legalize all drugs. Even though I'm writing this book in California at a time when medical and recreational marijuana is legal throughout the state, most of the people I tell about this proposal to legalize all drugs respond like Anslinger: "What about addicts? If heroin/cocaine/meth were legalized, wouldn't there just be more addicts?" What most of these well-meaning souls never consider is that the narrative of addiction was created by Anslinger and Hearst in order to convince the public that drugs needed to be regulated.

Behind Anslinger's putative claim that it's immoral to just let people remain addicts is a man who had become afraid of the very narrative he'd created. When the woman was screaming for morphine, easing her suffering was as simple as a run to the druggist, where a twelve-year-old Anslinger was able to legally purchase the drugs the woman needed. Over fifty years later, all he remembered was the scream—not the woman behind the scream. And he consoled himself with his belief that his prohibition of drugs was the only thing keeping the number of addicts under control, despite the clear evidence to the contrary.

The woman's morphine addiction was clearly creating a problem for her health, but at that time, it did not threaten her safety. She could safely purchase the drug she desired because of the Pure Food and Drug Act of 1906. She knew what was in the morphine she needed, and she was able to relieve her symptoms without the dangers that attend a modern-day drug deal.

When Anslinger sat on his panel on drugs for *Playboy,* he was confronted by William Burroughs. At this time, Burroughs was a middle-aged novelist who had suffered from an addiction to narcotics for fifteen years. On the subject of the effectiveness of drug prohibition in treating addicts, Burroughs stated, "I would also like to point out that my own problem with addiction was solved through medical treatment, while I was in

England and could have obtained all the junk I wanted on prescription. All the time I lived under Mr. Anslinger's fatherly protection in this country, I found it quite impossible to kick my habit. And I tried eleven times."

After Burroughs's statement, *Playboy* changed the topic.

Hari ends *Chasing the Scream* with a point I will echo here. In the 1950s, Anslinger faced a man he respected, a US congressman, who had a heroin addiction. Anslinger privately confronted the man about his drug use, urging him to quit, but the man said he couldn't quit and would find the drug no matter the risk. Anslinger's own antidrug campaign had restricted any safe and legal access to heroin, and he feared for the congressman's life. So Anslinger, the father of drug prohibition, provided the man with a steady, safe supply of heroin that he could pick up at a Washington, DC, pharmacy. The Federal Bureau of Narcotics even paid for the "prescription" until the man died. It would be years before a confidante of Anslinger's revealed that the congressman was none other than famed anticommunist Senator Joe McCarthy.[20]

Even the leader of prohibition realized that heroin maintenance was the most compassionate act he could perform when confronted with an addict he knew. I have found this to be true in my own life. When I was in grade school, I looked down on the strung-out addicts depicted in my D.A.R.E. workbooks, but it is easy to demonize a theoretical addicted person. When that addicted person is someone you know or love, the rules tend to lose their impact.

Given the failed history of prohibition and the current state of opiate addiction ravaging the country, the answer to "What about addicts?" is not to criminalize their behavior, but to support them in being healthy. The goal should not be to achieve some outdated notion of moral superiority through stone-cold sobriety, but to allow people healthy means of altering their consciousnesses. The current system of prohibition has deprived society of the legal opportunity to experiment with drugs in a moderate way. There is addictive potential in illicit drugs, just as there is in cigarette smoking and drinking alcohol, or in behaviors like gambling or shopping. There are also many benefits to using drugs, such as relieving stress and pain, bonding with other people, and even attaining a level of spirituality you may not be able to otherwise access. I suspect that the costs of prohibition far outweigh the costs of actual drug use.

Stories of addiction scare us, thrill us, and always hit just a little too close to home. And even still we demonize the subjects. "How could they do this to their families? To themselves?" The shift from pity to blame is subtle, but swift. You can see it at work in a pamphlet released by the US Public Health Service in 1951, titled "What to Know About Drug Addiction": "Usually, [drug addicts] are irresponsible, selfish, immature, thrill-seeking individuals who are constantly in trouble—the type of person who acts first and thinks afterward."[21]

It's true that the consequences of drug addiction, from losing a job to losing custody of a child, are great. But what's complicated about the consequences is determining what causes them: society's criminalization of drug use, the bad effects of some drug use, or the shame that comes with the stigmas of both. How have we entrusted our government to handle the addiction epidemic?

So far, no one has won the War on Drugs. I make the case that the War on Drugs has failed because it fundamentally fails to understand addiction itself. Rethinking our approach requires that we understand the experience of drug reward: what gives one the appetite for the drug and perpetuates the cycle of use.

Dehumanizing drug addicts does not solve the problem of addiction; in fact, it only makes matters worse. It further entrenches the racist origins of the drug war and gives the already affluent percentage of the population who have experienced less trauma peace of mind by allowing them to dismiss addiction as a problem of the troubled individual. Psychologist Carl Hart conducted an experiment that showed just how complicated addicted people's choices and behavior can be. In his study, he recruited crack addicts to live in a hospital for several weeks. During this time, he would offer each participant a dosed amount of crack, with the amount unknown to the smoker. After the initial dose, the participant would be offered either more opportunities to smoke throughout the day, or they could choose to collect a monetary reward as low as $5. The experiment concluded that when the initial dose of crack was fairly high, the subject would typically choose to keep smoking crack during the day. But when the dose was smaller, the subject was more likely to pass it up for the $5 in cash or voucher.[22] Subscribing to the popular conception that addicted people will choose any dose of drug over any other experience is the easy way out—and simply not true. It's not addiction that enslaves the mind; it's the persistence of emotional trauma and isolation. Even when they're around drugs, addicted people are not simply slaves to craving. They are more than capable of making rational choices.

The criminalization of drugs is the criminalization of their users, branding them with shame and depravity and driving them further into social and political isolation. In doing so, we reinforce jails, drug dealers, and violence. We fundamentally preserve the problem of addiction via its so-called solution. Instead, we need to accept that as long as drugs exist, they will be used. We need to understand drug reward, in every sense of the word. Ultimately, we need to question current legislation and drug-related policy in order to shift our focus to the socially isolated periphery.

3

IT'S MY PARTY

A YOUNG GIRL, THIRTEEN YEARS OLD, runs through a dense forest of birch trees. The year is 1939. Her hair is cut short, with blunt, heavy bangs pinned to the side. Her face is dappled in warm summer sunlight, her dress dotted with wildflowers. She and her friends have matching flushed cheeks, pink from exercise, and they laugh loud enough to fill up the empty silence of the wood. They yank wild berries from their hiding places in the bushes and pop the fruit into their eager mouths, staining their tongues and the tips of their fingers a deep, bruised purple. Here, in the rural Polish village of Wiśniowa Góra, the air is fresh and there is more than enough room to run.

The girl's name is Guta Kasz. She cannot imagine any other future than what she has always known. She will become my grandmother, but it will be eleven more years before she gives birth to my mother, and seventy-six more years before she will sit in her Beverly Hills living room, half-blind and smiling, telling me and a reporter how those summers when she picked berries in the woods of central Poland were the happiest times of her life.[1]

Guta Kasz was born the middle daughter of a middle-class family in Łódź, Poland. Her full name was Shayna Guta, but her family liked to call her Gita (which always sounded like an unattractive nickname to me) or Guta. Her older sister was Fredda, and her younger sister was Brenda.

Long after Fredda and Brenda's deaths, Guta would still feel like the middle child. Some things never leave you.

Guta's parents were Benjamin and Sara Kasz. Benjamin sold and installed radio antennas, while Sara took care of the home. The five of them lived in a three-room apartment. The family was "very" Jewish, celebrating Shabbat every week and going to the synagogue on the Jewish holidays. This detail would have serious consequences in 1939.

The Jews of Łódź, and Poland more broadly, had a history of facing antisemitic policies. Two generations before Guta was born, Jews were not allowed to settle in certain Polish cities. The generation before that was prohibited from owning buildings or selling liquor. But over the course of the twentieth century, Łódź turned into an industrial giant, the second-largest city in the country. Jewish factory owners, Jewish merchants, and Jewish industrialists played a key role in this growth. By 1914, Jews owned 175 factories in Łódź and made up a third of the city's population.[2]

The First World War decimated Łódź, along with many of its factories. The government did not provide any financial support to its Jewish factory owners to rebuild and even enacted some antisemitic policies in the period following the end of the war.

Yet the Jews of Łódź, including Guta and her family, managed to build a community. This was the community that Guta was born into in 1925. The boys in her neighborhood attended newly opened Jewish schools. Łódź's Jews could choose among three synagogues when they wished to go to temple. Most attended the Alte Shul, the orthodox synagogue with sparkling spires and a steel-blue dome. On Saturdays, Guta would meet her friends in the park or go see a movie. In 1939, a banner year for Hollywood, Guta might have seen *Wuthering Heights, It's a Wonderful World,* or *The Wizard of Oz* at the local cinema that summer.

Guta and her friends were all too aware of the anti-Semitism that permeated Łódź and blanketed all of Europe at the time. She knew which streets to take and which streets she should avoid if she wanted to stay away from the Polish boys and their beatings. She knew she was at her safest when she walked with other people, on the "good" streets, in broad daylight; but ultimately, if some leering Gentile wanted to attack her, they would do so, and there wasn't much she could do about it. Jews were less than half of Łódź's population, and that didn't count for nearly enough.

During the summers, the Kasz family drove twenty kilometers east of the city to the village of Wiśniowa Góra, home of the berry-filled woods. Mother Sara and her three daughters stayed in the rented spare room of a farmhouse. Father Benjamin visited them on the weekends. When I look at pictures of Wiśniowa Góra today, I see a farmhouse resting in the middle of a lush, green meadow. Woolly sheep graze in the foreground. I want my thirteen-year-old grandmother to have lived in a place this idyllic, like something out of a fairy tale. Maybe this is why I like to think of her as that girl in the forest. I want her to have had some knowledge of peace before her life changed forever.

On September 1, 1939, Germany invaded Poland. One week later, the German army occupied Łódź. Over the next few weeks, the German army issued the following decrees: Jews were forbidden from engaging in the textiles industry; Jewish businesses were seized by the Germans; Jews were not allowed to leave the city without special permission; synagogue services were forbidden; and Jewish-owned bank accounts were blocked. Among these decrees was an order forbidding Jews from owning cars or radios. But Guta's father, who had sold radio antennas, hoarded a secret radio the family huddled around, listening for news from the outside world. From then on, Guta rarely left her house. On October 20, 1939, she celebrated her fourteenth birthday with stern-faced German soldiers patrolling the streets.

Łódź was officially annexed to the German Reich on November 9. A week later, the Germans destroyed all of Łódź's synagogues, including the Alte Shul. Collapsed towers of the bombed-out synagogues lay defeated on the earth and were slowly buried by uncaring snow.

The Germans required that Jews identify themselves by wearing a yellow Star of David pinned to their clothing. They also required all non-German shop owners to place signs in their store windows that showed if the owner was Polish or Jewish. Perhaps the Jews were not surprised by what came next.

Friedrich Uebelhoer was the German governor of Nazi-occupied Łódź and neighboring Kalisz. Uebelhoer had served in the Imperial German

Army during World War I. He had a long, thin face, a receding hairline, and a bone-deep disgust for the Jewish people. That winter he sent the following confidential memo to his police force: "Jews must be placed in a closed ghetto. . . . We must succeed in drawing out all of the valuables squirreled away by the Jews. . . . It is obvious that the establishment of the ghetto is only a transitional measure. I reserve for myself the decision when and by what means the city of Łódź will be cleansed of Jews. In any case, the final aim must be to burn out entirely this pestilent abscess."[3]

On December 10, 1939, he ordered the construction of the Łódź ghetto. The Nazis established the ghetto in the northeastern section of Łódź. It was 1.5 square miles in size, and for the most part, it had no running water or sewers. Barbed wire surrounded the ghetto's perimeter, and special police units guarded all entry points. On February 8, 1940, the Nazis had finished the ghetto's construction and began forcing the city's Jews—about 160,000 people, including Guta and her family—to relocate to this small area.

Benjamin Kasz had a Gentile friend who was forced to vacate a small, two-room house in the ghetto. This is where the family—Guta, her two sisters, her parents, her grandmother, and a cousin—lived for four years. Their lives became severely compressed. The special police guarding the ghetto's perimeter had authorization to shoot any Jew seen crawling through the barbed wire fence or leaving the ghetto without permission. If a Jew was caught throwing smuggled goods or money over the fence, or receiving smuggled goods, they were shot on sight. If a Jew went to the fence after the 9:00 p.m. curfew, they were shot without warning. The few who disobeyed this rule were indeed shot and killed.

Guta and her sisters were always talking about food, how they didn't have it, how much they wanted it. Around them, the ghetto's residents died from starvation, cold, sickness, or exhaustion. This was, of course, the purpose of the ghetto. Throughout the early 1940s, over forty-three thousand people in the Łódź ghetto died—a quarter of its population.

Since Łódź had been such an industrial hub, the Germans used it as a major production center for their war effort. In May 1940 they established factories within the ghettos and forced the Jewish inmates to provide free labor. Factory workers worked ten- to twelve-hour shifts and received thin, watery broth for their meals. Guta was sent to work in a factory where she cut rags and sewed the pieces into rugs and blankets to warm the German soldiers who kept her imprisoned. Meanwhile, people around her died of hypothermia.

From 1941 to 1942, forty thousand more Jews from Germany, Austria, Luxembourg, and beyond were deported to the Łódź ghetto, along with five thousand Roma, who were placed in a segregated block within the ghetto. As more people crowded into the tight area, diseases like typhoid fever and tuberculosis spread. Food became even more scarce. Thousands more died.

Guta feared deportation at every moment. From January to September 1942, the Nazis had deported seventy thousand Jews and five thousand Roma from the Łódź ghetto to the Chelmno extermination camp. In September, the Nazis demanded that the ghetto's residents surrender all of their children under age eleven and their elderly over age sixty: twenty thousand were gassed in Chelmno. The Nazis deported two thousand patients from the Łódź hospital to Chelmno. When eighteen of these patients tried to escape, the Nazis shot them. That month, the ghetto's population was reduced by half. While trudging to the factory, Guta would see the police rounding up the inmates of the surrounding blocks. She never knew when they would come for her family's block.

However, between September 1942 and May 1944, the deportations stopped. Guta and her family were spared. They worked in the factories along with 90 percent of the ghetto's residents. They swapped information about the war effort with their neighbors, along with stories of thousands gassed in Auschwitz in the south and Treblinka in the northeast. Rumors of an uprising in the Warsaw ghetto reached their ears in 1943. Later, these rumors would be replaced by stories of the Warsaw ghetto being recaptured by the Germans.

By May 1944, Łódź was the last remaining ghetto in Poland. Seventy-five thousand Jews lived there, including Guta and her family. Miraculously, both parents and all three daughters were still alive, having survived starvation, cold, and disease. But in the next month the Germans resumed their deportations, sending three thousand to Chelmno and transferring the rest to concentration camps.

Guta's family was on the last transport out of Łódź on August 29, 1944. Their train car was so crowded that there was only room to stand for the 230-kilometer journey. As the train rumbled and bumped its way south, I imagine Guta wrapped her arms around Fredda and Brenda so they would manage to stay upright in the crush of people. Their mother, Sara, might have worn a scarf tied around her head, too exhausted to cry, while their father, Benjamin, held his wife's hand, staring mutely at the rusted walls of the train car. They were bound for Auschwitz. Guta was eighteen years old.

When they reached Auschwitz, the men and women were ordered to form two separate lines. Typically, new arrivals to Auschwitz could expect there to be a "selection," in which the SS doctors would pick out the elderly and women with young children to be sent to the gas chambers. But when Guta's family arrived, there was no selection. Guta, her mother, and her sisters stood together with the women. Benjamin stood with the men. They tried to keep eye contact with each other from their separate rows, but the mass of people was so crowded they lost sight of each other.

Luckily for Guta's family, there was no work at Auschwitz. The camp was overcrowded. The women were processed and assigned to a barracks in the men's section. Two hundred women slept in multitiered bunks. At night, men entered the barracks and raped some of the women. Guta heard their screams from the end of the barracks, where she and her sisters cowered in an upper bunk with their mother covering their heads as if to shelter them from the sounds. Guta and her family stood at attention for roll call for hours at a time, twice a day. After two weeks, their entire transport was shipped to Stutthof, a concentration camp in northern Poland.

Stutthof, Guta remembered, "was worse than Auschwitz." The women slept on bare floors, and lice spread throughout the barracks. Again there were droning roll calls. The guards in Stutthof would enter the women's barracks at night and rape them. One night, a drunk Nazi guard walked into the latrine while Guta was using the bathroom. He picked her up like a rag doll and carried her through the length of the barracks to the living quarters he shared with the other guards. Sara watched helplessly from one of the upper bunks, petrified with fear. Guta struggled in the soldier's arms. She was sure she would be raped or worse. Then she and the soldier passed the barracks supervisor, a Jew from Czechoslovakia. From the arms of the Nazi guard, she begged the supervisor to save her life. After he exchanged some words with the drunk guard, he told Guta to go back to her bunk. Guta raced back to where her mother silently wept, scared to death and utterly helpless.

Two months after her near-rape, Guta, her family, and about five hundred other prisoners were transported again, this time to Dresden, Germany, where they worked as slave labor for the munitions plant. Guta operated a machine in the basement. The women were housed in a large room with bunk beds. When it was time to bathe, the kitchen staff brought them buckets of hot water, which was cause to rejoice. At lunch they each received a bowl of soup. When Guta was done with her soup, she would try to return the empty bowl to the kitchen so she could sneak a glimpse into the men's quarters, hoping to see her father. A day came when she spotted him lying in a cot in the infirmary. Seeing that nobody was around, she went inside to speak to him, but he was still and cold. He must have died just minutes before Guta found him. She turned back, ran to where her mother and sisters were, and told them Benjamin was dead. They all started to cry hysterically but they had no time to grieve. They had to return to their factory work.

On February 13, 1945, the British Royal Air Force began bombing the city. The bombing, which lasted for two days, killed an estimated thirty-five thousand people.[4] When the bombing started, the SS guards came into the women's barracks and tried to force them to take cover in the basement. At first the women didn't budge. They were all long past caring whether they lived or died. It wasn't until a nearby explosion blasted shards of glass from the window that the women made a hasty escape to the basement.

The next day, the SS guards led the women through the city. Guta picked her way over the rubble on skinny legs. She watched desperate parents clutching their children as they fled the city. Her eyes landed on the corpses of two British pilots lying on the ground. She trudged on with her mother and sisters out of the city, into a barren field. After a day of waiting, the guards took the women back to the factory. The guards sent the women to work rebuilding the bombed post office, but after a few weeks, they received news that the Russian army was approaching Dresden. Guta and her family were put on another train.

Soon the train reached a section of track that British bombs had ruined, forcing the women to disembark from the transport somewhere near the Poland-Czechoslovakia border. When it was their turn to get off the train, Guta's twenty-one-year-old sister Fredda didn't get up. She was too sick and weak to rise, so her mother and sisters were forced to leave her behind in the train car. Guta never saw her older sister again.

The SS guards led the women on a death march. For days, they went without food. Some of them dropped dead from starvation, exhaustion, or both. One night, Guta and two other women sneaked out of the barn they were locked in and knocked on neighbors' doors, begging for food. A few people gave them soup and bread, earning the Czech people my grandmother's good graces for the rest of her days.

On the morning of May 8, 1945, Guta and the other women woke to realize that the SS guards had fled. Soviet soldiers were on the horizon, riding bicycles toward them. The women, despite how starved and weak they were, sprinted towards the Russians with shouts and whoops. The Russians gave them food and medical care, as well as clothes from the suitcases the SS guards had abandoned. Guta, now twenty years old, shrugged into her new clothes and hugged her surviving sister, her mother, and anyone else who was grateful to be alive. The past six years did not seem real; maybe they felt like nothing more than a bad dream.

The Russians put all of the women on a train back to Poland. Guta, her mother, and her sister were ready to go home, but while changing trains in Prague, they met other survivors who had just fled Poland. "Don't go back," the men warned, "they're killing the Jews." So the women stayed in Prague.

While Guta and her sister were walking down the street in Prague one day, they came across a group of survivors. One of them was named

Chaskel Kliger, and the second he saw Guta, he fell in love. I don't know if my grandmother's feelings were half as strong as my grandfather's. In all the time I saw them together, I never saw any real affection flowing from my grandmother toward my grandfather, or toward any other man for that matter. Of course, it is strange for anyone to think about their grandparents as sexual beings, but I think my grandmother was a specific case. Her greatest source of pleasure came from the fact that she could stretch the same emerald-green bottle of Bactine that she'd had since the '50s or that the only cleanser she used on her face was a bar of Dove soap.

But Guta needed a husband, and Chaskel was already devoted to her and had taken the steps to bind his life to hers as quickly as possible. He was fifteen years her senior and had been married before. His first wife was killed in one of the Nazi camps, and his two-year-old daughter was slaughtered with other children in the Łódź ghetto in 1939. I never heard him talk about the daughter and wife he lost in the war, but I believe that when he met Guta, he wanted to start over and have a family that wouldn't be ripped away from him. Guta, Chaskel, and their surviving relatives moved to the American occupation zone in Germany and settled in the city of Plattling. They sent Brenda to America along with other adoptable children, and she was settled with a family in Atlanta.

Guta and Chaskel married on December 16, 1947. Guta's mother, Sara, wrote letters to America, looking for her relatives who had immigrated to the States before the war started. The American Kaszes responded to Sara's notice and vouched for their Eastern European relatives to immigrate to the United States. Guta, Chaskel, and Sara applied for visas and arrived in New York in June 1949. Chaskel Kliger changed his name to Henry Peckanowski, which he would later Anglicize to Peck. They left the war, the camps, and their dead behind them.

I didn't learn the story of my grandmother's life until a year before she died. I finally convinced her to share her story, which she did in an interview with the Beverly Hills *Jewish Journal*.[5] My grandpa Henry had passed away in the '80s, and great-grandmother Sara died—or, as I like to say, she left her physical body—in the '90s. Grandma Guta was the only one who remained from that generation.

For years, all I had known about Grandma Guta's experiences in the Holocaust were the snippets I picked up like grains of rice dropped on the floor. Even though nobody ever told me not to ask her about those years, I knew she had suffered unimaginable loss. I also knew that, just a year after Guta had finally arrived in America, her younger sister Brenda died in Atlanta. (She had survived the Holocaust but accidentally swallowed a chicken bone and died of intestinal strangulation.)

Grandpa Henry also never spoke about his experiences in the camps. Instead he would check on me compulsively, paranoid that I would disappear, constantly asking *Where is Allison? Where is Allison? Where is Allison?*

Shortly after Grandma Guta died, I learned about Grandpa Henry's first family before he met my grandmother: a drowned wife, a murdered daughter, and, as I later learned, a son who had survived. This first family was a mirror image of the family he created with Guta. In September 1942, in the Lødz ghetto, the Nazis picked up Grandpa Henry's first daughter, two-year-old Pola, in their roundup of children and the elderly. She was massacred along with the rest. The Nazis took Grandpa Henry's first wife, Deborah, to a women's-only concentration camp on the shore of the Baltic Sea. When the war turned and the Allies descended on Poland, the Nazis at that camp took their remaining inmates out to sea and threw them overboard, drowning all of them. We believe Deborah was one of the drowned.

As for Grandpa Henry's first son, George Kliger, he retained his father's original surname. He was told to declare himself an orphan and was sent with other surviving Jewish orphans to America. He was adopted by a family in Minnesota and grew up to become a professor of humanities at the University of Minnesota. I did not learn about George's existence until 2016, the same year Grandma Guta died. It was George who told me about Grandpa Henry's first family, the ghosts that haunted my grandfather and likely fueled his constant need to know where I was, to know I was safe.

Nobody had to take me aside and warn me not to bring up difficult memories for my grandparents. I never wanted to do anything that might disturb the simplicity of our relationship, the easy symbiosis we lived in. Every day after school, I would go to Guta's squat, salmon-pink house on Le Doux Road in Beverly Hills, sit at the Formica table in her kitchen, and do my homework while she listened to talk radio station KFI 640. She would scramble eggs with onions or spread a pat of margarine on a slice of toast and set the plate before me. Only then would I realize I was hungry.

My mother worked long hours at her law firm, so I would be with my grandmother until after sunset. When my homework was finished, I would scribble short stories onto random sheets of crisp white paper or legal pads stolen from my mother's office. They were dark, disturbing thrillers about being kidnapped and left for dead, my grandfather's worst nightmare. But when I handed my drafts to Grandma Guta, she would stop whatever she was doing to sit down and read them. Then she would nod approvingly and tuck the drafts away into a manila folder she kept in one of her kitchen drawers. I knew they would be waiting for me when I wanted to revisit them.

And they were. While we settled her affairs after her death in 2016, I found some of the stories I had written as a child, still stored in her files. She'd held onto them all that time.

In 1980, the diagnosis of posttraumatic stress disorder (PTSD) was added to the third edition of the *Diagnostic and Statistical Manual of Mental Disorders (DSM.)*[6] Researchers began to work with veterans of the Vietnam War to better understand the disorder. At that time an estimated 30 percent of Vietnam veterans were suffering from PTSD, a higher percentage than any group of veterans in history, according to the National Center for PTSD in the US Department of Veterans Affairs (VA).[7]

Unlike soldiers from previous conflicts, Vietnam vets faced a negative reception when they returned home from war. Their sacrifices on the battlefield were never acknowledged. Forced to suffer in silence, many of these veterans started to experience flashbacks, crippling anxiety, and other symptoms of PTSD.

Besides the addition of PTSD to the *DSM,* the '80s also marked the beginning of two major developments for the field of neuroscience. Neuroimaging techniques like PET scans and MRI machines were just coming into use, and thanks to these tools, neuroscientists were able to identify the biological markers of stress and trauma. They also began to recognize the existence of stress hormone receptors in the brain. The existence of stress hormone receptors meant that the brain did not simply issue commands to organs like the adrenal glands, which produced stress hormones. It had to be a two-way relationship. The presence of receptors in the brain meant stress hormones also had to influence the way the brain operated and developed.

In the early '80s, a grad student named Rachel Yehuda found herself in the VA conducting research for her PhD in psychiatry and neuroscience. She was looking for the biological markers of this newly recognized diagnosis, PTSD. The VA, full of traumatized Vietnam veterans, was the perfect place for her to do this work. She learned about the existence of stress hormone receptors and decided to test the idea that the relationship between the brain and stress is dynamic. She tested the theory with rats by removing the adrenal glands from the brains of infant rat pups. The rat pups without adrenal glands developed brains that were 15 percent larger than the brains of the control group. It was clear that stress hormones affected brain development. Yehuda also started studying the levels of cortisol, the stress hormone, in vets who had PTSD. She found that, against all expectations, the vets with PTSD had lower levels of cortisol. It didn't make sense.

Yehuda was raised by observant Jewish parents in a Cleveland neighborhood heavily populated by Holocaust survivors.[8] After getting this surprising result from the Vietnam vets, she decided to look at Holocaust survivors. Did they also have lower levels of cortisol? Her research found that Holocaust survivors had similarly low levels of cortisol. In many ways, the Holocaust survivors suffered a PTSD very similar to the Vietnam veterans. They also had nightmares, flashbacks, and severe anxiety. The difference was that the Holocaust survivors did not have their equivalent of a VA, so after she completed her PhD, Yehuda established a clinic for Holocaust survivors at Mount Sinai Hospital in New York City.

It was at Mount Sinai that Yehuda and her research team found the subjects for a longitudinal study of Holocaust survivors and their descendants. From 1993 to 1995, Yehuda's team recruited forty Holocaust survivors, meaning people who had undergone any of the following experiences during World War II: imprisonment in Nazi concentration camps, being tortured or witnessing torture, or having to flee their homes or hide. Ten years later, Yehuda asked those forty subjects if they might refer their offspring to the study so she and her team could examine the intergenerational effects of trauma.

In 2015, Yehuda's book *How Trauma and Resilience Cross Generations* made its way around the major media outlets, sparking headlines such as "Study of Holocaust Survivors Finds Trauma Passed on to Children's Genes."[9] The study's findings were telling. Children born to mothers with Holocaust-related PTSD had brains that were more reactive to stress.[10] Yehuda's research was a contribution to the young and growing field of epigenetics. According to the tenets of epigenetics, traumatic experiences can affect the way your genes are expressed, turning off some genes and turning on others. Not only do these epigenetic changes affect the person who directly experienced that trauma; the changes also affect their children and their children's children. Also, I think they help one deal with high-stress environments in a way that reflects the upside of what may be a genetic modification caused by the trauma.

Parents who survived the Holocaust likely passed on more than PTSD to their children. In studies of the way that depression is passed down through the family tree, male mice who suffered extreme stress in infancy fathered female mice with "depression-like behavior."[11] Even if the mouse mothers were stable and nurturing, and the traumatized fathers contributed nothing to child care, the mouse daughters showed signs of depression. This trait persisted for two generations, passing on to the mouse grandchildren.

Given these findings on intergenerational trauma, nobody should be surprised that some of the leading thinkers on addiction are the descendants of Holocaust survivors. One such person is journalist Maia Szalavitz, a former cocaine and heroin addict, the daughter of a Holocaust survivor, and the author of *Unbroken Brain: A Revolutionary New Way of Understanding Addiction.*

Szalavitz's father, Miklos, was five or six years old when the Nazis began rounding up Hungary's Jews. In 1944, he was taken to Strasshof concentration camp in Austria along with his mother and two-year-old sister. Because of the Nazi policy to kill all women with young children—as well as the children themselves—in concentration camps, Miklos should have died. In fact, his family was on a transport to Auschwitz when the Allies moved in to liberate them. He was literally on the road to hell—the gas chambers.

When Miklos Szalavitz entered the first grade after the war ended, he was so traumatized that he could not speak. His teachers believed he was intellectually disabled. Indeed, the muteness that afflicted Miklos is a common result of traumatization. Dr. Bessel van der Kolk, an acclaimed neuroscientist and the author of *The Body Keeps the Score: Brain, Mind, and Body in the Healing of Trauma,* made a career out of studying the biological effects of trauma. He took PET scans of the brains of trauma victims while asking them about the trauma they had experienced. When the victims were asked to remember their trauma, the part of the brain known as Broca's area—one of the brain's speech centers—showed a white spot, meaning there was a significant decrease in the functioning of that part of the brain. Whenever the victim experienced a flashback, their Broca's area stopped working, and they lost their ability to speak.[12]

The stress Miklos endured not only affected his ability to speak; it also led to epigenetic changes, affecting the chemicals that regulate genes. Epigenetic changes do not change the DNA that transmits genetic information; what they do is change the structures around the DNA so that this genetic information is read differently. The trauma Miklos endured during World War II contributed to his depression and inability to speak, and he passed those epigenetic changes on to his daughter, Maia. Like the mouse daughters of Yehuda's study, she inherited her father's depression.[13]

Stress causes a decrease in an infant's dopamine receptors. Dopamine, the neurotransmitter responsible for the brain's pleasure and reward systems, floods the brain when you exercise, eat delicious food, or use just about any recreational drug. When dopamine decreases due to what researchers call "adverse childhood experiences" (ACEs), the dopamine incentive-motivation system is permanently disrupted.[14]

Changes to this system increase a person's risk of addiction. In one study, researchers found that rat pups who were separated from their mothers for just an hour a day in their first week of life were much more eager to take cocaine in adulthood than their peers who had never experienced maternal separation.[15] Cocaine provides the dopamine their brains cannot produce, supplying the answer to a question the rats don't even understand.

Not only do ACEs affect the dopamine system, but there are studies showing that infants in stressful environments have lower levels of other crucial brain chemicals, like the receptors for benzodiazepines, which soothe anxiety. "Benzos" like Valium and Xanax can easily be purchased on the street.

Infants who do not receive enough nurturing from their parents also show a decrease in serotonin, the neurotransmitter enhanced by selective serotonin reuptake inhibitors like Prozac and Lexapro. A study conducted with monkeys found that monkeys that had been separated from their mothers and raised by their peers had lower levels of serotonin than monkeys who had been raised by their mothers for their whole lives.[16] Furthermore, the peer-raised monkeys were more likely to abuse alcohol and to be more aggressive in adolescence.

When these crucial brain chemicals get out of whack during infancy, these children grow into adults who are especially fearful, anxious, or hyperactive. They are more sensitive to stress than their nontraumatized peers; as a result, they are more prone to abuse substances that will help them cope with that stress.

When I researched this chapter, I came across the story of Dr. Gabor Maté, an addiction expert based in Vancouver, British Columbia—and, you guessed it, another descendant of Holocaust survivors. For decades, Maté has worked with the addicted people in Vancouver's troubled Downtown Eastside neighborhood. His book *In the Realm of Hungry Ghosts: Close Encounters with Addiction* catalogues their stories, rife with alcohol-induced violence, dislocation, neglect, and physical, sexual, and emotional abuse—a veritable who's who of ACEs. When I read their accounts, I was not shocked by the severity of their addictions; instead, I was surprised that any of them had managed to survive.

Yet it was Maté's own story that stuck with me. He isn't addicted to heroin, crack, or methamphetamines. Instead, since his youth, he compulsively buys multiple copies of the same Beethoven overture, a habit that he cannot seem to break. (By the way, Maté has gone on to become the scientific advisor to what's becoming an internationally known magic mushroom company currently traded on the stock exchange.[17])

Maté explored his own addiction in *Hungry Ghosts* with Dr. Aviel Goodman, a specialist in behavioral addictions, specifically sex addiction.[18] Goodman noted that Maté apparently lacked the hormone oxytocin in his childhood. Oxytocin is the love hormone, the chemical responsible for the warm, fuzzy feeling you get when you hug someone you love or hold a puppy in your arms. It enables humans to form loving connections with each other and create lasting, intimate relationships. Infants who are not held enough by their parents experience steep drops in oxytocin and find it difficult to form strong emotional connections as they mature, which is, not surprisingly, another risk factor for addiction.

Goodman suggested Maté was not cuddled by his parents in his infancy, but he was able to hear, making his auditory processing his strongest means of forming emotional connections. Maté was born to Jewish parents in Budapest in 1944. When he looked back on his own childhood, he remembered:

> For the first fifteen months of my life my father was away in a forced labor camp, and for most of that time neither of my parents knew whether the other was alive or dead. I was five months old when my grandparents were killed at Auschwitz. Many years later, not long before her own death at age eighty-two in Vancouver, my mother told me that she was so depressed after her parents' murder that some days she got out of bed only to look after me. I was left alone in my crib quite often.[19]

While alone in his crib, the infant Gabor Maté's only comfort was the classical music his mother played in their home. His compulsive shopping addiction, therefore, was an effort to soothe himself, providing him with the oxytocin he was deprived of as a baby.

The study of intergenerational trauma is a growing field. More people are studying how one's environment and life experience affect their genes and the genes of the next generation. The body remembers trauma that happened two generations ago, which means you are affected on a cellular level by the stress that your parents and grandparents endured. This stress is not limited to large-scale tragedies like the Holocaust; it can be as macro as institutionalized slavery and as micro as domestic violence within one's family. In his book *It Didn't Start with You,* Dr. Mark Wolynn goes into scientific detail about the way your parents and grandparents will affect how your own genes are expressed: "In your earliest biological form, as an unfertilized egg, you already share a cellular environment with your mother and grandmother. When your grandmother was five months pregnant with your mother, the precursor cell of the egg you developed from was already present in your mother's ovaries."[20]

I haven't taken a science class since the '90s, but I imagine this process in terms of a *matryoshka,* a Russian nesting doll. You open one doll to find another, smaller doll inside it, and another, smaller doll inside that one, until you get to the doll of the baby, as small as the tip of my pinky finger. If the largest doll is affected by a traumatic event, like the Holocaust, that experience will affect the smaller dolls nestled within it.

There has been untold suffering in the world, of course: institutionalized slavery, Chernobyl, hurricanes, earthquakes, genocide—you get the picture. Most people will have suffered the impact of intergenerational trauma. However, this does not mean that people who have suffered abuse or misfortune are doomed, along with their children and their children's children. As with so much else in life, a lot depends on your perspective.

I didn't know this at the time, but I was lucky to have been born in Los Angeles in the late 1970s. I was lucky to have been raised by an overprotective mother, a paranoid grandfather, and my dark, wry, resilient Grandma Guta. I have a memory of her from the night of the 1994 Northridge earthquake, which struck California's San Fernando Valley with a quake measuring 6.7 on the Richter scale. I was spending the night at Grandma Guta's house in Beverly Hills, only sixteen miles from the epicenter. At around 5:00 a.m., my shaking bed woke me up. I'm a native Angeleno; earthquakes are de rigueur. But this one was violent. As I looked out through the sliding glass door to Grandma's little backyard, it looked like lightning was flashing.

I trotted on shaky legs to my grandmother's room down the hall. She was already up. She told me to grab some candles from the kitchen. I retrieved them and snuggled into her bed. The house was dark except for the flickering candle, silent except for her muttering to herself. The room illuminated in a flash from behind me. I turned to look out my grandmother's bedroom window, facing the backyard, to see transformers explode into sparks that tore at the night sky. I was nervous and jumpy, but Grandma Guta laughed.

She struck a match, lit a candle, and produced a deck of cards. We played until the sun rose.

4

JUMPING MOUSE

WHEN I WAS LITTLE, my dad told me the story of Jumping Mouse, a magical little rodent from Native American mythology, who sets out for a far-off land only to lose his sight and smell along the way when he gives his senses to other animals who have lost them and can't function without them. All along, he maintains hope, encouraged by his friend, the magic frog who gave him the power to bestow others with these abilities. Jumping Mouse continues on his journey toward his dharma and is rewarded when the magic frog transforms him into a healthy and powerful eagle so he can finish his journey.

Grandma Guta hated my father immediately, she said, but she also had a soft spot in her heart for him, which lasted far longer than my parents' four-year stint as a married couple. Grandma took in his tangled, rabbinic beard, his tanned face, and his shifting hazel eyes as the markers of an amoral hippie with the ability to have two wives and a girlfriend in the same San Fernando Valley. Subconsciously, she probably associated him with hypocritical religious people she'd known in the ghetto. In addition to these already pretty bad associations, my dad had to contend with the fact that he really looked like the kind of person that the Establishment—and a recent European immigrant—would associate with serial killers like Charles Manson. Of course, my dad could have changed his look after the Manson Family's Tate–LaBianca murders scared Angelenos that summer of '69. As chance would have it, a bookshelf in Guta's house was later macabrely decorated by a book that had a goosebump-inducing, hair-raising, blood-red, handwritten *Helter Skelter* adorning its black cover.

I used to think my dad was the beginning and the end of humanity, the alpha and omega. Before his girlfriends disrupted our friendship, I was his best bud. Even though my parents divorced before I turned two, he was the one who drove me to gymnastics practice, toting a clunky camcorder to record my tumbles. Charismatic, gregarious, bounding with enthusiasm to the point that I had to ask him to quiet down so I could do my homework, the dad of my youth was Dr. Jekyll. I tried not to share too much of my adoration with my mother and grandmother, the women who raised me. They noticed, however. They always watched me so closely.

I must have been five or six years old one day when Dad and I were sitting in his kitchen. He was teaching me about manifesting physical realities, something he'd learned from his friend Ram Dass. He met me at eye level, like he was a child, too.

"The teachers tell us we contain the complete power of the universe within us," he said. "In fact, we are so powerful that it can be frightening. But it doesn't need to be."

I didn't understand him yet. He sensed my confusion.

"The point is that because we have a universe within us, our thoughts have power," he explained. "Whatever we think of, we can achieve. By recognizing your own power, you can manifest anything you can imagine."

This sounded good to me. "How about a basket of puppies?"

He sat back on his heels and stroked his chin, as if deeply contemplating the prospect. "I don't see why not."

Under his guidance, I tried to channel the energy of the universe within me as I pictured my basket of puppies. I even imagined the type of puppies—mainly chocolate labs and golden retrievers—because I didn't want to end up with something I hadn't expected. Dad watched me focus on this image in my head; then he watched me run out the front door, looking for that basket. I couldn't believe it when it didn't work. But actually, it did; as Dad says, "Mohammed went to the mountain. The mountain didn't come to Mohammed." Soon I was lucky enough to always have a few dogs on hand. Currently, I have a pack of them, plus four cats, a hamster, a bearded dragon, a chameleon, their prey, and crickets that every night chirp super loud but are deeply reminiscent of my nights on Rembert Lane in Coldwater Canyon, in a world away from the city, dominated by the noises of nature, the howls of the coyotes.

"This kind of thing takes practice," he said.

I sincerely believe in the power of manifestation. I have had miraculous outcomes throughout my career, and the fact I have cool children is also a miracle of manifestation. (Although I am not into bragging about them—bad mojo.) I used to imagine them, and here they are, better than anything I ever expected. I think my dad ascribes his success to his powers of manifestation, and I think he created a myth around his own origins to explain his rise from poverty. How else does someone survive the childhood he lived?

I know Dad was born in Cleveland, Ohio, in 1941. His parents, Arel and Pearl Margolin, already had a son, who must have been at least eight years old when Dad was born. I don't know much about Arel's family except that they were Russian Jews; they had to fake an American birth certificate for Arel to immigrate at six months old. Pearl was an orphan. In Arel's official job he was a drill sergeant in the army, but he supplemented his income by promoting underground boxing events around town. The nation was slowly waking up from the Depression, and in Cleveland anyway, the men who had been so ruled by poverty could treat money as callously as it had treated them. They placed bets, won and lost wages, and swung their fists at each other instead of at their wives. Arel was the unspoken organizer of these rings, and he had a man in the police department whom he paid to turn a blind eye to the proceedings. Not long after Dad was born, Arel got a tip from the city sheriff that the police were setting up a raid on one of his rings and had Arel's handcuffs polished and ready. With the heat on him, Arel moved his young family to a place where anyone could disappear: the San Fernando Valley.

The Valley of the '40s and '50s was 260 square miles of lawless country. Out of curiosity, I looked up pictures of the Valley from this time period, and it is as desolate as anything you might imagine. There was nothing to indicate human life but the dirt roads cutting through miles and miles of shrubland and orange orchards. People lived so far apart from each other that a man could have three different families in three different towns without any danger of his wives finding out.

Without their Cleveland connections and Arel's side income as boxing promoter, the Margolins were dead broke—part of a tribe I like to call the "Lost Jews of the Valley." When I try to imagine Dad's childhood, it looks like something out of *The Grapes of Wrath*. In actuality, there must have been moments of levity. Dad used to tell me about how he used to ditch school all the time to dance on *American Bandstand*. It was part of the reason why he could barely write when he graduated.

When my father's brother Ralph was old enough, sometime in the early '50s, he left the family to join the armed services. The GI Bill was still around, and Ralph planned on using the money to pay for law school. The United States was in the midst of the Cold War; the threat of nuclear warfare hung over everyone's heads. The military charged forward in its arms race to outpace the nuclear capability of the Soviets. After Ralph finished his time in the army, he enrolled in the local college. Despite his scattered education, Ralph graduated and earned a place at UCLA's law school.

Meanwhile, Dad was working at his father's paint store. During this time, Arel started the Valley's first free temple, a place for the lost Jews to congregate. My dad wasn't religious at all when Arel opened the temple. He was a young man of sixteen when his brother entered law school. At this time everything seemed to be on the upswing for the Margolins.

Ralph was at the center of the first tragedy. While at UCLA, the once-vibrant and active young man started to complain of fatigue and weakness. Ralph dropped weight from what had already been a compact frame. The doctors diagnosed him with leukemia. Unfortunately, Ralph was one of the tens of thousands of workers who had been exposed to atomic bomb testing at a Nevada test site, and he had contracted cancer from the resultant radiation.[1] Radiation, like communism, was an invisible enemy, and in the end, it turned out to be even more deadly. Ralph hadn't even been a serviceman when he was poisoned; this was something that happened during ROTC training! The cancer acted rapidly, consuming him within a couple of months.

That same year, Dad's father went into surgery with heart complications and died on the operating table. The surgeon made a mistake by using "dirty blood," or at least that is the limited information I have been told. I do know that after Dad's father died within weeks of his brother's passing, he went to the free temple Arel had started.

He sat in the temple his father had built, questioned the existence of God, and wondered what the point was of being a good Jew when you could die so suddenly. From what I understand, Dad didn't pursue any kind of spiritual life for another fifteen years.

There is evidence that trauma experienced in childhood can stunt emotional and intellectual growth.[2] If this is true, then it makes sense that my father has always seemed more like a peer than a parent, someone who never emotionally progressed beyond adolescence. I used to wonder about the man he might have become if not for the untimely loss of his father and brother when he was sixteen. He's described his dad to me as a good, kind man. About his brother, he only likes to say that Ralph was so cheap he would sit at a parking meter until it ran out. This might have been Dad's way of coping—to press these important figures into two-dimensional shapes. Their untimely, tragic deaths served the superman origin story he told himself. Tragedy was no stranger to the people of the Valley, and what doesn't kill you eventually makes for a good story to tell at cocktail parties in the Hollywood Hills. I imagine this difficult beginning added to Dad's internal myth of himself as a David up against the Goliath of death and poverty.

Dad started working at Leed's Shoes to help make ends meet. He applied and was accepted to Valley College. Occasionally, he would go to events where the famous LA attorney Barry Tarlow was speaking. Tarlow was a graduate of Harvard Law School who was famous in the '60s and practiced law almost until his death in 2021. I think my dad viewed Tarlow in a more inspirational light than his brother who died in law school, idolizing the handsome, successful lawyer. Still, Dad probably would not have gone to law school if he hadn't become friends with someone who told him about Southwestern College's night school law program, which, at that time, accepted people out of junior college.

Dad's mother, Pearl, was his only living relative. She died in the early '80s. I don't remember much about my paternal grandmother, except that she once made green Jell-O for me and Dad. I'm not sure why I didn't realize at the first bite that I hated it; I never had Jell-O again except maybe one or two Jell-O shots in college. After we left Pearl's Fulton Avenue apartment off Ventura Boulevard, I hurled green vomit out of my Dad's car window while we drove down the boulevard and headed over the canyon. Although Pearl wasn't a kind woman, she depended on Dad for financial support for the rest of her life. It was one of many points of contention between my parents. Dad was always nice to her, always coming to her rescue, even though she was emotionally abusive toward him. Apparently, none of his efforts ever softened his mother's treatment of him.

I used to wonder about my dad's habit of dating younger women who never seemed to particularly care for him. Although there's no way to confirm this, I think the deaths of his father and brother put him in a state of arrested development. He always dated younger women because he had never matured emotionally. In addition, I wonder if Pearl's mistreatment of my dad influenced him to pursue emotionally distant women. Mom's descriptions of Pearl depict a hard woman who was impossible to please. Surely, the loss of her husband and oldest son must have left its mark on her. Their deaths had certainly affected my dad, stagnating his development, I'm convinced. However, for the longest time, I could not imagine why my dad would return to anyone who had been so mean and callous to him, even if that someone was his mother. I could not understand how or why someone would return over and over again to a mother who was neither maternal nor particularly kind.

From my father, I have inherited hazel eyes and an olive complexion—the same tanned skin that gave the police officers of the San Fernando Valley the impression that Dad was Hispanic and therefore deserved to be harassed every chance they got. I guess it's odd to suggest that my Eastern European Jew father was subjected to a midcentury version of stop-and-frisk given the police violence we are more familiar with today, but the fact remains.

Somehow Dad made it into the associate's degree program at Valley College. By his own admission, he could barely read or write when he applied to law school. It seemed like a miracle when he was accepted. He loves to illustrate how ill-prepared he was for law school with the story of getting back his first exam. When the professor announced the highest grade in the class, she made a point of saying, "This is the highest grade in the class, and it had *four* words misspelled in the first sentence." When she proceeded to read the paper, Bruce realized it was his exam and called out to the professor to claim responsibility. At that point, the professor smiled and commented, "Don't worry. When you become a real lawyer, you'll have a secretary to type up your papers."[3]

I think the certainty behind that "when" is what convinced Bruce he could be a lawyer after all. He realized that the secret to being a good criminal lawyer was telling a convincing story in plain language to the judge and jury.

Even though his youth had been difficult, Dad had good timing. He started law school in 1964, just one year after the first state marijuana arrest was made in California. When Bruce enrolled in school, major changes were being made around search and seizure laws, starting with the *Mapp v. Ohio* case in 1961.[4] Prior to *Mapp,* the decision of whether or not to follow the exclusionary rule—which allowed the exclusion of evidence seized illegally—was left to the states. The Supreme Court decision in *Mapp* applied the exclusionary rule to all of the states as part of the due process ensured by the Fourteenth Amendment. This meant that for the first time, local police had to have warrants to search and seize an individual's property.

Five years later, the Supreme Court ruled on *Miranda v. Arizona.* Miranda was an alleged kidnapper whose confession was suppressed by the police. After the Supreme Court ruling, police were required to read a list of "Miranda rights"—including the right to remain silent, in accordance with the Fifth and Sixth Amendments—to the people in their custody. At the same time that the Miranda doctrine and exclusionary rule were put in place, what would become known as the counterculture was growing in popularity. From the Haight-Ashbury neighborhood in San Francisco to Hollywood and beyond, more and more young people were scoring pot and lighting up. My dad, not realizing the serendipity of his timing, entered the practice of law when the cops didn't even know the law well enough to pretend they were following it.

By the start of the '60s, more young, white, middle-class people were smoking pot than ever before, even though marijuana possession was still a crime. America elected John F. Kennedy, who was rumored to be a fan of pot and LSD, to the White House. It was also fairly common knowledge that President Kennedy received regular shots of B-12 and methamphetamine in order to quell back spasms and maintain his rigorous schedule. He shared his doctor—Dr. Max Jacobson, who was better known as "Dr. Feelgood"—with everyone from Truman Capote to Marilyn Monroe.[5] And as marijuana became more popular, this new generation had questions: "If the government has been lying about how dangerous marijuana is, then what else are they lying about?" This was the same government that had gotten them involved in a senseless, endless, bloody war in Vietnam, if they came back at all. Families didn't recognize their empty-eyed sons, many of whom had developed heroin addictions while serving Uncle Sam.

This was also a time in US history when LSD was legal and marijuana possession was a felony. At the start of Tom Wolfe's nonfiction book *The Electric Kool-Aid Acid Test,* Stanford University graduate and *One Flew over the Cuckoo's Nest* author Ken Kesey was imprisoned for marijuana possession. Kesey and his cohort of "Merry Pranksters" were leading a series of "acid tests" in San Francisco.[6] The only reason why the legal statuses of pot and LSD changed is because of the actions of the Harvard professor turned "Pope of Dope" Timothy Leary. In 1960, Leary had his first experience with magic mushrooms while on vacation in Mexico.[7] That fall, he would assemble the members of the Harvard Psilocybin Project, which included poet Allen Ginsberg and fellow academic Richard Alpert (who would later change his name to Ram Dass).[8]

The Psilocybin Project came to an abrupt end in 1962. For two years, Leary and Alpert studied the effects of LSD on curious Harvard faculty and graduate students, but Harvard sacked both Leary and Alpert after discovering the men had been giving psychedelics to undergrads.[9]

Leary and Alpert took their own journeys—one became an enlightened yogi, and the other became "the most dangerous man in America"—but they spread a similar message: "turn on, tune in, drop out." On August 8, 1964, almost six months to the day after their historic appearance on *The Ed Sullivan Show,* the Beatles smoked their first joint.[10] Their dealer was folk singer Bob Dylan. To smoke pot or drop acid, to eat mushrooms or drink peyote tea, was to be young and cool and hip in the '60s. It was a part of the angst of that generation: they wanted to separate themselves from the very society they desperately wanted to change.

The people of Los Angeles and the rest of California were no exception. Across the city and the state, rock stars, hippies, major Hollywood players, and average Joes were getting busted for marijuana possession. Actor-turned-politician Ronald Reagan was elected governor of California in 1966 after running on a platform to lock up all hippies, junkies, commies, and other undesirables. Even though an estimated 65 million Americans were smoking pot by 1969,[11] marijuana possession was, and has remained, illegal at the federal level since the Marihuana Tax Act of 1937. That act was struck down because of Timothy Leary, of all people. In 1969, Leary was caught trying to cross the US-Mexico border with two joints in his pocket and was arrested. He made a Fifth Amendment appeal that succeeded. It was a brief win for drug users everywhere. Just one year earlier, the US government had made LSD illegal out of concerns for the growing numbers of young people who, under Leary's guidance, were tuning in and dropping out.[12]

By the time Dad graduated in 1967, the laws in California had changed so much—and were so ill-equipped to appropriately handle the rising counterculture—that the police simply could not keep up. This meant that when Dad opened the offices of Bruce Margolin, Esq., he was in a perfect position to get the marijuana possession cases of the rich dismissed. "It was like taking candy from a baby," he would say. By 1970 his practice had eight lawyers and twenty-five employees on staff, and they were raking in tens of thousands of dollars without even breaking a sweat. They had fifty cases a day on their calendar, and Dad was flying all over the country to make court appearances. It seemed that the money, the clients, and the fame would never end. But this was also a monkey on his back, not just because of his working-class roots but also because of his anticapitalist hippie idealism.

With all this success, the next logical step must have been for him to run for office. Politics seemed the thing to do for any hotshot lawyer. What's more, Dad knew he was different. He wasn't like those other stiffs on the ballot, no sir. He was going to run on a marijuana legalization platform at a time when marijuana possession was a felony.

He ran for state assembly, a Democrat hoping to represent the 57th district. Shockingly—and perhaps in a testament to his charisma and popularity at that time—Dad came dangerously close to defeating the twenty-six-year incumbent, a Republican named Charles Conrad. Dad lost by less than five percentage points. I don't know for sure, but I imagine the campaign stressed him out and made him claustrophobic. I used to hear stories about Dad's infamous excess of energy, how he would kick the walls to wear himself out before bed. Even though he is well into his seventies, I still see that same inertia, the drive telling him to go, go, go. So when I consider that inner chaos, I can understand that the pressures of running his firm and running a campaign might have gotten to him.

His girlfriend recommended a psychiatrist named Harry Segal. Dr. Segal was another Jewish guy who had become moderately famous in LA's hippest circles. He was as into Eastern medicine as all of Dad's friends were, and he gave Dad two books at the end of their first session: Carl Jung's *Man and His Symbols* and Ram Dass's *Be Here Now.* "I know where you're going," Dr. Segal told Bruce. "I just wish I could come with you." Dad took this as a sign to quit his practice and travel to India. Other factors also encouraged him to leave: 1) The Long Beach district attorney's office used an undercover cop to try to catch Dad accepting cocaine as a form of payment. My dad has never done a single line, let alone take drugs of any kind as currency. He is actually pretty straight, both in business and in personal behavior. So he didn't fall for the trap but was understandably freaked out when he learned of the setup. 2) Dad received an unusually macabre package in the mail: a custom-made, ornately decorated miniature wooden coffin containing a dead rat with a knife through its heart.

Dr. Segal would eventually quit his practice, too. I have a clear memory from around 1986: a glass house in the Hollywood Hills, Persian rugs, and Dr. Segal wearing a magician's cape and doing tricks. Later, he would have his own residency at Hollywood's famous Magic Castle. I saw his performance the first time I went.

Whether or not Dr. Segal's advice was sound, within a month, Bruce quit his practice; said his goodbyes to his girlfriend, dog, and home in the Valley; and flew to the Greek islands. He lived for almost a year in self-imposed exile, doing a lot of yoga and essentially committing *Be Here Now* to memory. He met Leonard Cohen. He learned different kinds of meditation on an Israeli kibbutz. He entered every house of worship he stumbled upon while traveling through Turkey. Finally, in 1971, he landed in Bombay, India.[13]

Dad had been away from Los Angeles for eight months before he met Ram Dass, author of the book he'd been toting across continents. When he tells the story of meeting Ram Dass, he says he manifested the yogi's presence, something he learned from *Be Here Now*. It was the same process he would try to teach me years later when I failed to conjure a basket of puppies out of thin air.

After Dad completed a ten-day silent meditation course in Bombay, he traveled to New Delhi to stay at the Palace Heights Hotel. When he checked in, he spotted Ram Dass's name scrawled in the guest book. Ram Dass had done the same silent meditation course five times for a total of fifty days before he and Dad arrived at the same hotel.

Others might call it a lucky coincidence, but Dad was convinced that he had conjured Ram Dass. He left the man a message, and they met that night. Ram Dass suggested Dad go see the Maharaji Neem Karoli Baba, and that's what he did. That's where Dad got his new yogi name: Badrinath Das.

After ten days with the Maharaji, Dad began to think about returning to the States. He flew back to LA around Christmastime, went back to his house in Studio City, and tried to figure out his next move. About a month later, he got a phone call from Ram Dass: "Timothy Leary is in jail. Can you help him?"

Much has been written about Tim Leary and his 1970 escape from the California Men's Colony. The authorities finally caught up with Leary in 1973, detaining him in Kabul, Afghanistan. Once Leary was back in the States and behind bars, it was Ram Dass's idea to hire my dad for the trial. Dad defended the former Harvard psychologist pro bono.

The Leary prison escape case is what made my dad famous, even though he had already experienced a good deal of success for a poor kid from the Valley. After this episode, Dad started hanging out with Leary and Ram Dass and other key figures of the '70s. He became the LA director of the National Organization for the Reform of Marijuana Laws (NORML). Later on, he would defend people like the porn star Linda Lovelace and a few of the Hells Angels. It all started with Leary.

Dad's argument was unique. After talking it over with Leary in prison, they both decided it was best to claim that Leary was suffering from LSD flashbacks at the time of his escape. In court he argued that the LSD had changed Leary's brain so much that the man now lived in an altered reality or "meta-consciousness."[14] Inventive as it was, Dad's defense failed; the judge found Leary guilty on the escape charge.

Still, the case made national headlines. The woman who would later become my mother was finishing her first year of law school when the decision came down. A couple of years later, in the summer of 1975, she saw my dad in person for the first time at the LA city attorney's office. Despite his wild beard and eyes, Mom must have been impressed by Dad's reputation. Either way, they got together quickly and were married within the year. Another year after that, I was born.

5

LATIGO CANYON

I THINK WHEN YOU ARE YOUNG you can confuse the man with the persona he gives off. In the case of my mom, I think she conflated the idea of my dad with the television lawyer Perry Mason, who was a champion of justice. It turned out that Dad wasn't as friendly as Perry Mason. Also, although I don't consider age differences to be a problem per se, Dad was nine years older than Mom; and this detail did not endear him any further to her parents.

A far more important detail was Dad's wandering eye. Mom knew early on that he was a bit of a womanizer, but she tried to ignore it, along with every other warning sign. Whether she knew he was seeing other women all throughout their engagement was another matter.

I once asked Mom, "So why did you decide to marry him?"

After she rolled her eyes and muttered things about how I "make a federal case out of everything" and needed to "let it go," she finally came clean and confessed she just wanted to get out of her mother's house. Within a few weeks of meeting my dad, she moved her belongings from her parents' home on Le Doux Road in Beverly Hills to Dad's home in Latigo Canyon. They lived there as happily as possible for about a year before the wedding, which took place in 1976. My grandparents hated their prenuptial cohabitation, but Mom had made up her mind. She started working at Dad's law office and every day became more entrenched in his life. Then, four days before their wedding—an intimate ceremony held in Mom's parents' backyard, with only fifty guests besides the rabbi—the Latigo Canyon house burned to the ground.

It should be noted that Mom never liked that house. Latigo Canyon is a remote area near the mountains of Malibu, fairly removed from the city and other human life. To get to their house, you had to drive for several miles on a dirt path through dense forest. What the area lacked in human beings, it more than made up for in wildlife. Mom would often find rattlesnakes in their pool. The house itself was a different matter entirely. Dad, having gone from rags to riches by his twenty-fifth birthday, poured his energy into building his house on a hill, an ode to glass and concrete that was about as warm as a winter morning. Mom hated the house with a passion.

The week before their wedding, Mom and Dad went on a short trip. Neither of them remembers where they went or why, but when they returned, their house was engulfed in flames. There are several theories; my mom thinks it was arson.

I asked her, "But why would anyone want to set the house on fire?"

"How should I know? I think it was the housekeeper."

"Why the housekeeper?"

"Your father might have forgotten to leave her check," she said. "Plus, she was crazy." Either way, she interpreted the fire as a singularly negative sign: "It was an omen."

After the fire, the wedding, and the marriage, Dad rebuilt the house in Latigo Canyon. I remember him leading me on a horse down the winding paths just out of sight of the house. My mom loves to bring up an accident from when I was five years old. While moseying along the path, my horse spooked at a snake and threw me. I almost cracked my skull in half. Dad would live in that house with girlfriend after girlfriend—years passed. I never heard him mention the fire until after he sold the house.

It wasn't until I revisited a couple of Dad's recent interviews that I ever heard him even mention the fire. In one of them, his interviewer was Zach Leary, the son of Dad's infamous former client Tim Leary. In the interview, Dad mentions his time with Ram Dass, how he got the Leary prison escape case in the first place, and how he did the case for free. I already covered all this in the previous chapter, although I omitted one detail about his "payment." Apparently while Leary was locked up at the California Men's Colony, before he escaped, the prison guards taunted him. Once he escaped, he left a poem in his cell: "Follow me to freedom. In the days of Hitler, you enslaved the Jews. In the days of Rome, you kept Jesus. Follow me and you can be free, too."[1] Dad said this poem was his "fee."[2] Sadly, the poem was burned in the fire.

At the time, it seemed to me that the fire arose out of nowhere. In his interview with Zach Leary, he talks about the poem and other memorabilia he'd gathered after his life-changing sojourn to India, and he says he lost all his treasures in a fire at his Malibu home. Here, my ears prick up. He never mentions the timing of the fire, less than a week before his wedding to my mother, which she identified as yet another red flag. However, he does identify a kind of warning in the fire: "That was Lord Shiva checking my ego." Zach agrees with him, and the interview continues.[3]

Maybe I should not be surprised that two such different people interpreted the same event in different ways. It would be so simple to use my dad's explanation as more evidence of his inherent narcissism. My mother's possessions had been in that house, too, not that he mentions them. He is definitely self-centered in the way that a lot of New Age/*Be Here Now* types cite spirituality as an excuse for neglecting the people in their lives. More likely, Dad was worried about materialism because he thought that was his biggest issue, when in reality, he had more of a problem with the way he treated others. I could also take Mom's "omen" as a symptom of her chronic anxiety, the kind that keeps her chasing after my youngest even though she's well into her sixties, and that drives her to check on me several times a day.

Or maybe this event, which happened a year before I was born, sticks in my memory because it's illustrative of a pattern. My mother sees the worst, like the wrath of a spiteful God aimed at her and those she loves, and my father sees a lesson meant just for him. As the sole child of this particular union, I wonder at the two sides of myself: optimistic, chatty, and convinced the universe is conspiring to aid me on the one hand, while my neurotic other half lingers in the background.

6

A BRIEF HOPE, QUICKLY EXTINGUISHED

NOBODY CAN KNOW FOR CERTAIN whether this would have actually happened, but for a brief period in the 1970s, it seemed that the federal government might legalize marijuana. Not medical versus recreational or any other caveat; legal weed from sea to shining sea.

It's also important to mention that every era of United States history seems to be characterized by a drug of some kind. In the late 1800s, everyone was a morphine addict. The 1990s were characterized by heroin. These associations also change depending on geography and drug supply and demand. As should now be clear, however, the instinct to alter consciousness via one form or another has been consistent throughout history and around the world. The question of which drugs become a "menace" and which ones are encouraged tends to come down to money and politics, not inherent good or evil.

Joan Didion said the '60s ended on August 9, 1969.[1] That was when the Manson Family murdered Sharon Tate, a gorgeous blonde actress and the young wife of director Roman Polanski, along with four others. Tate was the most famous casualty of the Manson murders, which involved Hollywood mainstays like celebrity hairstylist Jay Sebring, Voltyk Frykowski, coffee heiress Abigail Folger, Steven Parent, and Leno and Rosemary LaBianca, who were killed in their Los Feliz home the day after the Tate murders.[2] Across the city, anxious celebrities, wannabes, and citizens read the headline in an extra edition of the *Los Angeles Times:* "Second Ritual Killings Here." "That could have been us," the paper's readers whispered. Sales of guns and guard dogs increased in the following weeks.[3]

Although most wouldn't agree with me, I think 1969 was also the beginning of a moment of hope for the marijuana legalization movement. Over the next few years, the legalization movement would progressively see more indications that the federal government would legalize marijuana. Then, once it seemed that legalization was not only likely but inevitable, everything fell apart.

For one thing, the spirit of the times had started to take a dark turn in 1969. The rumblings were quiet at first. On October 6, 1966, California outlawed possession of LSD.[4] Already, the level-headed adults were starting to question where their acid-fueled, pot-smoking kids would bottom out.

They got their answer in the fall of '69 with the death of Diane Linkletter, the daughter of television personality and *Kids Say the Darndest Things* host Art Linkletter. Linkletter's youngest child, Diane, was the bright-eyed, brunette girl next door. It became national news when this seemingly happy twenty-year-old girl stepped out of the kitchen window of her sixth-floor apartment in West Hollywood and died from complications of the fall. Her father, who had been known for his paternal charm and cheery disposition, began waging war against drug use, especially among children. Linkletter claimed that an LSD flashback had triggered Diane's death, and he singled out Timothy Leary as the man responsible for his daughter's untimely end. Toxicology reports did not show drugs in Diane's system, but Linkletter needed a culprit, and the tide had already started to turn against everything associated with LSD.

President Nixon—who was authorizing aides to cover up the Watergate scandal at the same time as he was denying the findings of the Shafer Commission, which issued a report calling for the decriminalization of marijuana possession—signed the Controlled Substances Act (CSA) into law in 1970, making marijuana and LSD Schedule I drugs. The CSA divided the different drugs into numbered "schedules," with Schedule I being the most dangerous and the least medically beneficial.

Luckily for marijuana advocates, the Nixon presidency didn't go so well. After the Watergate scandal and Nixon's subsequent near-impeachment, he was succeeded by his vice president, Gerald Ford, who proved to be an unpopular president. The country reacted in the next election by choosing Democrat and peanut farmer Jimmy Carter to be president.

The transition from Nixon to Carter coincided with a shift in the country, too. Many good books have been written on the influence of drugs on the cultural consciousness—and the individual consciousness. For example, would the findings of Freud have been possible if not for his use of cocaine, which he called a miracle drug? Some might say he would have come to his conclusions anyway, but the dreams he had ultimately led to his findings on the ego and the superego.

When the Manson Family trial got underway, many were struck by how closely Manson and his followers resembled other run-of-the-mill hippies of that time. Manson showed up to court on July 24, 1970, with a freshly carved "X" on his forehead and a handwritten note that read, "I have Xed myself from your world." He may not have been aware of it at the time, but Manson had also "Xed" out the orgiastic excess of the '60s with his murderous cult. The backlash would be swift and lasting.

So much of this book depends on the ability to hold in one's mind two seemingly irreconcilable images at the same time: what we remember, and what actually was. The truth of the moment, any moment, is often darker, more complex, and yet simpler because it is honest. For example, there is the man that Bruce might remember himself to be from that time, a self-portrait, and then there is the man who lived the day-in-and-day-out of it all. We can gather faint impressions of the man from stories and newsprint and hope that a faithful representation appears.

The year 1969 was the beginning of the end, not just for Bruce but also for the collective that made up the counterculture: the hippies, stoners, and dropouts. The spirit of the decade had ventured into a more sinister place. This descent started with the Manson murders. What is a man who has spent his life fighting for everything he's gotten supposed to do in the face of assured success? Bruce floundered. Even with the money, the car, the house, and the clients, a sick restlessness seized him.

7

PARANOIA AND POLICY

AS SOON AS I HEARD A KNOCK at the door, I jumped up and crouched behind the sofa in the waiting room of my father's West Hollywood office. There I stayed hidden next to the dust bunnies as the secretary opened the front door. I listened to their "hi's" and "how are yous?" I listened to them walk into the back room, and I never came out from my hiding place until the room was completely still, until all I heard was the low drone of the big tropical fish tank and the faint sounds of traffic leaking in from Sunset Boulevard. That's when I would finally crawl out from behind the couch and resume my activities, usually coloring or reading a book.

In 1982, I was five years old, and both of my parents were receiving death threats from their clients. I overheard one conversation my dad had where a client threatened to kidnap me; hence my new insistence on hiding from every client who walked through his door.

My childhood was characterized more than anything by paranoia. My mother never let me out of the house by myself. My grandparents were always checking in on my whereabouts. For the longest time, I preferred to spend time with my dad because he was so laid back and had such a hands-off approach to parenting. He was my co-conspirator and friend more than he was my guardian. It wasn't until I learned about the kidnapping threat that I realized there was reason to be nervous.

In 1984 there was an incident where one of my dad's clients climbed up onto the roof of his house and whacked his then-girlfriend on the head with a baseball bat. While the client was on probation, the court had mistakenly charged him on an old case and sent him to prison, but he believed my dad had screwed him over. Once he got out, he came to my dad's house on Swall Drive and attacked the girlfriend. My dad wasn't present for the attack, and once he heard about it, he went on the run. For the next two years, I gathered he was hiding out in the Sportsman's Lodge on Ventura Boulevard.

I based my first published short story on the incident. A burglary goes wrong and the girlfriend ends up dead, murdered by a man wielding a baseball bat. It was published in the Beverly Hills Education Foundation booklet. I would look at my name in print, Allison Brandi Margolin, and feel more of a thrill at being published than anything else.

For me, growing up in the '80s was like growing up in an echo chamber of fear and anxiety. In Southern California, we had a lot to contend with. There was Richard Ramirez, otherwise known as the Night Stalker, who killed, raped, and invaded the homes of random Angelenos in '84 and '85. The AIDS epidemic was kicking off. Every day there were news stories about people lacing food with toxic drugs, serial killers and rapists prowling in backyards, the sense that things were freewheeling out of control. If you were a child in the '80s and '90s, fear was probably a part of your daily vocabulary.

For example, as a child I learned about the Manson murders through reading my grandmother's copy of the book *Helter Skelter,* whose title was printed on the cover in letters that looked like dripping blood. After I heard that the Manson Family had once lived in Laurel Canyon, I could never drive there without feeling a shiver go through me. My fear was unjustified; the members of the Manson Family had either been imprisoned, killed, or disappeared into the general population by the time I learned who they were. In fact, I would later learn that the Manson cult had actually been based in Death Valley in the northern Mojave Desert, far away from Laurel Canyon. But my fear remained, even though I had never encountered "the family" myself. You never knew who could be hiding in those hills.

Paranoia—be it the childhood paranoia of a small girl fearing kidnapping, or the kind of macro-anxiety that can seize a nation—affects public policy in an undeniable way, especially when drugs are involved.

The first legislation in the United States involving marijuana was the 1937 Marihuana Tax Act, passed by Congress after a young man named Victor Licata in Tampa, Florida, chopped his family to pieces with an axe. When they covered the story in the press, they said that Licata had been smoking "marihuana cigarettes" for over six months,[1] attributing the slaughter of his family to the crazy-making marijuana, the loco weed. Although Licata was declared unfit to stand trial for reasons of insanity just two weeks after the massacre and was committed to the Florida State Hospital for the Insane, the news continued to report that pot had driven him mad. Never mind that there was already an investigation into his troubling mental state before the slaughter.

Harry Anslinger, the first commissioner of the Federal Bureau of Narcotics and the true father of the drug war, wrote about Licata in a 1937 article titled "Marijuana, Assassin of Youth." He retold the story of Licata while giving his testimony at the congressional hearings for the Marihuana Tax Act. He used the public fear around the Licata story to push for the passage of the Tax Act, which didn't outlaw pot; it put a tax on the sale of cannabis. More importantly, however, it gave the FBN a purpose for existing since alcohol prohibition had ended. It wasn't until 1969 that the Marihuana Tax Act was overturned in *Leary v. United States*. By then the new drug creating a panic was LSD.

When I was growing up, the drug creating a panic was crack. There were stories of the "crack epidemic." In 1986, there was a story of another young man whose life was ruined by drugs. University of Maryland basketball star Len Bias overdosed on cocaine on June 19, 1986, the morning after he was drafted to join the NBA champion Boston Celtics.

Democratic Congressman Thomas "Tip" O'Neill of Massachusetts used Bias's death to mobilize the House Democrats. Together they assembled a bill that would become the Anti-Drug Abuse Act of 1986. That act mandated a minimum sentence of five years without parole for the possession of 5 grams of crack cocaine. To earn the same length of sentence for cocaine possession, you had to be caught in possession of 500 grams, which is, to be blunt, a shit ton of cocaine. The 100-to-1 disparity of cocaine versus crack would lead to the incarceration of more Black and Brown men, men who looked like the dead basketball star. Bias, it should be said, died from a cocaine overdose, not from crack. It is disturbingly easy to find a scapegoat in a drug and find yourself caught up in the wave of public opinion. It is harder to look at the nuances of a situation.

Let's begin with the man who started it all: Victor Licata. Licata was the son of Italian immigrants. He had a preexisting history of mental illness and was likely experiencing the throes of psychosis when he massacred his family. Mental illness, it seems, was a family trait. One of the brothers he killed was a diagnosed schizophrenic. On his father's side, he had a granduncle and two cousins who had been institutionalized for mental illness. And, as the prison psychiatrists learned while examining him, his parents were first cousins.

As for where Licata got the marijuana he had become "addicted" to over the previous six months, the state drug and narcotic inspector said he was looking into "several places" where Licata might have bought the joints. But the chief detective downplayed the drug's role in the slaying; in his opinion, the marijuana probably hadn't been what drove Licata to psychosis. Still, the police chief made the following statement in the October 18, 1933, issue of the *Tampa Times*: "Maybe the weed only had a small indirect part in the alleged insanity of the youth, but I am declaring now for all time that the increasing use of this narcotic must stop and will be stopped." And two days later, the *Tampa Times* issued an editorial titled, in all caps, "STOP THIS MURDEROUS SMOKE." Even in that editorial, however, the reporters had to concede that the pot might not have mattered: "It may or may not be wholly true that the pernicious marijuana cigarette is responsible for the murderous mania of a Tampa young man in exterminating all the members of his family within his reach—but whether or not the poisonous mind-wrecking weed is mainly accountable for the tragedy its sale should not be and should never have been permitted here or elsewhere."[2]

It would be several years before Harry Anslinger learned about the Licata case. In early 1937, Anslinger was casting about for horror stories involving the plant that he could use as ammunition to push through the passage of the bill that would become the 1937 Marihuana Tax Act. On February 1, 1937, Anslinger got a letter from the chief inspector of the Florida State Board of Health. Once he read the contents of the letter, which detailed the particulars of the Licata case, Anslinger responded to the chief inspector with gratitude and a request to send all similar cases his way.

Anslinger would use the Licata incident to drum up political support for an act that Congress wasn't interested in passing. The bill wasn't popular. If passed, it would put taxes on the plant that had industrial uses for fiber, birdseed, and varnish oil. The tax act was meant to bring in money, not to prohibit personal marijuana use. Anslinger also cited other instances involving the loco weed, most of them saying the drug was the reason Black men were taking advantage of white women sexually. These horror stories were enough to mobilize Congress.

Victor Licata hung himself in 1950. Despite the struggles of people like Licata, Ronald Reagan began deinstitutionalizing mentally ill people while he was governor of California. The policy spread nationwide, especially after Reagan was elected president. From 1955 to 1994, about 487,000 mentally ill patients were discharged from state hospitals, which were closing everywhere.[3]

Psychiatric drugs developed in the '50s, such as Thorazine, were the first pills that could demonstrably treat mental illness. In the '60s, the government started to criticize the decidedly poor treatment of mental patients in state-run hospitals. It was in this vein that Ken Kesey published the novel *One Flew over the Cuckoo's Nest* in 1962.

The 1960s and 1970s were a tumultuous time. Not only did the events of that period affect literature and art; the period itself was affected by its politics, the Vietnam War, and the civil rights movement, all of which continue to influence federal and state legislation. After John F. Kennedy was assassinated in 1963, Vice President Lyndon Johnson became president. During his first State of the Union address in 1964, he proposed a set of initiatives to combat poverty in the United States, "an unconditional war on poverty." These initiatives were "designed to improve education, skills, and resources of low-income individuals and families to help them expand their productivity and ability to make ends meet and enhance their lifelong economic outcomes."[4] Johnson signed the Economic Opportunity Act of 1964 into law, which authorized government agencies to direct community-based social programs to promote health, education, and employment.[5] This was intended to expand economic growth and build a better America. But the war on poverty did not last long.

After Johnson's first term ended, he defeated Barry Goldwater to win the presidency in 1964. Because he was not elected to office for his first term, the Constitution allowed him to run for reelection in 1968, but eventually Johnson decided not to seek the Democratic nomination. Hubert Humphrey, the Democratic nominee, lost the election to Republican Richard Nixon. As president, Nixon promised to decrease federal expenditures. He did so by cutting off funding to inner cities, creating a vicious cycle: the lack of funding meant a lack of education, leading to more poverty, gangs, violence, drugs, and so on.

Prior to this time, the American public did not think there was a need to regulate drugs, but the cycle kept getting worse. In 1970, Nixon kicked off the War on Drugs by signing the Controlled Substances Act into law, which "places all substances which were in some manner regulated under existing federal law into one of five schedules. This placement is based upon the substance's medical use, potential for abuse, and safety or dependence liability."[6] Drugs became seen as a threat to racial purity. The belief was that the more drugs there were in society, the greater the possibility of racial integration and the elimination of social, cultural, and racial barriers.

Nixon's War on Drugs continued until 1974, when the Watergate scandal forced him to resign, and Gerald R. Ford became president. Ford's domestic policy was geared toward the economy because the United States was in a recession. After his proposal for a tax hike failed, he then proposed a tax cut of $16 billion. He fought with Congress to limit expenditures, but unfortunately for Ford, the Democratic-controlled Congress believed that "economic recovery necessitated additional government expenditures; it kept sending spending proposals to the White House, most of which Ford vetoed. For the rest of his term, Ford waged a war with Congress over the appropriate balance between tax cuts and government expenditures."[7] These policies continued to affect the inner cities; there continued to be insufficient resources, and the cycle continued.

After Ford, Carter became president. Within six months, he asked Congress to decriminalize marijuana possession, and he said his administration would also investigate the penalties for possession of cocaine. Under Carter's proposal, possession of small quantities of marijuana would result in a civil fine that would not create a criminal record.[8] Concurrently, Carter appointed Peter Bourne as special assistant to the president for health issues. Essentially, Bourne oversaw the federal government's approach to the nation's drug problem. He also advocated for the decriminalization of marijuana, although he wanted increased penalties for harder drugs.[9] In a 2000 interview with *Frontline,* Bourne explained the administration's rationale:

> *The view then with the Carter administration was that you should not have penalties that are more damaging to the individual than the problem that you're trying to solve. We have no influence over what penalties the states set, but the decision that we made in the Carter White House is that, as far as federal law was concerned, the possession of less than an ounce of marijuana means that you're a user, not a seller, and it should be made a misdemeanor. It would still be illegal, but it would be something more like a traffic ticket. If you had more than an ounce and you were clearly a trafficker, then there would be more severe penalties, and it would remain a felony.*[10]

After the Carter administration, Ronald Reagan took office. Under Reagan, drug policy was less of a public health issue and became more political. The government revoked public programs, and the cycle continued. While Reagan was president, profits from US sales of illegal drugs were used to fund the right-wing Contra revolution in Nicaragua, even though some street-level dealers involved in the operation were arrested and incarcerated. A report from the US Department of Justice Office of the Inspector General refers to articles in the *San Jose Mercury News* by Gary Webb:

> *Oscar Danilo Blandón was a cocaine trafficker in Los Angeles who provided the profits of his sales to the Contra revolution. According to the articles, Blandón, along with Norwin Meneses, turned "Rick Ross into L.A.'s first king of crack." The articles noted that in 1986 the Los Angeles Sheriff's Department (LASD) raided more than a dozen locations connected to Blandón's drug operation but found virtually no drugs at any of the locations. The articles reported speculation that the CIA compromised these LASD raids, perhaps because of Blandón's ties to the Contras. The articles reported further that while Blandón was eventually prosecuted in 1992 by federal authorities and "admitted to crimes that have sent others away for life," he was released from prison after 28 months in jail, and was paid by the DEA for his cooperation. Moreover, Blandón received permanent legal resident status in the United States.*[11]

Rick Ross, poor and illiterate, was sentenced to life imprisonment under California's three-strikes law. Fortunately, while Ross was locked up, he learned how to read. He studied the law and found a loophole that served as the basis for an appeal that led to his eventual release.

In 1994, the tragic murders of Kimber Reynolds and Polly Klaas led California voters to enact California Proposition 184, the three-strikes law that would become one of the most all-encompassing sentencing laws in the country.[12] Kimber Reynolds was the eighteen-year-old daughter of a wedding photographer in Fresno, California. She was killed during a robbery in 1992. The killer was a repeat offender, a "career criminal" who had just been released on parole.[13]

Then, a year later, twelve-year-old Polly Klaas was kidnapped at knifepoint during a slumber party at her mother's house in Petaluma, California. She was later strangled and killed by her abductor, Richard Allen Davis. Davis, like the man who killed Kimber Reynolds in Fresno a year earlier, was a recent parolee. Four months before he kidnapped Klaas, Davis had been released on parole from the California Men's Colony in

San Luis Obispo after serving eight years for kidnapping a friend of his girlfriend's sister.

After two high-profile murders by recent parolees, California voters were all too eager to pass the three-strikes rule, with 72 percent of voters approving Proposition 184.[14] The proposition ensured a life sentence in prison for offenders convicted of three violent or serious felonies. California's list of violent or serious crimes, however, included more crimes than other states. Firearms violations, burglary, simple robbery, arson, providing hard drugs to a minor, and drug possession all fell under the umbrella of violent or serious crimes.

For a time, the voters felt reassured, but a 1997 study found that the state's three-strikes law "did not decrease crime or petty theft rates below the level expected on the basis of preexisting trends."[15] In 2012, California passed the Three Strikes Reform Act.[16] This was after the California Department of Corrections released a report showing how the law had disproportionately affected people of color. Over 45 percent of the inmates serving life sentences under the 1994 three-strikes law were African American.[17]

PART 2
EVIDENCE AND CROSS-EXAMINATION

8

THIS IS YOUR BRAIN ON DRUGS

THE SKY ABOVE FELT CLOSE enough to touch, even though it was light-years away. We lolled back in the grass like we were kids—which, at twenty-one and twenty-five, we basically were—having spun around in circles until the world around us went wild while we collapsed on the grass. The air felt heavy enough for me to taste it on my tongue. I turned my head toward Steve, whose compact form was usually abuzz with some anxiety or a pain I couldn't begin to imagine. I wondered if he felt the same things I did, if the grass under his arms and fingertips was a sensory delight for him as well, if the stars moved overhead in slow motion for him, too. I wasn't worried about anything, not the three additional points I should have gotten on my final LSAT score, not the anxieties I felt about entering Harvard Law School the next month. I only wanted the warmth in my belly to continue, to radiate through my chest, my arms, my legs, past the tips of my fingers and toes and to blanket the world. This was some excellent ecstasy.

I was in limbo for a summer, no longer a Columbia undergrad, not quite yet a Harvard law student. The world, it seemed, was on the brink of a tectonic shift. It was the last year of the century, the new millennium loomed, and people were starting to talk about Y2K with the same vigor they'd use in discussing Mayan calendars and the end of the world in 2012. None of this mattered to my parents, however. They practically forbade me from taking a gap year—which, to me, would mean twelve months of partying and a reprieve from the marathon study sessions that had kept me locked in Columbia's library all day and all night. Their opinion was that I'd gotten into Harvard Law School; better go ahead and enroll before the higher-ups thought better of the decision.

So now I was attempting to compress as much of the relaxation of a gap year as I could into two and a half months. My only objective was to sleep and spend time with friends. My mother is the one who introduced me to Steve. He was a nice Jewish boy from a good family, and our mothers knew some of the same people. I met him when he and his mother showed up at a party at Brad Kern's house. The Kerns were my mom's neighbors in Coldwater Canyon, and the Kern patriarch was a plastic surgeon who shared a practice with my best friend Kim's dad. (There might only be three degrees of separation between everyone in Beverly Hills.) Steve came from money. He was in medical school. Mom didn't love him immediately; she probably barely registered his presence, which, to me, was a plus. Later on, she'd degrade her relationship with Steve from polite acknowledgment to stoic tolerance. I think the only reason she didn't block him from passing the gates of our home is because I tolerated the string of jerks she'd brought into our lives with minimal opposition.

I met Steve at the right time. When other people learn that I went to Columbia in the mid-1990s and steered clear of anything harder than Jägermeister and pot, they can scarcely believe it. There were drugs all over that campus. But besides an alcohol-fueled freshman year, I hadn't done much of anything. Because neither of my parents drank, I grew up knowing nothing about alcohol; so the very first night I drank, when I was about sixteen or seventeen, I downed twelve shots of vodka. I was so sick the next day that the negative associations kept me in check, for the most part.

My first year at Columbia, my grades were so miserably average that I realized I would have to spend more time studying if I wanted a shot at getting into Harvard Law. While the kids around me did coke and heroin and E, I was living like a monk in the library. My idea of a hot Friday night was to stay in researching trivia about the Beatles and the urban legend about Paul McCartney's death and the band's subsequent cover-up. I chose to immerse myself in drug culture as much as possible without doing anything myself—the ultimate voyeur. I was obsessed with zines that glamorized IV drug use, and I pored over drug-related photos, such as an iconic shot of Jaime King shooting heroin into her inner thigh, for inspiration. I wanted so much to be part of what I perceived to be a glamorous set of models and artists, writers and beatniks that were shooting up; but I never wanted to jeopardize my academic standing.

I was a political science major with not-so-secret writing aspirations. When I toured Columbia's campus with my dad when I was fourteen, I connected with the campus's beatnik aesthetic. In my mind, writers lived in New York, a place so deeply unlike my native Los Angeles. Once I arrived as a freshman, all of my intuitions about Columbia and New York City proved correct. I was a weirdo among weirdos for the first time, and I thrived in that community. I had fun, I went to parties, and I avoided drugs besides pot. In the back of my mind I always knew that I wanted to go to Harvard Law School, and there were some childhood fears about drugs damaging brain cells that maintained their grip during my undergraduate experience.

The title of my senior thesis at Columbia was "The Seeds of Change/ The Roots of the Status Quo: Why the Drug Legalization Movement Has Not Taken Off." It was 1999, and I thought drug legalization was long overdue. It's interesting, but even though my father was the director of NORML in Los Angeles and a well-known member of the legalization movement, I don't remember talking about my thesis with him. I interviewed my dad's friend and colleague Dale Gieringer, a leader in NORML and one of the authors of Proposition 215, which legalized medical marijuana in California in 1996. I dedicated a subchapter of my thesis to the politics of NORML. But the only appearances my father makes in my thesis are as my father, not as a legalization advocate or well-known lawyer.

My thesis argued that marijuana legalization had failed because the movement had been so splintered. The medical marijuana advocates didn't want to affiliate with the "stoner" recreational marijuana advocates. None of the marijuana advocates wanted anything to do with the "hard" drugs like heroin, cocaine, and its close relative, crack. The legal marijuana movement's strategy was to normalize the plant as much as possible, and it would have been difficult to proclaim marijuana a benign substance without using other, more "dangerous" drugs for contrast. Marijuana smokers were your neighbors, your doctors, your friends, each one an Everyman.

The Everyman argument barely qualifies as a side note in my thesis. I mention that legalization advocates drew a distinction between the soft drugs, like pot, and the hard drugs. At the time, that distinction seemed less important. But while flipping through the thesis more recently, I realized this classification of hard and soft drugs was the same reason why my famous stoner father judged my cocaine use so harshly. Maybe he had internalized NORML's argument.

I earned high marks for my thesis and used some of its arguments to write my application to Harvard Law School. I later wrote my third-year thesis, "On the Right to Get High,"[1] based on that essay. I wrote that thesis in a newly built '90s-era law school dorm on the corner of Shattuck and Telegraph in Berkeley. If I had owned a television, I couldn't have finished it. I wrote the thesis under the auspices of a professor/practitioner who would become my life mentor and who continues to help me to this day. In "On the Right to Get High," I argued that the Controlled Substances Act is unconstitutional because there is no rational basis to regulate drugs according to the CSA paradigm. In addition, even assuming the CSA has a rational basis, the science behind the classifications is absurd.

My father, it should be noted, thought I was insane to take on such a provocative subject for a Harvard application. But I was accepted to Harvard, and I firmly believe it was partly because of this essay. I finished college, graduated, and moved home for the summer. With no responsibilities for the first time in years, I was ready to gain firsthand knowledge of the "hard" drugs that had fascinated me for so long.

The summer of '99 was my first truly free moment to even bother to experiment, so Steve's arrival in my life seemed fated. We started dating almost immediately. I smoked weed and was very open about it. He and his friends would also smoke, but they were closeted about this particular indulgence. It seemed they had a love-hate relationship with herb, so while they admired my forthrightness, they would never be as public about their own drug use.

People with serious drug problems seem to have a general anxiety about marijuana smokers, especially when those smokers are as candid about their use as I am. This might be an issue of logistics. Other substances are easier to mask: cocaine, Valium, and ecstasy are all odorless. There is also an anxiety that any association with public stoners will affect other people's reputations. Even though Steve and his friends liked me—and possibly even admired me for being so open about using herb—they must have worried that my candor would taint their images by association.

Personally, I had always been intrigued by the stories of people like Stevie Nicks and Drew Barrymore. I had a battered copy of Barrymore's addiction memoir *Little Girl Lost* on my bookshelf. I was fascinated by LA women who used drugs and partied and lived glamorous lives, and I studied them like an anthropologist who was also a fan. The first time Steve offered me E, I realized that this was my chance to live the life of my heroines. It also helped that I didn't have the usual school-related anxieties that summer or any responsibilities. I have to admit I also loved the idea of being a Harvard Law student dating a medical school student who did drugs and had wild parties all night.

My first hit of E in the parking lot of the Shoreline Amphitheatre was a moment of consecration. I was stepping out of the role of grade-A, type-A student into something far more romantic. I took the hit in the parking lot before climbing into Steve's car and pulling out into the night. We drove up the 5 through cow country, dirt country, and northern California scrub desert. By the time we reached 1015 Folsom, a now-closed club in San Francisco, the E hit. I remember the shift from heavy darkness to the bright light. These memories are probably affected by the dilation of my pupils from the E. More light flooded in than I anticipated.

I remember my first E experience pretty clearly even though other parts of that summer are hazy. I felt so rooted, like I was really in my body for the first time. I was an intellectual youth and almost never thought of my body as much more than a vehicle to carry my brain from place to place. All of my concern was in the realm of my anxious, hyperactive mind. I worried constantly about my intelligence, concerned about whether I was smart enough to compete with the types of people who would be at Columbia or Harvard. I worried that there was something about human behavior that I was not able to completely comprehend, as if everyone else had found the secret to being comfortable with themselves and I was still trying to figure things out. But when I took E, those concerns faded away, and I got to experience the moment. I felt connected to my body. I felt the air on my face. I saw the depths of color in the sky. I was content.

My moods would crescendo to the heights of pleasure and happiness when I was with Steve and then plummet to incredibly dark despair while I recovered alone in my childhood bedroom. During these moods, I would jot down thoughts in my journal. The mental energy I would usually devote to my schoolwork had to go somewhere, so I took to rigorously analyzing my relationship with Steve. I have always been a workaholic: if there was no assignment before me, I would find something in my own life to pick apart. Gradually, my times with Steve would evolve from me simply hanging out with him and his friends and trying various psychedelics, to me tripping and looking at Steve, tripping and wondering what Steve was thinking about, tripping and trying to see if he liked me as much as I liked him.

We were boyfriend and girlfriend at the time, but my father had always told me that men were born cheaters; it was your job as the woman to keep him happy enough that he would ignore his baser instinct. As fucked as that perspective is, it made a home in my mind. I approached my relationship with Steve the same way. I made myself as pliant as the grass we lay upon, acquiescing to Steve's every desire except for maintaining my weed habit. Some things were sacred. The E helped me be the kind of girl I thought would keep Steve's interest. Now I guess we'd call her the "cool girl"; she can party with the boys but stay lithe and sexy, she's cool with threesomes, she loves going out every night and does not fantasize about staying in with a Carole King biography and the latest issue of *People*.

Even as I partied with Steve, I felt something wasn't right. I wondered why I had to do psychedelics to go out when it seemed that other people didn't need hallucinogens to have a good time. Was there something wrong with my brain?

Ever since I was young, I'd feared that using drugs would affect my intelligence. Even if you weren't alive in the '80s, you probably know about the fried-egg commercial: A frying pan sizzling with oil fills the frame. A metallic thud echoes in the background. A man's voice, both young and worldly, says, "This is drugs." An invisible hand drops a cracked-open egg into the pan, where it fries. The man continues, "This is your brain on drugs." He pauses, letting the egg sizzle before asking, "Any questions?"

This ad from a Partnership for a Drug-Free America came out in 1987,[2] when I was about ten years old. I remember watching it for the first time and not understanding how my brain was supposed to be a fried egg. I also remember thinking that the egg looked pretty delicious. Even if I watch that ad now, I feel the same way I felt as a kid—bewildered and a little hungry.

Four years before the fried-egg commercial came out, the Los Angeles Police Department and the Los Angeles Unified School District joined forces to create an antidrug education program for the city's elementary school students. In 1983, I was one of the students in the Drug Abuse Resistance Education program.[3] The message of D.A.R.E. was black and white: *If you use drugs, you will die.* This was part of the same messaging we were getting in the '80s from First Lady Nancy Reagan, who popularized the antidrug phrase "Just Say No." These messages never became more nuanced.

It didn't help matters that all of the D.A.R.E. spokespeople struggled with drug addiction themselves. I knew, along with the other kids in my class, that Corey Haim, famous for his role in *The Lost Boys,* was using cocaine and crack while promoting D.A.R.E.[4] It soon became public knowledge that Drew Barrymore, another D.A.R.E. spokesperson, was addicted to cocaine during her tenure with D.A.R.E. In 1992, Patti Davis, daughter of Ronald and Nancy Reagan, would publish a memoir detailing her own pill addiction. She would also write that her mother, "Just

Say No" Nancy, was using tranquilizers four times a day and was certainly dependent on pills.[5] My classmates and I didn't know about the drug use happening in the White House, but we were kids living in Los Angeles in the '80s, just like Haim and Barrymore. It seemed odd to ignore what was common knowledge—that the people representing D.A.R.E. were all using drugs.

Dad was fascinated by the D.A.R.E. program. At that point, he'd been a director of NORML's LA chapter for almost a decade and a criminal lawyer for even longer. I remembered him receiving kidnapping threats from unhappy clients—most of whom were trying to get out of drug charges—so I'd always associated the drug scene with the *Helter Skelter* vibe. Not to mention the client who had cracked a bat into the skull of one of Dad's girlfriends. All I had learned from D.A.R.E. Officer Mora in my school was that drug users were bad, and it would be in my best interest to steer clear of anybody in that scene. This was a difficult position for me to maintain considering that the scents of patchouli and pot followed my father wherever he went. I knew my father wasn't like the drug users Officer Mora was talking about. Also, one of my dad's clients whom he seemed to be constantly defending was a lifelong heroin addict who was always doing some kind of work in the office; and though I didn't know it at the time, I later discovered many people around me were on drugs in one way or another. It doesn't matter who you are or where you come from; all types of drugs are prevalent.

My initial idea of drug users was very much influenced by the D.A.R.E. curriculum. I imagined gaunt faces, track-marked arms, tremors—all the signs of the visibly strung-out users who were illustrated in my D.A.R.E. workbooks. I was distressed, to put it mildly, that my father made a living defending people like this.

Just say no. That is the message that all the D.A.R.E. curricula boiled down to. Good kids, good people, did not use drugs. I always saw my father as a wacky figure. He did yoga, he took the name Badrinath Das, and he was always going on "sabbaticals" from his law firm to jet off to India. For the most part, I looked at him with affectionate bemusement and let him live his life. At times he'd irritate me. Sometimes I would get annoyed by the smoke rolling off of his clothes and breath and by the pseudo-hippie, free-spirit persona he inhabited. How anyone could believe he was so antiestablishment and such a man of the people when he lived in a fabulous house in Beverly Hills was beyond me. I remember thinking of him and his friends while reading about the phonies in *Catcher in the Rye*. All I needed to do was swap out martinis for pipes.

His ideas about drugs and the law might have influenced me because I learned about them so early. My D.A.R.E. graduation happened in eighth grade, and there was a competition among the students for who would give the graduation speech. I wrote an eloquent speech about how using drugs would jeopardize my future journalism career. This speech pleased the D.A.R.E. officers, and they chose me to speak at graduation. I remember taking the microphone and looking out at the officers in their uniforms and my classmates in their acid-wash jeans. I opened my mouth . . . and launched into a takedown of the fried-egg ad. My prior speech had been a Trojan horse, and now I was ready to deliver my real message.

"It is not as simple as 'Just Say No,'" I said. "Different drugs affect different people in different ways. I mean, it's not like marijuana is the same thing as cocaine. Why are we lumping these two things together?"

Never mind that back then I actually probably thought that a single line of coke was deadly. This was about a year after Len Bias died. Media coverage of his overdose made it seem like this healthy NBA draft pick had died of a heart attack after smoking a hit of crack cocaine. I definitely believed that a line of cocaine could give you a heart attack because of the media spin around the Bias incident. In reality, Len Bias overdosed after ingesting cocaine orally.[6] Taking drugs through the mouth is actually one of the most dangerous ways to take it, because it takes so long to digest that you may not realize you're overdosing until it's too late.[7]

But I had anecdotal evidence that weed wasn't nearly as dangerous; otherwise, how could Dad be healthy enough to do all that yoga? The issue with the D.A.R.E. thing was that they lumped all drugs in together. Pot was equally bad as heroin, as far as Officer Mora was concerned. I knew that wasn't true. And I knew that young Drew Barrymore and Corey Haim were going to rehab as preteens even as they worked as D.A.R.E.

spokespeople. It was phony. Also, I started thinking about how doing drugs really causes different states of mind. Although at that time I had no interest in altering my consciousness, I was preoccupied by the mind, learning, and thinking. And though I was not even on the verge of artic- ulating my thoughts on the subject because I was just beginning to form them, I did know that sending people to prison for thinking in a certain way—even if that way of thinking was not supported by everyone, even if you were so-called addicted to bringing about that way of thinking—was not right.

9

NO ONE NEEDS TO
DIE AT THE VIPER ROOM

I WAS SIXTEEN YEARS OLD when River Phoenix died on the sidewalk outside LA nightclub the Viper Room in 1993. I had always felt a kinship with the young actor, starting with his role in the 1986 Rob Reiner film *Stand by Me*. I conflated Chris Chambers, the character River played in that film, with the actual person River was—someone who was smiling on the outside and crying on the inside, the protective "big brother" sort with his own internal wounds. River was a sensitive weirdo, and so was I. After watching *Stand by Me,* I followed River's career and clung to any detail that made me feel closer to him. I stopped eating meat because he was an animal lover, an environmentalist, a vocal vegan, and an ambassador for People for the Ethical Treatment of Animals.

The release of the 911 call made by River's brother Joaquin (then going by "Leaf") began to wake everyone up to how little we knew about him: "My brother's having seizures. You must get over here, *please.* You must get over here, *please.* . . . Now I'm thinking he's had Valium or something. You must get here, please, because he's dying."[1] The kids in my school who had spent time in the club scene all thought River had overdosed, because either they or one of their friends had seen the young actor drinking or snorting cocaine at some point; so between these rumors and

Leaf's mention of Valium in the 911 call, I was confronted with the fact that someone with such a clean public image, whom I had idolized for having so many qualities that I desired for myself, could die so suddenly from a drug overdose.

The coroner's report confirmed all the rumors: River Phoenix had died of a drug overdose after ingesting a speedball,[2] the same mixture of cocaine and heroin that had killed comedian John Belushi over a decade earlier. He started seizing and was dead within twenty minutes.[3] Toxicology tests showed "acute multiple drug intoxication" and "lethal levels of cocaine and morphine," the metabolized version of heroin.[4] River had ingested eight times the lethal dose of cocaine and four times the lethal dose of heroin.[5]

I was bewildered. How could such a sensitive and talented person, who ate tofu and advocated for animal rights, who publicly frowned upon drug use and claimed it wasn't for him, take enough hard drugs to kill himself many times over? How could it happen in front of so many people he was close to? His girlfriend, his brother, and his sister were there, as were some of his famous friends, including Johnny Depp (who owned a share of the Viper Room at the time) and Flea from the Red Hot Chili Peppers. He had performed on stage with the band playing that night. He was surrounded by people who knew him and cared about him. My coming to terms with this tragedy and realizing how it had come to pass would take years of thought and my own deep dive into living as a drug user.

The extent to which River Phoenix's relationship with drugs was kept secret was a reaction to the heavy judgment society places on drugs and drug users—a judgment that is even harsher when the user is a rich celebrity.

I, along with everyone else, was fascinated by the apparent double life River led. Although River's family tried to keep the focus on his environmentalism in the aftermath of his death, the wider public could not stop discussing the usual questions people have when someone overdoses. How could someone with so much to live for die so suddenly? How did we miss the signs of his addiction?

About a week after the coroner's report, family, friends, and industry professionals attended a memorial service for River on the Paramount Pictures lot. River's mother, who was calling herself Heart, gave a long, rambling speech about how she always knew River would use the "mass media to change the world" and "be our missionary" to spread the word about protecting the environment. She then shared a vision she'd had in which River negotiated his time on Earth with the Divine Creator. God kept urging River to go to Earth to be born, and River kept resisting before finally giving God twenty-three years. Heart smiled at the assembled mourners and said River was back with God; he had never wanted to be in the world anyway.[6]

There was a long silence among the group that could have been interpreted as solemn reverence or mute confusion. Heart asked others to share their memories of River. A few people spoke, giving the usual "he's in a better place now" spiel or "River's in heaven, blah blah blah, it was his time, blah blah blah," as his ex-girlfriend Suzanne Solgot put it.[7] The actress Martha Plimpton, who had dated River for over a year and even attended the Oscars as his date, was irritated, too: "You would have thought he was ninety and had died in his sleep. The people who were saying this felt tremendous guilt that they had contributed to his death."[8]

Finally, from a corner of the room, director John Boorman blurted out, "Is there anybody here who can tell us why River took all those drugs?"[9] The question shocked Heart and upset River's younger sisters, Summer and Liberty, who ran out of the room.

Boorman's question is something I hear repeated whenever anyone overdoses, but especially when that person has a certain level of money or fame. They ask how they could have missed the person's struggle with a drug addiction, how they could have missed the signs, why they didn't do more when the person was alive. How could someone who seemed to have the world at their fingertips throw it all away? Even Heart, days after the memorial service where Boorman dropped his bomb of a question, conceded that the director had a point. "It's what everyone was thinking. Why, when you're living this dream, when you can have any car, any house, any girl, you're so famous—why? Why?"[10]

Now when I read Heart's question, it seems a little naïve. What young, rich, successful person is ever satisfied with what they have? In fact, what young person ever possesses the perspective to realize that the world is opening up before them, that they can have anything they wanted? I was never a famous actor, but when I was in my teens and twenties in Hollywood, I remember walking down the Sunset Strip amid the glittering lights and glowing neon club signs. Rarely did I pause to think about what a beautiful and fleeting time that moment was. And if I did catch myself in a moment of gratitude, my next thought would be how I could make the moment shine even brighter.

I overcame my drug addiction, but I kept following celebrities' struggles. As I got older, I thought increasingly about the role secrecy plays in addiction and how it could land people in serious trouble. One aspect of addiction that few people discuss enough is the loneliness involved. There is no better way to highlight that issue than with the rich and famous—the ones who always seemed to be surrounded by fans or friends but who are privately suffering. Nobody understands what it means to keep your addiction quiet the way a celebrity does. It may seem odd to write about celebrity overdoses in a book calling for drug law reform, but the lives of celebrities highlight a key problem that comes with prohibition. People will rarely seek help when they are afraid of the consequences for their personal or professional lives. Instead they will keep their addictions a secret for as long as possible. By the time other people learn about their addictions, the problem is far more severe than it might have otherwise been. In the end, it doesn't matter how rich or famous you are. Nobody is immune to addiction, and there is something we can learn from the stories of celebrities' struggles with drugs, starting with my childhood crush, River Phoenix.

When Boorman asked why River had taken so many drugs, Samantha Mathis—River's girlfriend, and the costar of his last completed movie, *The Thing Called Love*—answered as best she could: "River was so sensitive. He had so much compassion for everyone and everything that he had a weight on his heart." While I think Mathis had a point about River's sensitivity—the young actor once ran out of a restaurant because his then-girlfriend Martha Plimpton ordered seafood—I can point to a number of other reasons for River's problems with drugs and alcohol besides his tender heart.

River's parents, John and Arlyn Bottom, were hippie dropouts. Arlyn gave birth to River Jude Bottom on August 23, 1970, on a peppermint farm in Madras, Oregon. With baby River in tow, Arlyn and John traveled around the West and Southwest, all the while smoking pot, dropping acid, and eating magic mushrooms for about two years. Interestingly enough, two separate acid trips led the couple to seek religion and quit using drugs. Arlyn had a vision of a golden hand that "seemed to rip away the darkness."[11] John was lying in a field and heard a voice saying, "Why don't you receive me?" John said a tall man appeared who declared himself to be a Christian. The man, John said, "had two Bibles. One was an antique. I was a history student. I felt God knew what would interest me. At first, I cried. Then I quit drugs and smoking."[12] They started searching for greater meaning and a religious home. And in 1972, they found that home in a new cult named Children of God.

A former Christian minister named David Brandt Berg founded Children of God in 1968. Then the cult was called Teens for Christ. Within three years, they had grown from fifty to fifteen hundred people and had taken on their new name. Berg was a very literal interpreter of biblical scripture. He took 1 Corinthians 6:12—"All things are lawful to us"—to mean he had carte blanche to do whatever he wanted.[13] The Children of God believed in sexual liberty, thinking that all forms of sexual expression (except gay male sex) were holy, if they were motivated by love. Berg was clearly obsessed with sex. In a 1973 letter, the fifty-four-year-old wrote: "Come on Ma Burn Your Bra. We have a sexy God and a sexy religion with a very sexy leader with an extremely sexy young following! So if you don't like sex you'd better get out while you can still save your bra! Salvation sets us free from the curse of clothing and the shame of nakedness!"[14] A former member described the cult's stance on adultery this way: "You could do anything in God's name if you did it in love. That included sharing sexually with other people. We were taught that the ultimate sacrifice that a man could make to God was to share his wife with another man."[15]

The Children of God even encouraged sexual experimentation among young children. In 1974, a lengthy investigation into the Children of God revealed that the group was run by Berg from where he was living in Europe, issuing orders through his "Mo Letters" ("Mo" was short for Moses). Berg's practices were not only unorthodox; as the investigation uncovered, they also bordered on the criminal. One time Berg married a young woman and forced the wedding guests to watch their first sexual intercourse as husband and wife. This particular detail reminded me of a few stories I'd heard from my father about his hippie days and the weddings he would attend that included "public consummation ceremonies."

There were also rumors that Berg encouraged his followers to molest their own children.[16] "[Berg] believed that one of the best ways for kids to learn about sex was by having it with their own parents," a former member said. "There was a memorandum about this sent out. People were supposed to read it and burn it."[17] Because the practices were so questionable, Children of God only stayed alive through a code of secrecy. Members were not supposed to tell nonmembers what they did. And the 1974 investigation concluded that the Children of God were safe from prosecution because of the First Amendment.[18] I imagine that incest and child molestation weren't part of the welcome brochure when the Bottoms stumbled upon a Children of God commune in Crockett, Texas, in 1972. John and Arlyn were easy sells, immediately disavowing their previous lives in the outside world and relinquishing all of their worldly possessions to benefit the cult.

When I read about their time in Children of God, it was clear to me that John and Arlyn were searching for greater meaning in their lives; but their philosophy on religion leaves a sour taste in my mouth. My father and his friends were also hippie types, the kind of people whom David Brandt Berg sucked up like a morally bankrupt vacuum.[19] The difference was that my father never depended on me to financially support him in the way that River's parents would. I cannot imagine the stress that would cause for a kid.

As seems to be the case with any group of people who have a holier-than-thou attitude, my father and his friends were very hypocritical, especially about drug use. My father would smoke weed all the time, and I believe his friends were also doing cocaine, but he judged me harshly for using cocaine in my twenties. They were supposedly antimaterialistic people who focused on peace and love, but my father had a house in Beverly Hills and a luxury car. Similarly, River's parents would privately condemn their son's drug use or say he had to go back to living off the land, even as they pushed him to make more movies and make more money to support their family. When I read about River's childhood, I can't help but see the similarities between John and Arlyn and my father. Even hippies can be repressed, especially if they get wrapped up into the teachings of a problematic figure like David Brandt Berg.

Although John and Arlyn had already given up drugs before joining Children of God, another benefit of the cult was its promotion of a drug-free ethos. While the Children of God had loose ideas of sexual liberty, they were vehemently antidrug. Another member of Children of God remembered John and Arlyn telling him that one reason they had joined the cult was to stay off drugs.[20] In a later interview, River would recall a story from the Children of God sermons: "We heard Janis shot airplane glue into her veins the night she died, that's the kind of stuff the pastor would tell us. 'Cocaine—the devil's dandruff,'" he said.[21]

Interestingly, although River had certainly had several experiences with hard drugs at this point, he would maintain his granola public image, his only concession to harmful substances a pack of cigarettes he would buy and then smoke in "guilty little puffs" aimed at the ceiling. "I think I might wait 'til I'm 70 and then do it all at once," River said. "Just stay ultra-healthy 'til I'm 70 and then just go, 'Waaaaaa-ooooo!'"[22] This ties into something else River might have learned from his early childhood in Children of God: how to keep secrets.

Children of God believed in spreading their word through missionary work, but the cult was careful about who it welcomed into the fold. The Bottoms bopped around Texas and Colorado for a few months before they were trusted to proselytize in South America. First, they went to Mexico and Puerto Rico for almost two years, and they kept traveling south until they settled in Caracas, Venezuela. During this time River became fluent in Spanish and the family grew by two more, a girl named Rain Joan of Arc and a boy named Joaquin Rafael. John Bottom was rewarded for his piety with a title: archbishop of Venezuela and the Caribbean.

The Children of God did not pay their archbishops. To bring in money, John and Arlyn set the kids to work busking. Towheads River and Rain sang in the streets, becoming known to the locals as *los niños rubios que cantan,* or "the blond children who sing." If it was ever a hardship for five-year-old River to be the breadwinner for his family, he didn't dwell on it. "We [sang] because we needed money, but we also wanted to pass along love," River said. "That was where I learned to give a lot of joy and happiness, from singing."[23] This pattern of River financially supporting his family would continue for the rest of his short life.

The Children of God's practices became more disturbing while the Bottoms continued their work in Venezuela. Berg was guiding his flock toward a new method of bringing more followers into Children of God, based on another Bible verse, Matthew 4:19: "Follow me, and I will make you fishers of men." Somehow Berg took this verse as a directive to the women of the church. They should bring new men into Children of God by having sex with them. A 1976 Mo Letter described the new practice, which Berg called "flirty fishing," in greater detail: "What greater way could you show anyone your love than to give them your all in the bed of love? How much more can you show them the Love of God than to show them His Love to the uttermost through you?"[24]

This practice pulled the wool from John and Arlyn's eyes. They left the Children of God almost immediately afterward. Arlyn said, "The guy running it got crazy. He sought to attract rich disciples through sex. No way." John was more reluctant to condemn Berg: "He may have been a sexual pervert, but he is still a better man than a lot of people."[25]

The Bottoms stayed with a friend they had made, a Catholic priest named Padre Esteban, for about a year before John and Arlyn decided it was time to return to the States. Padre Esteban arranged for the family to travel by cargo ship in October 1978. During that trip, the Bottom children witnessed the ship's crew killing fish by smashing them on the sides of the boat. Horrified, they swore off meat forever and convinced their parents to do the same. A few months later, they completed the transition from vegetarian to vegan. Veganism and other environmental concerns became the family's new gospel after Children of God, which they were determined to leave in the past.

All told, the Bottom family was part of Children of God for four years, from 1972 to 1976. In that period, John and Arlyn quickly became leaders in the cult. They founded a colony in Caracas, and John oversaw nine or ten other communities throughout Venezuela. The children contributed, too, keeping the family afloat with the money they brought in by singing in the street.

Later, River would be evasive about his odd childhood in interviews, making up stories or exaggerating details so information would conflict. When a journalist came to interview him on the set of the last movie he worked on (but did not complete), *Dark Blood,* River joked with director George Sluizer: "Oh, George, let's see how much I can lie to him." When he talked about his parents' work in Children of God, he would call them "missionaries," not "cult members," even though he was completely aware that that's what they were. Perhaps it was an extension of River's acting to fabricate or obfuscate the details of his upbringing. Perhaps it was a way for him to repress a stressful and occasionally traumatic childhood.

In a 1991 interview with *Details* magazine, River would confess that he first had sex when he was four years old: "But I've blocked it out. I was completely celibate from ten to fourteen."[26] A friend of River's confirmed this: "Yes, yes, yes, he was molested. It began with other friends in the same commune/cult, and it escalated."[27] River's acceptance of his childhood molestation, as if it were a normal thing for a toddler to have sex, sends a chill down my spine. I would not be surprised if this kind of thing happened in many of the hippie communes. There was a reason why my mother always kept a close eye on me when I was around my father's friends.

Molestation like River's was a fate that many of the children in Children of God suffered. *Charmed* actress and #MeToo activist Rose McGowan was also raised in Children of God. She recalled her childhood (and the cult's practice of promoting sex between adults and children) for biographer Gavin Edwards, author of *Last Night at the Viper Room,* the most recent account of River's life: "Their whole thing was that children are very sexual beings." She said Berg preached that God made children capable of enjoying sex for a reason. "I was not molested because my dad was strong enough to realize that hippie love had gone south," McGowan said.[28]

The cult's promotion of sexual liberty and bed-hopping among adults, and its encouragement of incest and approval of sexual expression among children, created a perfect storm for child sexual abuse to happen. However, by River's own confession, he was not celibate from the time he was first molested at age four until age ten. The Bottoms left Children of God when River was seven, which means his abuse continued for three years after they left the cult.

In answer to Boorman's question about why River took all those drugs, some of River's biographers point to the childhood abuse he was subjected to. They point to River's unreconciled trauma—both from having to support his growing family as a young child and from the molestation—as the thing that drove him to abuse drugs. I am sure trauma played a role in River's addictive behaviors. Indeed, there is plenty of research showing that adults who have suffered from childhood emotional, physical, or sexual abuse are far more susceptible to alcoholism, drug abuse, and depression than their nontraumatized peers.[29]

However, I am more inclined to agree with Gavin Edwards's assessment of the situation. By all accounts, River was a kind and sensitive soul. His childhood experiences may have only made him more aware of the potential for pain and beauty in life: "Despite being repeatedly molested, he ended up a joyful person anyway, full of love for the world. He was certainly self-aware enough about what happened—he told good friends about it, although he chose not to share it with the world. Even if River were alive today, he might not be able to explain how his experiences in Venezuela formed his adult self. The human spirit is a mysterious thing: traumas that flatten some people bounce off of others. Pain and hope get tangled into uncuttable Gordian knots."[30]

Whatever his reasons were, River kept this part of his life to himself and the people close to him. I have a few theories, but my strongest has to do with what he absorbed from his time in Children of God and the way his parents continued their code of silence around the cult years after they had left. Even after River's overdose in 1993, when reporters asked Arlyn, then going by Heart, about Children of God, she refused to discuss it. A *Gainesville Sun* reporter named Bill DeYoung spoke to Heart after the memorial service in Florida. She gave him a ten-minute taped interview, which was surprisingly forthcoming for her. But when DeYoung called Heart to go over the quotes he would use, this time she was critical, saying they made her "sound stupid." Heart put DeYoung on speakerphone so everyone could hear. "It was spooky," DeYoung said. "When I got to the part of their childhood and I mentioned Children of God, Heart stopped me. 'We don't want our name anywhere near the Children of God,' she said. Then she [added], 'Oh no, we don't want that. Take it out.'"[31] Even after River's death, Heart was careful about the face she presented to the public and wanted to ensure that any stories about him played down his drug addiction and instead showed the healthy environmentalist, the gifted actor, the kind spirit.

If there is one thing that can drive a person to using drugs, I think it must be the idea of splitting up the personality, dividing oneself into neat little boxes. Around some friends, River partied. Around others, he ate tofu and played guitar. Not only was he living multiple lives, but these lives were at opposite extremes: devil or saint, vegan or heroin addict, the only genuine guy left in the world or an actor. River learned from his family and childhood to compartmentalize, and this skill would serve him in his film career.

I first saw River in the coming-of-age film *Stand by Me*. What I remember of River is his emotional draw, even at such a young age and in an ensemble of young actors who would each go on to have their own success. Reiner remembered once asking River to remember a time an adult disappointed him for one scene. River apparently walked away, thought for a few minutes, and came back ready to perform. That was the take that went into the movie, and when I rewatched it to write this chapter, I was struck again by the naked emotions on display, tears of hurt and anger. Reiner said, "Obviously, there was something very hurtful to him in his life that he connected with to make that scene work. You just saw that raw naturalism. I've seen the movie a thousand times—and every time I see that scene, I cry."[32]

It was on the set of *Stand by Me* that River first started experimenting with drugs, smoking marijuana with costar Corey Feldman after discovering a crew member's bong. When they asked the man what the bong was, he answered them and let the kids, who were about fourteen at the time, try it out.[33] River and Corey coughed a lot and didn't get the appeal—or at least that's what Corey said. River seemed to have acquired a taste for it, however. Later, while the cast was staying in a Manhattan hotel for a press junket, Corey said he smelled marijuana coming from River's room. River played this off, denying it entirely.

The Bottoms, now known as the Phoenixes, also had a family friend named Larry McHale who served as a sort of nanny for the family. Larry drove River around to see his friends, all of whom were adults. Once, after a day trip to the Magic Mountain theme park, one of Larry's friends pulled out a baggie of cocaine. Another of Larry's friends, Pat Brewer, said, "River looked very unsure, [cocaine] was something new to him. I remember saying, 'I wouldn't give any of that to the kid.' But then River insisted on having his share. I think he was trying to prove himself in the group and felt peer pressure."[34] River didn't enjoy his first cocaine experience. He started wheezing and went to be alone in the garden. But over the next few weeks, Larry and River would come back to Brewer's house to talk about music and play guitar. Over the course of these visits, River became increasingly comfortable with using drugs.

No matter what went on behind closed doors, River was already cultivating a straight public image. When *Stand by Me* became a surprise hit in August 1986, he became a celebrity. For his ten weeks of work shooting the movie, he made $50,000, but after the movie became a hit, his fee skyrocketed to $350,000 a picture. His star was on the rise, and he started giving more interviews. It's in these conversations that we see River's public antidrug position. Even though he certainly was smoking pot at this time,

River told *People* magazine, "I've tried marijuana a few times but I don't like it. I get really boring on marijuana. It makes me dull."[35]

One facet of adolescence is the trying on and discarding of different personas, experimenting with changes in your hairstyle, the kind of music you listen to, even the way you speak in the pursuit of your "true" self, the identity that most fits what you want to show to the world. In an ill-advised attempt to discover the "real" me, whom I imagined to be a dark, brooding intellectual, I dyed my hair an inky black in college. The color was not a good choice for someone with an olive complexion, but I can't help but feel affection for that younger self when I look at my sullen school photos. This tenderness is one of the surprises I've discovered in adulthood, and one that River would never find. When I read his conflicting stories in interviews, and I see how he manipulated the story of his upbringing or, later, the realities of his drug use, I realized this adopting of characters was as much a reflection of his youth as it was a testament to his skill as an actor. *Stand by Me* was all the more powerful because of how it so poignantly captured the agonies of that space between childhood and adulthood. River's performance in the film marked the beginning of a new phase in his career—one of fame, wealth, and increasing drug use.

I think the importance of being fulfilled in one's personal and professional lives isn't discussed enough. When I was a young lawyer in my twenties, I remember running on sheer adrenaline during my working hours. Every moment felt urgent. I was aware of the stakes if I messed up. The pressure associated with the fact that people's lives were in my hands (whether or not they went to jail) was the driving force in my work life. But once I got home after a busy day, I would no longer feel that urgency or even the relief that one might imagine. I wanted to do something that would bring a fraction of the heightened nature of work into my personal life. So I turned to cocaine. I imagine that as an actor who had to conjure up vivid emotions for the camera, River may have also struggled with returning to himself after a day on set. In 1989 he spoke to DeYoung about how movies allowed him to lose himself: "It just feels so good, it's such a great escape, you know, it really is. It's a great fantasy. It has nothing to do with the idea of movies, it's just getting lost. Having an excuse to get that far out of your head is just a really good feeling."[36] He could have been describing what it was like to use drugs, not just to act in movies.

River's films ranged from the mundane—*Explorers, Little Nikita*—to the sublime, like *Running on Empty,* for which he earned an Oscar nomination. He attended the Academy Awards ceremony with his then-girlfriend, the actress Martha Plimpton. The young couple looked like the epitome of grunge cool, with River's flowing golden locks and Martha's slicked-back short hair, which she'd cut for a role. But soon after the ceremony, the couple broke up after years of fighting about River's drinking and drug use. Martha wanted River to get sober; River did not. Martha would later say, "When we split up, a lot of it was that I had learned that screaming, fighting, and begging wasn't going to change him. He had to change himself, and he didn't want to yet."[37]

When not in LA, River lived in a growing pseudo-commune in the college town of Gainesville, Florida, as far away from Hollywood as he could get. John Phoenix hated that his kids were in show business, and he wanted the family to get away from the center of it all. He'd get drunk on Scotch and start calling Hollywood "the great Babylon," where "they care for money and nothing else." "It's an evil, bad place," he'd say.[38] Not only did John hate Hollywood, but he resented Arlyn for keeping the kids in the Hollywood machine. River, always the peacemaker, tried his best to balance the conflicting wishes between both parents. As the family's primary breadwinner, he couldn't outright quit acting, but he placated John with the promise that after a few more movies he'd quit for good. They'd go back to the land. In the meantime, father and son bonded by getting roaring drunk.

Martha Plimpton came to stay with the Phoenixes in Gainesville one summer and recognized the changes in River, who now was drinking every night, smoking the local marijuana strain known as Gainesville Green, snorting cocaine, and tripping on mushrooms.[39] "River and his father were *always* having breakthrough conversations where River would tell his father about alcohol, about their roles. But the next day nothing would change. River would say to me, 'Well, it's not *that* serious, it's not *that* bad.'"[40] It was the first time Martha recognized the troubling ways that River drank and did drugs, and it worried her: "He really liked getting drunk and high, but he didn't really have a gauge for when to stop."[41]

I think the real turning point in River's drug use, and in his career as an actor, was while shooting *My Own Private Idaho.* His work in *Idaho* marked his ascendancy into the rarefied air occupied by a select few actors, like Daniel Day-Lewis or Leonardo DiCaprio. Ethan Hawke—who acted alongside River in River's first feature film, *Explorers*—had this to say about River's turn as a narcoleptic teen prostitute: "You remember the Daffy Duck cartoon, where Daffy's trying to do all this stuff in front of the audience and the cane keeps coming and dragging him off? And finally he does this big magic trick and kind of lights himself on fire and he gets a standing ovation, and as he floats up and away, he goes: 'It's a great trick, but you can only do it once.' I thought that about *My Own Private Idaho:* We got to watch River light himself on fire. And he did."[42]

River's friend, actor Keanu Reeves, delivered the script to him around Christmas of 1989, after schlepping it on the back of his motorcycle from Canada to Gainesville.[43] Filmmaker Gus Van Sant had written the script about two teenage male prostitutes, scraping by to survive on the streets of Portland. One was a good boy fallen from grace, played by Reeves; the other was a boy born and bred in hardship, played by River.

While working on *Idaho,* River fully immersed himself in the role, from the way he walked and spoke to his sexual behavior and further experimentation with slamming heroin. Van Sant hooked Reeves and River up with some of his friends, either former or current street boys familiar with the Portland scene, to research their roles. River, especially, dove headfirst into researching the lives of street boys. Mike Parker, a twenty-three-year-old former runaway and friend of Van Sant's, was River's primary source of information. Parker would take River to a gay club called The City and would point out the young male prostitutes to River. He told River he used to attract johns by "looking young and innocent as possible, giving bursts of uncontrollable laughter," and shuffling his feet shyly. River picked up the mannerisms like a natural, mastering "all the marketing tricks," as Parker would say.[44]

It was while researching *Idaho* that River also got into harder drugs. He first became interested in the technical act of shooting up through watching Van Sant's first movie, *Drugstore Cowboy,* on New Year's Day 1990. Soon afterward he tried pharmaceutical-grade morphine and heroin. That fall in Portland he smoked heroin a few times, too. Another adviser for *Idaho,* a former addict and hustler named Matt Ebert, said River told him he'd never done heroin before when they did it together for the first time. "I remember thinking, 'He's lying,'" Ebert said.[45] But River wasn't the only person using heroin on the *Idaho* set. Ebert said there was "rampant heroin use" among the cast and the crew. River, Ebert noticed, was developing a problem with it. "River started with heroin out of malaise, and because it's a delicious drug, but then the reason changed."[46] River began using heroin from curiosity and as a way to get into his character's head, but as time went on he started becoming addicted.

A lot of people were doing heroin in the '90s. Some of my classmates at Columbia were shooting up in the dorm room next to mine; it was almost as common as cocaine or even pot. In August 1993, just a few months before River would overdose outside the Viper Room, the *New York Times* reported that heroin use was spreading across the United States. Increased production of opium poppies led to a rise in supply, which in turn allowed the heroin sold on the streets to be of higher purity than ever before. According to a DEA official quoted in the article, the heroin of the early '80s was only about 3 or 4 percent pure; the average purity of heroin in 1993 was 35 percent.[47] Heroin with a greater purity could get people high by safer means, like snorting or smoking. People were afraid of sharing needles in a post-AIDS world, and many would have stayed away from heroin if asked to shoot up. Snorting heroin, however, was a friendlier way to ingest it. Soon heroin became a club favorite, especially as a way to mellow people out who had used cocaine or crystal meth. River's interest in injecting heroin made him different from the users described in the *New York Times,* but the point is that heroin was readily available, and people were mixing it with cocaine to create speedballs.

Something else people don't seem to realize when they talk about the popularity of heroin in the '90s is the romanticism around it at the time.

"Heroin chic" became a movement in fashion that glamorized languorous images of strung-out models. Kate Moss set a new standard for beauty that focused more on waif-like thinness than the fit models of the '80s. A 1993 Calvin Klein ad that featured her hip bones jutting out was credited with starting the heroin chic trend. It is impossible to know for sure, but one can guess that River's character as "a sensitive," his impulsive nature, and his history of trauma made him a prime candidate for drug addiction. And the Kate Moss ads surely had some impact.

After River died of a cocaine/heroin overdose in 1993, Nirvana member Kurt Cobain killed himself while on heroin in 1994, overshadowing River's passing. Even as the kids around me were tacking up posters of Cobain and wearing mourning garb, I kept thinking about River's death. I recognized much of myself in him; I was also the person who turned to vegetarianism out of sympathy for animal suffering. Although my upbringing had little in common with River's time in Children of God, I knew what it was like to grow up in a repressed, antidrug household. My father, a consummate stoner, was vehemently opposed to alcohol, and my mother just wasn't into drinking or taking drugs. The first time I drank alcohol in high school, I got sick because I knew so little about drinking and because, like River, I had an all-or-nothing approach to life.

In the spring of 1999, a good friend of mine was robbed at gunpoint while out in the city. She was terrified of going to the police station by herself, so she asked me to go with her. However, I told her I was studying and couldn't take time away from that to accompany her to the station. It was one of the more ruthless decisions I've ever made, and my friendship with her has never been the same since then, rightfully so. On the flip side, when I started partying with my first husband, I couldn't stop the way other people seemed to be able to. I could never imagine going out to a club without being high on cocaine or ecstasy. For a long time I wondered what was wrong with me, why I needed drugs to have a fun night. Now I realize that, as a young lawyer dealing with the high pressure of trying to quickly understand a lot of complicated material, I needed to do drugs just to shut off the work part of my brain. Not to mention the fact that going to clubs sober is not very fun for most people, myself included.

From my adult vantage point, what really strikes me about River's death is how much his public image as a tofu-eating blonde angel ultimately led to his downfall. Over and over in interviews, River maintained his stance against drugs, even as he continued to cycle between extreme behaviors. From his family home in Gainesville, River spoke about Hollywood's cocaine culture with disgust: "People look at you if you have a *cold*. You feel you can't blow your nose. It depresses me."[48] What's interesting about this quote is that River does not seem to have an issue with cocaine use per se; just other people's assumption that he might be using cocaine. This would make sense for River, who wanted to be free to do his thing without judgment.

For what it's worth, he would always have sympathy for people who struggled with drug addiction. When Corey Feldman, one of the other stars of *Stand by Me,* was arrested for heroin possession in 1990, River was sympathetic: "It makes you realize drugs aren't just done by bad guys and sleazebags. It's a universal disease."[49] He also was a good friend to the people in his life who were looking for sobriety, sometimes calling a drug counselor named Bob Timmins to help his addicted friends, although he never asked for help for himself. Timmins said, "He called me twice in the last couple of years to ask me to intervene with friends. And he made it passionately clear that he was committed with his time and money to making sure these people didn't die. In one case he drove [a famous rock star] to a clinic in Arizona."[50]

River's drug use and drinking also allowed him to connect with his father John, who had been living in an estate River purchased for him in Costa Rica. John lived in Costa Rica alone while the rest of the family lived in Gainesville, and he had become a fixture in his neighborhood bar. When River came to visit his father in 1990, apparently the two of them stayed up late talking about their drinking habits and addictive behaviors. Scott Green, a member of the Gainesville rock band Aleka's Attic, later said he'd talked about these conversations with River: "[River] thought he might have inherited his dependence from his father but he didn't think it was in any way his father's fault."[51] This cognitive dissonance might have been willful ignorance or an example of an actor buying into their own act. But in the period between 1990 and his death in 1993, even an actor as good as River had to admit he had a problem.

After River finished shooting *Idaho,* his drug habits continued to expand to include heroin, Valium, and any other drug he might want.[52] Eventually his work started to suffer. While shooting a movie called *Silent Tongue,* some of the filmmakers wondered if he was acting while high.[53] But they kept their concerns to themselves, and River was always kind. In between shoots he'd bide his time by partying in LA. His drug use led to the end of his relationship with Suzanne Solgot. She said, "He didn't want me nagging him. Pointing out the contradictions between his public stands and what he was doing to his body."[54]

After his breakup with Solgot there was little to keep River out of trouble. Martha Plimpton would say that he'd call her at random times. "He'd often be high when he called, and I'd listen for twenty minutes to his jumbled, made-up words, his own logic, and not know what the fuck he was talking about," she said. "He'd say, 'You're just not listening carefully enough.'"[55]

River showed clear signs of intoxication while shooting his last completed movie, a drama called *The Thing Called Love.* It was bad enough that his talent agent, Iris Burton, called Heart to come to LA and speak to her son. For the first time, even Heart could see that River was not well. But she didn't confront him; she just watched anxiously as he gave a hollow performance. When *The Thing Called Love* was released after River's death, film critic Roger Ebert noted, "the world was shocked when River Phoenix overdosed, but the people working on this film should not have been. . . . This performance should have been seen by someone as a cry for help."[56]

River was clean and sober when he started shooting what would be the last film he worked on, a thriller called *Dark Blood.* When production began in rural Utah, River was coming off a relaxing trip to visit his father in Costa Rica, where he celebrated his twenty-third birthday. The mystical vibes of this desolate part of Utah really appealed to River. He'd lie on the porch of the house he was staying in and yell out to UFOs, "Take me, I'm ready! What else is out there?"[57] He was doing well on the film until they got to a scene that featured a dead snake. River, the vegan and self-proclaimed savior of the Earth, had a meltdown and locked himself in his trailer. Iris called River and heard him rave, "Iris, they're killing snakes. They want me to work with murdered snakes. They poisoned them. Or strangled them. I don't know. . . . They're liars, fucking liars, all of them. They killed the snake. *They're murderers! Murderers!*"[58] Iris had to fly to the set to keep her client calm.

The last two weeks of the shoot were to happen in Los Angeles. Following the snake incident, director George Sluizer let River go back to LA a day early. River proceeded to get back into drugs. On Saturday, October 30, River arrived at the *Dark Blood* set looking haggard. He'd been partying all night and had taken a Valium to bring him down enough to work. Sluizer noticed, "He was not one hundred percent in control of his body movements. But there was no problem with his acting and so there was no reason for me to intervene."[59]

That fateful night, River went out with girlfriend, Samantha Mathis, and two of his siblings, Rain and Leaf (now known as Joaquin). They arrived at the Viper Room at 12:27 a.m. The club was packed, and Johnny Depp was playing with his band P on stage. At 12:45 a.m., one of River's friends (the same one whom River had twice driven to rehab) handed River a drink with a dissolved speedball in it. River knew the drink had something in it, but he didn't ask what, and he drank it in one gulp. Immediately, River felt sick. He asked his friend, "What did you give me? What the fuck is in it?" He threw up on the table before slumping in his seat, unconscious.

Discussions about recreational drug use never seem to include information on the importance of routes of administration. Eating a drug will have a different effect from injecting it or snorting it or any other route of administration. When you consume a drug orally by eating or swallowing it, the drug hits the bloodstream very quickly. Depending on the potency of the drug, this rapid release can put people at risk for heart problems or potential overdose.

With a stimulant like cocaine, the blood pressure rises and the heart rate quickens, leading to possible heart attacks immediately or other issues over time. In a 1982 interview with *People* after John Belushi's speedball overdose, UCLA professor and drug expert Dr. Ronald K. Siegel commented on the different routes of administration for cocaine and cocaine hydrochloride, or crack. According to Siegel, it takes approximately three minutes for a person to feel the effects of cocaine when snorted, compared to about fourteen seconds when injected intravenously. Crack cocaine can be smoked, providing the quickest hit: six seconds on average.[60] For people who have developed a tolerance to cocaine, it's preferable to find a more potent and quicker hit.

Siegel also mentioned the increased risk of seizure with higher doses of cocaine, caused by changes to the brain's electrical currents, and he discussed how cocaine had become the "drug of commerce" in the entertainment industry. He explained, "I see slightly more females than males [using speedballs]. They all tend to be in the same professional positions— actors, actresses and movie production people. . . . It is very socially acceptable in [Hollywood] and almost required."[61]

The route of administration also affects how dependent an individual becomes on a drug. A 1994 study found that people who injected cocaine had the highest levels of dependence, while those who used cocaine intranasally had the lowest levels of dependence.[62] This study did not include a review of cocaine dependence when it is ingested.

We do know that consuming a drug orally has a longer onset time and a longer duration. This is why, when it comes to using marijuana, beginners are encouraged to try smoking the plant first before eating edibles. When you eat an edible, the THC takes longer to cause a reaction because it has to pass through the stomach and liver. But when the THC gets metabolized by the liver, it turns into 11-hydroxy-THC, which has an easier time passing the blood-brain barrier, creating a more intense high that lasts for a much longer time than other routes of administration for marijuana.[63] On the other hand, smoking a joint has a more immediate effect, since the THC goes straight to the brain; but it does not create a lasting high (unless, of course, you keep puffing away).

Another important yet rarely mentioned aspect of addiction is the concept of "set and setting." The set is the mindset or mental state a person brings to the drug experience, and the setting is the environment they are in when they use drugs. Both the set and the setting will affect a person's high and even their drug tolerance. For example, if you think alcohol makes people violent, there is a higher chance of you becoming an aggressive drunk.[64] This iteration of the self-fulfilling prophecy bears out with all drug use, from stimulants like cocaine and methamphetamine to depressants like heroin.

There are different ways to interpret how setting affects a person's high. First, there is the physical location of the individual's drug experience. When trying a new drug for the first time, it is always best to be in a comfortable, safe environment, not necessarily at a large social event like a concert or a club. There is also a social aspect to consider. One study found that having external rewards or stimulation outside of drugs, like recognition from peers or the love of a pet, can make people less susceptible to developing a problematic relationship with drugs.[65]

In short, the issue of addiction goes far beyond any one drug. The way the drug is administered and an individual's set and setting all play major roles in whether that person will form an addiction.

When River initially lost consciousness in the nightclub that night, his girlfriend Samantha Mathis didn't know what to do. If she called an ambulance, River would get help, but he would also become a story in the tabloids, bolstering his reputation as an unreliable actor. Instead, Mathis called a friend to come help.

River woke up and stumbled out the side door of the Viper Room at around 1:00 a.m. He immediately collapsed on the sidewalk and started having seizures, his head smacking against the concrete. His sister Rain sat on his chest, trying to hold his body still. Leaf watched in a state of panic, but didn't call 911 until 1:10 a.m. River had already stopped breathing when they arrived four minutes later. Onlookers in Halloween costumes were surprised to recognize the now-still body as River Phoenix, while the actor, musician, and friend to all who met him died on the Sunset Strip.

What strikes me as particularly senseless about River's death is that he might have survived if the people around him had felt comfortable calling the emergency responders earlier. He may have survived if Narcan[66] had been in use and available at that time. He may have survived if there was one doctor on staff at the Viper Room. There were two opportunities where the people around River could have called emergency responders and perhaps saved his life. After all, Cedars-Sinai Medical Center was just a mile and a half away, a five-minute drive at midnight. When River passed out at the table inside the club, instead of worrying about what the other clubgoers would think, his friends could have dialed 911. And again, when River collapsed on the sidewalk and started seizing, a club bouncer told Leaf he should call for help. "He's fine," Leaf said, watching anxiously.[67] By the time Leaf finally made the 911 call that would be played over and over across the country, it was too late.

I understand that the players involved were all young. River was the oldest, at age twenty-three. Part of what this story's about is that it's one of those accidents that happen to the young, especially when they're rich and famous and have access to any mind-altering substance they could want. Nobody knows what they would do in that situation until it happens to them, but young people certainly don't always know the best way to handle an emergency. The law protects people who report witnessing public overdoses,[68] but the combination of stigma and fear can paralyze people in the moment.

The fact remains that the speedball River ingested that night was not the only thing that killed him. I believe that if the people involved had not had to worry about the consequences for River's image, his reputation as a good boy, they might have called for help sooner and saved his life. But I also believe that if supervised drug use were legal and clinics existed as they did between 1912 and the early 1920s[69] throughout the United States, many lives would be saved, including River's, because the prevalence and existence of these clinics served to destigmatize the use and abuse of heroin. It is the stigmatization—which comes, in large part, from the criminalization—that kills people.[70]

Given these differences in society, River might not have died at the Viper Room that night.

In the memorial service at the Paramount lot that November, Samantha Mathis was present, along with Leaf and Rain and the rest of River's family; his talent agent, Iris Burton; his past directors like Rob Reiner from *Stand by Me* and Gus Van Sant from *My Own Private Idaho;* and former costars like ex-girlfriend Martha Plimpton, who appeared in *The Mosquito Coast* with him, and Bradley Gregg, who had played the older Chambers boy in *Stand by Me*. While the mourners gathered to deliver their platitudes about River being free now that he was in a better place, it was Gregg who interrupted the proceedings. He shouted, "River didn't have to die to be free!" Then he stood up and repeated himself: "River didn't have to die to be free!"[71]

10

FLYING THROUGH THE WEEDS OF THE AUGHTS

BEFORE I HAD CHILDREN OR DOGS or had met the man who would become the steadiest comfort of my life; before I had the responsibilities of a law practice, a staff, a family that depended on me; before I had stacks of unread newspapers and glaring accusatory red numbers telling me of missed phone calls, unread text messages, unanswered emails—I had some freedom. And in that small window of freedom in the summers after college and during law school in the early 2000s, sensing the stale breath of obligation on the horizon, I devoted what free time I had to the pursuit of pleasure.

The beautiful thing about growing up in Los Angeles is being exposed to a wide variety of ethnic groups: Mexicans, Central Americans, Armenians, Persian Muslims, and Jews, representatives from every Asian nation. However, I was so secluded, so cloistered in high school, that even though I'd gone to Beverly Hills High with the Persian Muslims who first introduced me to the art of smoking opium, I didn't meet them in high school. My then-boyfriend Steve, four years older, had to introduce us years later.

We all met in the summer of '99—or was it the summer after? Now I have a hard time remembering. Steve's friends H. and R. were nice. They had one of those little townhouses in Beverly Hills, the kind that always feels a little haunted and makes you wonder if anyone actually lives inside of them. R. would ignite the flame of a Bunsen burner and set a teapot over the fire—a detail I remember because I always found it ruggedly charming that they eschewed the functioning stove. We'd sit in little wooden chairs around the kitchen table under the soft light of a floor lamp. We drank black tea with leaves that settled on the bottom. One of the boys told me the caffeine and sugar in the tea raised the blood pressure, therefore improving the high.

H. breathed life into the pipe before passing it around, wisps of faintly sweet-smelling smoke drifting over our heads. Steve told me H. and R. brought the opium in through the rugs they imported. I never asked where it came from, but the handful of times I found myself seated at that kitchen table, I remember the opium being very mellow, making my limbs heavy and my mind tranquil after the hyperactive buzz of the club scene from the night before. Steve and I found this late-night communion around the opium pipe far better than the alternative way we found to come down from the coke and grasp what snatches of sleep we could: a tablet of Xanax.

I still wonder at the message H. and R.'s parents were trying to convey when they brought the young men back home: *You're enjoying the liberties of America too much and too often. We're packing you away to Iran, where you will remember how to live a life of duty and deprivation*—a concept that seemed so foreign to me. I didn't know H. and R. well. They were friends you pick up when your life becomes oriented toward a certain hedonistic sun, caught in the same orbit. But I remember our "opium teas" were the best, most peaceful, and doubtlessly safest drug experiences I ever had in my twenties.

In many ways the image of the white girl corrupted by a foreign man and his drugs is what spurred passage of the United States' first drug ban: an 1875 ordinance banning the operation or visitation of opium dens in San Francisco, as discussed in chapter 1. At first the authorities didn't care what went on in Chinatown's smoke-filled opium establishments, as long as the only people patronizing them were foreign, working class, or anyone else deemed below their notice. But once stories got out about middle-class white girls reportedly being lured into these so-called "dens of iniquity" and forced into languorous, sensual orgies with the Chinese who operated them, the hand-wringing and moral panic spread far beyond the bounds of Chinatown. One grand jury spread tales of "white girls between the ages of thirteen and twenty [who] are enticed into these opium dens, become regular habitues, and finally are subject wholly to the wishes of the Oriental visitors."[1]

More stories of this sort made their way into the local newspapers. An undercover reporter with the *San Francisco Examiner* wrote of "two white girls, neither of whom were over 17 years of age" and dressed as if they were going to a "Sunday picnic," being seen entering one of the neighborhood's opium dens.[2] A police captain made an interesting comment that, I think, gets at the heart of the issue: "It is only we detectives who know the extent to which the opium habit has caught on amongst the high-toned women in San Francisco. And the trouble is that the *high-spirited and most adventurous women* seem to succumb first." (Italics added.) This ordinance was not just meant for the Chinese laborers, but also for the women who sought out excitement, who donned frilly dresses and went into smoky lounges unseen by the watchful eyes of their fathers. The ordinance was an attempt to withhold pleasure from white women who dared to seek it.

Images that made their way into the papers of white women lying in opium-induced stupors next to the out-of-work Chinese did not deserve the hysteria they produced. From my perspective, each group lived under its own oppressive yoke, although to varying degrees, of course, with the Chinese facing economic hardship along with the xenophobia that would lead to the Chinese Exclusion Act of 1882. Meanwhile, it's possible that the middle-class white women might have been seeking frivolity for frivolity's sake, but I don't think this is so. A few years after the ordinance in San Francisco, Henrik Ibsen would produce his play *A Doll's House,* wherein Nora tells her husband Torvald that she has been "performing tricks" for him for their whole marriage to keep him amused and enraptured; and before that, she performed tricks for her father, to keep his love and, ultimately, his protection. "That's how I've survived," Nora tells her husband before she leaves the home she made for him. "You and Papa have done me a great wrong."[3]

I don't see a difference in the expressions of the white women and the Chinese laborers in the photos of these opium dens. They all have the same downtrodden, introspective quality, as if the opium they're smoking may not even be for pleasure but for respite from the daily challenges of their lives. They found this oasis in the opium dens of Chinatown, much as I would in that Beverly Hills townhouse over a century later. The laws have changed, but human nature has not. Everyone has a right to seek out what pleasure they can, what sacred retreat is available, including mind-altering substances. The vast majority of drug users never develop a substance abuse problem, which means the average drug user is someone who uses recreationally, to stimulate the mind, to heighten a social experience, to expand consciousness—in other words, for the sheer pleasure of the thing.

The government and its War on Drugs heightened the issue, framing the drug laws that would be drafted as a means to protect the public from dangerous and addictive substances that would steal people's free will away. The drug laws, starting with the Pure Food and Drug Act of 1904 and continuing through the Controlled Substances Act of 1970, were, on their face, about protecting the public. In reality, there were far more complicated political machinations at work, including such factors as the inherent racism of the politicians and the social and economic climates of the country. But the point was that the government was reframing itself as a patriarchal force, from cold and administrative law and order to the image of kindly Nancy Reagan sitting beside her presidential husband, urging America's young people to just say no.

So thorough was the messaging that the majority of the American people did not realize their cognitive freedoms were being checked. As attorney Richard Glen Boire puts it, "the so-called war on drugs is not a war on pills, powder, plants, and potions, it is war on mental states—a war on consciousness itself—how much, what sort we are permitted to experience, and who gets to control it. More than an unintentional misnomer, the government-termed war on drugs is a strategic decoy label; a slight-of-hand [*sic*] move by the government to redirect attention away from what lies at ground zero of the war—each individual's fundamental right to control his or her own consciousness."[4]

While I was organizing the research for my Harvard Law thesis, I discovered Boire's work on formulating a legal basis for the idea of cognitive liberty. He describes cognitive liberty as "a right to freedom of thought, to independent thinking, to autonomy over [one's] own mind and brain chemistry, and the right to experience the full spectrum of possible thought."[5] Now this view has apparently been adopted by some in the American Medical Association. In a 2020 journal article, AMA members Mark Tyndall and Zoë Dodd write: "We don't often think of personal drug use as a human rights issue, but, arguably, it is one. In 2016, Human Rights Watch and the American Civil Liberties Union released a report on the criminalization of drug use in the United States, the summary of which concluded that 'enforcement of drug possession laws causes extensive and unjustifiable harm to individuals and communities across the country.'"[6]

The people impacted by the criminalization of drug use are poorly organized and often hidden, as drug use is illegal and highly stigmatized. People using drugs face numerous barriers with regard to employment, housing, food security, and health care, while spending much of their time in the criminal justice system. Despite these barriers, drug user groups can be a critical force for change, and there are good examples of how people who use drugs have changed drug policy. The Supreme Court of Canada's decision to keep North America's first legally sanctioned supervised injection site open was largely due to the advocacy of drug users in Vancouver.[7]

If personal drug use is a human right, then addressing drug use and addiction will require a much broader approach. The best interventions proposed and practiced in the medical community will always be limited within the confines of a system in which drugs are illegal and the people using them must turn to sources that are entirely unregulated and often toxic. An ethical response to the opioid overdose crisis must include providing a strong social support system, breaking down stigma and discrimination, improving access to addiction treatment, and promoting harm-reduction interventions. Physicians and physician groups can play a major role in all of these areas by including social support in their treatment plans, actively breaking down stigma by treating patients with respect, offering evidence-based addiction treatment, and promoting harm reduction. These interventions could greatly improve health care outcomes and reduce opioid overdose deaths. In addition, physicians should be at the forefront of challenging drug laws and a criminal justice system that inflicts so much harm on patients and their families. If we do not recognize and address the drivers of drug use, challenge destructive drug policies, and tear down the pillars of structural violence, we will not see real change.

I got to meet Dr. Boire somewhere in a small, bucolic town off the 580, near Berkeley. I remember the golden light of a Berkeley fall, the smell of hay, and the kind of academic trailers you see around the East Bay housing at UC Berkeley. It was 2001; the country was at war, and the Patriot Act was about to pass. Some days it seemed only Dr. Boire and myself were thinking about drug reform. But then again, if not for the efforts of drug law reformers before me, I would not have been at Berkeley in the first place. I applied for and was accepted into the Berkeley Exchange, a visitor exchange scholar program, to study what was then the first statewide drug policy reform since the 1970s: California's Proposition 36, which allows eligible nonviolent drug offenders to avoid prison and the state's mandatory minimums (predetermined minimum sentences for certain crimes)[8] by entering a drug treatment program instead.[9]

This law passed due to the efforts of many drug law reformers before me who continue their work to this day. My favorites among them personally and professionally include Mikki Norris and her husband Chris Conrad,[10] a marijuana expert witness we frequently used to defend cases during 2004–2018 when Californians were allowed to defend marijuana cultivation and sales with personal use and collective use/sales. The law also partly owes its passage to Ethan Nadelman[11] and George Soros. The drug law reformer who is my current favorite is LA's very own controversial-for-no reason Cat Packer,[12] the head of the LA Department of Cannabis Regulation. She and I spoke on behalf of Proposition 19, the initiative that failed to pass in 2010 that would have legalized recreational marijuana. That measure would not have decriminalized marijuana or retroactively expunged records like Proposition 64 did, which ultimately did pass. And I was fortunate to have major drug law reformer Peter Barton Hutt as my very own advisor for my law school thesis. He has been the pro bono legal advisor to the Multidisciplinary Association for Psychedelic Studies[13] since the '80s. Hutt pleaded the case of homeless addicts in the only US Supreme Court case to ever deal with the subject.[14] He also recently arranged for his famous firm, Covington and Burling, to assist pro bono with a civil rights case we are currently handling that touches on environmental justice, cannabis, white supremacy, and Vietnam veterans.

The freedom, the right, to explore the full spectrum of possible thought, as if the mind were a vast ocean and you the captain with eyes set on the horizon—isn't this sort of intellectual curiosity another subcategory of pleasure? Why have we ceded this right to explore our own consciousness, and to experience that thrill of self-discovery, to a governing body? In my Harvard Law thesis, I ask, "What is the point in giving up the rights of nature, what is the point of living in a society, if to do so you must give up the right to control your own body and mind?"[15] These questions were woven into my argument that the Controlled Substances Act is unconstitutional because, as discussed in chapter 8, there is no rational basis to regulate drugs according to the CSA paradigm; and further, even assuming the CSA has a rational basis, the science behind the classifications is absurd. Marijuana is in Schedule I, but all plant substances are, because plants cannot be dosed into equal measurements and therefore cannot be scheduled. Cocaine is Schedule II.[16]

I wonder if the drug laws are not simply racist, classist, or a needless drain on national resources. I wonder if they are a way for the government to impose restrictions on what has always been a part of the human experience—using drugs, for whatever reasons a person chooses (as long as they are not harming anyone else). We should consider reframing the conversation from looking at how drugs can negatively impact our lives to how we can actually use drugs in a positive way, to increase pleasure and to aid in medical advancements.

Of course, there are other ways to pursue pleasure in life: food, sex, love, puppies, cashmere socks on a cold winter morning. I wonder if these pursuits don't just bring us back to the moment, if they mainly just remind us that all we have is whatever we are experiencing in the here and now. The silk of a cat's ear, the crisp bite of an apple, the kind of long, belly-aching laughter that brings tears to your eyes. And there is more, be it the inhale of sweet smoke in the dead of night or the spark of a joint between running errands. With all the hardship that awaits, why not find joy where we can?

My window of freedom was closing faster than I imagined. By the early 2000s my career really started to develop. After the six months I worked at my dad's firm, I quit and decided to open up my own practice with the help of Jeffrey Sklan. He always had different practices going on, from criminal to civil and everything else. Jeffrey started paying me to appear on his behalf at his clients' criminal court dates, in order to build my own practice. It developed quickly from there to say the least.

For my first appearance, I ended up in Torrance, California, working on a meth ring case. One of the defendants in that case also had a bunch of forgery cases, and I got him probation on those cases while I was handling his meth ring case. I was doing everything possible to try to keep him out of jail while he had all these cases going on. I actually won a not-guilty verdict in Torrance, which got me a referral to a client named Stephanie Landa. (Stephanie and her family later introduced me to my husband, Jon Lachman, who at the time was close friends with Stephanie's sons.) Stephanie was a sixty-year-old who had just taken a plea in federal court for a prison sentence of forty-one months for manufacturing marijuana, in violation of 21 U.S.C. 856(a)(1). Her sentence was based on federal mandatory minimum sentencing guidelines.[17] I had been working on the mandatory minimum and sentencing guidelines issue since college, when I published my first article about it in *Helvidius,* the Columbia undergraduate political science journal. On the federal level, sentencing guidelines consist of factors that Congress has determined, through the US Sentencing Commission, should also have an impact on sentencing. Under current federal law, mandatory minimums are still the law of the land for drug crimes, but the sentencing guidelines have been found to be advisory.

The district court in *Landa* held as follows:

> *This brings us to one last point of possible downward departure. Four years ago, Ms. Landa was hit by a car and thrown against its windshield while crossing a street. She suffered a dislocated shoulder and was bedridden for six months. She underwent surgery. Ten corkscrews were used to reattach muscles in her shoulder with the result that use of her arm has been largely restricted. Additionally, her rotator cuff was split and her front tooth was knocked out. She has permanent nerve damage in the neck. She has been in and out of surgery and therapy and consultation for yet more surgery. It is true that most of her medical needs could be met by the Bureau of Prisons. Nonetheless, given Ms. Landa's ongoing and serious need for specialized medical attention and the likelihood that her need for close medical attention will continue into the future, the Court concludes that a two-level downward departure is warranted (U.S.S.G. § 5H1.4, p.s.), at least when this factor is considered in combination with Ms. Landa's responsibilities for her teenage son and elderly parents. This reduces her guideline range to 41 to 51 months. Beyond that, her motion must be deemed as not presenting extraordinary circumstances.*

I took her case and applied for a writ of habeas corpus to vacate her sentence. I ended up going onto the Northern District Court with her on the issue that one of the codefendants had a conflict of interest with the prior lawyer handling the matter, and about this downward departure. At the time, the federal district court and the Ninth Circuit had just ruled *United States v. Booker,* 543 U.S. 220 (2005), which held that the sentencing guidelines were advisory, whereas before they had been mandatory. Her forty-one-month sentence was handed down under those mandatory guidelines, but her judge had said that if he hadn't used the guidelines, he would have given her a lower sentence. The biggest issue in the case was whether the holding in *Booker* applied to habeas corpus proceedings.

By that time, the Supreme Court held that the *Booker* holding applied only to procedural due process and not habeas corpus, so our petition was denied. There the court held:

> *Landa contends that United States v. Booker, 543 U.S. 220, 125 S.Ct. 738, 160 L.Ed.2d 621 (2005), is retroactive to her case, and the district court granted a Certificate of Appealability on that issue. However, the unambiguous language of Landa's plea agreement encompasses an agreement not to appeal or collaterally attack her conviction or sentence for any reason other than ineffective assistance of counsel. In addition, Landa failed to raise the voluntariness issue in her opening brief and therefore has waived that issue. Accordingly, her plea agreement is valid and precludes us from addressing the issue of Booker retroactivity. See United States v. Nunez, 223 F.3d 956, 958–59 (9th Cir. 2000); see also United States v. Cardenas, 405 F.3d 1046, 1048 (9th Cir. 2005) (holding that the changes wrought by Booker do not render a guilty plea unknowing or involuntary).[18]*

11

JULIET

IN 2017, MY DAUGHTER JULIET, then eight or nine years old, went on a vacation with her father to Disney World in Orlando, Florida. Shortly after their trip ended and my daughter was settled back into her life with us, I learned that her father was accusing my husband of making hash oil in our house. Hash, an abbreviation of the Arabic *hashish,* is a concentrated form of cannabis. The process of making hash oil can be incredibly dangerous, especially if the manufacturer does not know what they are doing and they are using a volatile solvent, like butane. A couple of months before this accusation from Juliet's father, whom I've chosen not to name in these pages, there was a news story about a home blowing up because of improper hash oil manufacturing. That family used butane. Because of how dangerous this process can become, it is standard procedure for Child Protective Services to take children out of such environments. My daughter's father accused my husband of making hash oil because he hoped the accusation would earn him custody of Juliet and would, ultimately, hurt me.

I had not been at all romantically involved with her father since 2010. At the time of the Disney trip, that was seven years prior, and I had no idea why Juliet's father was suddenly making a hash oil accusation. He then took that accusation to the family courts. He had opened a paternity case shortly after Juliet was born. Over the course of going back and forth with her father in this legal battle, I would learn that the source of the accusation was an innocent gesture from Juliet. Apparently, while walking down the tourist-riddled streets of Orlando with her father, Juliet saw a Cheshire Cat statuette in the the window of a knickknack store. She bought the little piece for my husband, which made Juliet's father extremely jealous. From that sweet gesture, it escalated into something so distressing. Her father came up with the idea—which he in no way believed—that my husband was endangering Juliet's safety by making hash oil in the home. For the record, my husband does not manufacture hash oil in our home. However, Juliet's dad understood its dangers, and he knew if he could convince the courts, he could take Juliet away from me.

I struggled to write this chapter on the subject of parental drug use and the intervention of Child Protective Services for reasons I did not expect. I realized pretty quickly that the one thing that connects all parents is anxiety, the question at the center of everything: am I screwing up my kid? Even when the kid gets older and strikes out on their own, the anxiety continues. My mother calls me several times a day, sometimes several times an hour, asking me if everything is all right, how my kids are doing, how I'm doing. She's always been overbearing—a helicopter mom before we had that name for it—and I used to resent her constant involvement. That is, until I had my own kids. Now I understand. The anxiety never goes away; the worry doesn't stop.

Now imagine that this universal insecurity among parents was exposed by a government organization. It's the end of a normal day in your household; you've gotten up at a quarter to six, made sure the kids were washed and dressed and fed, carted them to their schools—which are thirty-five minutes apart from each other, because there is no justice in the Los Angeles educational system—and now it's creeping toward 9:30, but you're still in sweatpants and need to make it to the office for a 10:00 a.m. meeting with a potential new client, and so you throw something on and try to convince a stranger of your competence as a lawyer, even though sometimes you can tell this person has no intention of ever hiring you, and now there are other standard office issues to deal with, and oh, wait, somehow it's 2:00 p.m., which means it's time to pick up the first kid and juggle phone calls on the way to picking up the second kid, and traffic from Santa Monica is Dante-esque but it's okay because the kids are fighting over who gets the iPad, even though they both have iPads, so there's no scarcity of iPads, but fight they must until you get to the house because this is a blessed day without after-school activities that require carpool arrangements, and your coworkers are waiting for your input on this motion or the wording of this writ, and now the client from this morning has more questions but still doesn't want to hire you, and the oldest kid is whining about her multiplication tables even though you've explained that there's no way around memorizing those things if she ever wants to get to middle school, and there's food to arrange and to eat and the youngest is hopped up on a Coke you gave him just to get him to be quiet, so now he's zooming around the house and riling up the dogs, and your husband has a look on his face that can best be described as "resigned exasperation," but the oldest is now climbing into bed, which means the youngest is soon to follow, and it's almost 11:00 and now you can't stop pacing around the house, which is dark and silent for the first time, and even though there was a time during your party-girl phase in the early 2000s that your night would have just been getting started, now those nights are more than a decade behind you and you have to be up in six hours, so you smoke a bowl in the bathroom until your mind slows down enough for you to close your eyes, before the cycle repeats itself in five hours and fifty-three minutes.

This is just an average day for you. I mean, it's an average day for me. I imagine there are other parents who can relate to the pace, the moments of despair in the face of a shrieking toddler followed by the instances of pleasure when you catch that same toddler giving his sister a hug. In California, the nightcap of a joint, a vape, a hit or two on the bong after the kids go down is standard procedure. It's no different from a glass of wine or a covert cigarette, a few scoops of ice cream, perhaps all three if the day has been particularly trying. Most parents can enjoy their moments of decompression without worrying that they will be reported to Child Protective Services and potentially have their children taken away; or at least most white parents, most middle- or upper-class parents, most parents with some sort of privilege will never fear that their nightcap will be used against them in family court.

Yet that's exactly what happened to me, and frankly, I was lucky. As a lawyer, I know the law; as the daughter of a superb family attorney, I had the best representation anyone could ask for. I was the right race (white) and had the right background (upper middle class), and there was no evidence supporting my ex's accusations that I had smoked weed throughout my pregnancy with our daughter and was unfit to care for her. I was lucky. I ended up getting awarded 80 percent custody, and it was pursuant to a settlement with Juliet's father. Many other parents without the blessings of race, class, and education on their side don't find the same fortune.

So I realized upon writing this chapter that I would have to expand the telling of drug use, the law, and families beyond my perspective to show the greater problem. I need to talk about the couple in California who owned a marijuana dispensary and whose neighbors reported the smell of pot smoke from their house. They had to attend months of parenting courses before they regained custody of their children. There's the mother with an opiate addiction who nodded out while taking her child on a run to Target. There are the "crack moms" who became scapegoats for all of society's ills in the '80s and '90s. And there is my story, which is where I find I must start. My case is closed, my daughter is now a happy and healthy thirteen-year-old, and for now, there is some peace between her father and me.

Although I am known most for my work as a lawyer, as a child I dreamed of being a writer. At Columbia, I took creative writing courses under established authors like the memoirist Dani Shapiro. I remember being taught the traditional structure of the story: the setup, the struggle, the dark night of the soul, followed by the triumph and resolution. This skeleton tends to inform the way most stories are told and is the best way to compel the reader to continue, or so I was taught. That said, my story, like the others in this chapter, may have a setup and a struggle; there may be moments where all appears to be lost, and even some rare glimpses of triumph. Rarely, however, is there anything like a resolution. That is because, when it comes to proving your capability as a parent, there may be a beginning, but there is no definitive end, no closure that would satisfy anyone.

Other than my own kids, I have not historically been a "baby person." I never was the type to coo at the squishy faces and shiny eyes gurgling at me from the comfort of their bassinets. Even today as the mother of two, I regard other people's infants with a cautious distance. I'm never going to be the person who begs to hold the baby. I'm always going to be standing a few feet away, exchanging skeptical glances with my dogs. Still, I badly wanted to be a mother. Like so many of the other major decisions I've made in my life, it wasn't a slow burn so much as a pin pulled from a grenade. It happened when I was deplaning from a flight in one of the smaller airports around Los Angeles (it might have been the Burbank airport), and in the midst of travelers and commuters milling around the gate, my eyes landed on a baby in a carrier. All at once, I wanted a baby of my own. I needed a baby of my own.

My first husband had ended our marriage some months before and practically threw me out of the house. At no point during my time with Steven did we ever consider adding a baby to our routine of partying and working. Once he divorced me, it took me awhile to accept that our marriage really was over. I spent that time, a divorced woman at twenty-six, pondering away in my childhood bedroom. Maybe my new focus on having a child was reactionary, but my mind was made up.

I hurtled into the pursuit of a child with single-minded energy. This was back in 2007, when there were articles all the time, as there still seem to be articles all the time, about Angelina Jolie and her brood of adopted and biological children. We were starting to hear the word *surrogate* in the conversation around fertility treatment. More importantly, I knew a few guy friends who had earned several hundred bucks by donating their sperm to banks. I decided that a husband was not the way to go. It wasn't like I saw stellar examples of marriage in any of the branches of my family tree. I would be better than everyone else and get a sperm donor, have my baby, and skip the whole husband business altogether.

I met Juliet's father through work. He was almost ten years older than me, a lawyer, and tall. I hired him to make some appearances for me through the firm, and one day we hooked up. It might sound terrible to say this, but the encounter honestly did not mean much to me. I saw him as something slightly higher than a sperm donor: a "sperm donor plus." He served a purpose and he was available, and I didn't want much beyond that. Now, over ten years later, I know that Juliet's father saw this arrangement as a build-up to something more. At the time I didn't realize this, or maybe I was too involved with my own concerns to care. Oddly, he became a comfort to me. And, about two months after we started hooking up, I found out I was pregnant. I ended things with him a month later.

I turned my focus toward motherhood. I curbed my coffee and herb intake. I did little beyond going to court and returning to my West Hollywood apartment to curl up in a ball and absorb television.

Throughout the duration of my pregnancy, Juliet's father was hostile. He didn't really believe in his heart that we had been fucking for procreative purposes. He was cold and distant when he came to the office. Sometimes I would wake up to long, scathing voicemails he'd left while he was on Ambien. For some reason, I accepted his vitriol as something I deserved, my penance for hurting his feelings. I had strung him along, or so he thought, and in the back of my mind, I hoped he would exhaust himself before the baby came. Although I still saw Juliet's father as a sperm donor plus, I knew our baby would probably want to have some kind of relationship with her father. And in 2008, I had other things to worry about: other people's drug problems that became legal problems.

As soon as Juliet was born—a month early—and was transferred to the NICU, the DEA called me in the hospital to say a client of mine had a warrant out for him on a federal case stemming from a traffic stop in downtown LA eight months prior that resulted in the recovery of a few hundred OxyContins. They seemed to have no idea that I was so fresh off giving birth to my daughter that I could barely walk from my hospital bed to the bathroom just a few feet away. I don't remember what I said at that moment, but the bewilderment resurfaces. I wondered how they could be talking to me about my client and the opiate case when I was so exhausted and my daughter was still under observation.

Though I was no longer in practice with my dad and wouldn't officially be in practice with him again until a nine-month period in 2010–2011, I had him surrender my client to federal court, because the DEA indicated the federal court would not wait for my daughter to come out of the NICU, and if my client did not appear, I would expose myself to accessory charges.

Childbirth is hell; as a society, we can agree on this. However, childbirth is even more fraught when your child is born a month early. The doctors put her under observation, and I tried to keep my anxiety from spinning out the worst possible scenarios. My mother would bring me food from the outside world that she hoped would cheer me up. I was in the midst of a controlled collapse, trying to keep my terror at bay so I'd be well enough to take care of Juliet when the doctors deemed it safe. I felt completely helpless.

During this time, Juliet's father weaseled himself back into my life. He began staying at my place during Juliet's two weeks in the hospital, and he didn't leave for three months. During those roughly ninety days, he transitioned from being unhelpful to actually problematic. He didn't help pay for any of the baby's diapers, bottles, food, or clothes. He rarely even held Juliet during that time, but he seemed very interested in touching me and trying to encourage me to have sex. When I wouldn't do that, he would start screaming at me, saying I wasn't referring him any clients and how could he help pay for the baby if he wasn't making any money? To my horror, I realized he was jealous of the attention I was giving our daughter. He seemed to take my diligence—the very diligence that taking care of a newborn requires, like the constant feeding, the soothing, the efforts to sleep when the baby slept, even though all I ever wanted to do was watch her, to make sure she was still breathing—as an affront to him. He wanted a parenting plan, something that said he'd get Juliet for X number of hours every week, even though we lived together and he had access to her whenever he wanted. Eventually I realized that I would be better off caring for the baby by myself than trying to delicately navigate Juliet's father's moods and the baby's health issues. I ended the relationship, again. And that's when the real trouble began.

Juliet's father filed an ex parte notice, which is a way to get around the legal requirement that both parties in a case must be present when they give an argument before a judge. When an attorney files an ex parte, they get to notify a judge about any motions or hearings without the other party's involvement. It's a dirty trick typically reserved for contentious cases. The worst part of the ex parte is that the other party usually cannot find out what they have been accused of unless they have contacts in the court. And if they do discover their alleged crime, they only have twenty-four hours to assemble a defense. In this case, my position as an attorney and my mother's history as a family lawyer allowed us to learn what Juliet's father had accused me of.

He claimed that I had overdosed on Marinol, a form of THC approved by the US Food and Drug Administration (FDA), while pregnant with Juliet. He also accused me of smoking pot throughout my pregnancy, and he claimed that I only took Marinol—a medication that is sometimes prescribed for nausea—to cover up the THC already present in my body. Later, I would learn that his mother, also a family lawyer, had given him the idea to file an ex parte notice. She told him that paternity cases were anonymous, which I suppose he took to mean that he could lob whatever accusations he wanted at me without either of us suffering professional repercussions. He must have thought that I would be most worried about the impact on my career, and he was leaving room for me to come running back to him. He never seemed to consider that the worst thing for me would not be a blow to my career but potentially losing custody of my infant daughter because of false claims.

If there ever was any lingering doubt in my mind about my fitness as a mother, the rage I felt then—which is reemerging just in my telling of this story—proves that I would do anything to protect my daughter. And that quality should be a priority for social workers deciding on which kids need to be removed from their homes.

My mom helped me quickly assemble a defense. In less than twenty-four hours, I gathered declarations vouching for my character and defending me against the Marinol overdose accusation from friends and witnesses to our terrible relationship. I asked Dr. Eidelmann, who had written my recommendation for medical marijuana, to write a declaration. I asked my friend David, of whom Juliet's father had been irrationally jealous, to write a declaration. I even asked the neonatologist who was treating Juliet's seizures for a declaration. You see, even though Marinol is legal and medical marijuana has been legal in California since the 1990s, the stakes were high.

Around the same time Juliet's father filed his ex parte in 2009, Californians were losing custody of their children for similar accusations of smoking or otherwise ingesting cannabis. Even after recreational marijuana was made legal, as recently as 2017 there was a case reported in *LA Weekly*[1] of dispensary owners, both of whom had medical marijuana licenses and ran LA-based cannabis businesses, who were arrested in front of their kids. LAPD found a can of butane and some ovens that can be used to make cannabis concentrates but were never operational. Three months after the initial arrest, the county placed their sons, ages two and eleven, in the custody of the mom's grandparents. A judge determined that the couple's levels of THC hadn't been reduced as was ordered by the court. It took seven months of court-ordered drug tests, Marijuana Anonymous meetings, parenting classes, and therapy before the couple regained custody.

Before Proposition 64, there was no state legislation protecting parents' use of medical marijuana. Proposition 64 did provide some protection: "California courts can no longer rescind or restrict a parent's custodial rights solely because they have recommendations for medical marijuana."[2] But still, as is often the case, it was left up to the discretion of the social worker.

In that same *LA Weekly* story, Jennifer Ani, a family law attorney who helped write Proposition 64, said many social workers did not understand that cannabis use alone cannot pose a real threat to a family: "I had one social worker tell me that the father was going to get high and drop the infant."[3]

I could not understand the motives of Juliet's father for filing the ex parte beyond spite and malice. He had never really shown much of an interest in Juliet when she was a baby. Many times, I was up half the night with her while he stayed fast asleep without giving any indication that he felt he should do anything. When he made his accusations, none of this mattered. It was unnerving how simple it was for him to accuse me of abusing Marinol or of smoking pot during my pregnancy. Fortunately, the judge dismissed the ex parte, but if I had been a different person—maybe someone with a lower income or a woman of color—I don't know if he would have. Again, I was lucky.

Even though he dismissed the ex parte, our judge still ordered us to come up with a parenting plan, what the courts call a custody arrangement or schedule. Juliet's father would have visitation on Tuesdays and Thursdays from 5:00 to 7:00 p.m. and on Sundays from 10:00 a.m. to 12:00 p.m. After about eight months, he got more hours on Sundays, watching Juliet from 10:00 a.m. to 7:00 p.m. After this increase in his hours, I began to notice worrying behavior from Juliet. She would come home from her Sunday visits with her dad in an agitated state: twitching, throwing tantrums, and crying throughout the night. I would ask him about Juliet's emotional health, thinking maybe I should try to get a monitor to supervise their visits or reduce the hours on Sunday. He dismissed my concerns and said Juliet always came back without a scratch. I filed an ex parte seeking a reduction of his Sunday hours. My ex parte was denied.

The next year, at the end of August in 2010, he and I agreed to increase his time once more to include one overnight per month. I still worried about his competency as a parent, so on the nights he had custody, I would spend the night. I never thought he would hurt Juliet on purpose, but I worried that he would be negligent. He also had a troubling habit of taking Ambien before he went to sleep every night. I couldn't stand the idea of Juliet waking up crying to a parent who wouldn't wake up—or even worse, of Juliet having an accident while he was knocked out.

Naturally, he thought my presence during these overnight visits was a critique of his parenting. This pattern of unease continued until Juliet was about two years old. That's when I met my current husband. Fueled by what I assume is jealousy, Juliet's father tried again to take custody of her. Only this time his accusations were far more serious.

———

When we talk about the War on Drugs, we almost never talk about the impact it has on families. And that is because the face of the War on Drugs has always been stereotypical images of strung-out addicts and their Machiavellian dealers. If children are mentioned at all, it's in terms of protection—the idea that law enforcement is the only thing standing between innocent children and their negligent, drug-addled parents. There is no room for nuance, no mention of the overwhelming percentage of drug users who never develop an addiction or the fact that, by and large, more children suffer from a parents' abuse of alcohol—which is perfectly legal and has the highest rates of addiction—than of any other drug.[4]

Lurking behind this mindset of removing children from their addicted parents is the "addiction as disease" ethos that colors so much policy. When we think of the "drug user," it is the addict that comes to mind. Rarely do we recognize the recreational or social drug user who might enjoy marijuana at night or try MDMA or cocaine while partying with friends.

These images are reinforced by stereotypes created by politicians and reinforced by the media. The film *Reefer Madness* is one example, along with some pulp fiction of the '50s and '60s, like N. R. De Mexico's 1969 cult classic *Marijuana Girl*. The drama of *Reefer Madness* was so over the top, the consequences of cannabis consumption so outlandish, that few took it seriously. There are some people, like former Attorney General Jeff Sessions, who seem to have taken the film's message as law, but most Americans have a more nuanced understanding of marijuana use. A 2017 Pew poll showed 61 percent of Americans believed in legalizing marijuana, compared to 12 percent of Americans in 1969.[5]

As public opinion shifts, so does the nation's view on pot-smoking parents. A 2017 article from the *Washington Post* featured more and more parents "coming out" about their marijuana use.[6] One would hope that as the stigma around using marijuana goes away, so too will the harsh penalties for parents who indulge.

But pot is one of the tamer substances when it comes to questions of child custody. Pot use does not have the same bite as, say, the crack epidemic of the '80s and '90s and that most reviled figure, the so-called "crack mom." The first image of the crack mom appeared on *ABC News* in July 1986. America met Jane, a woman with an addiction to freebase crack who had given birth to premature twins, each weighing just over two pounds. Jane would lose custody of her twins.[7] The story aired just one month after the *Washington Post* published an article with the title "Mothers' Drug Abuse Spurs Infant Addiction, Panel Told,"[8] based on the findings of Dr. Ira Chasnoff, the director of Northwestern University Hospital's Perinatal Center for Chemical Dependence. Chasnoff and his team of researchers found that children born to mothers who used cocaine during pregnancy were 15 percent more likely to die from sudden infant death syndrome, compared to infants who had not been exposed to cocaine in utero. That study also found some evidence of cocaine use affecting the outcome of pregnancy, whether or not the baby was carried to term, and the neurological effects the newborn may suffer from. However, the researchers also said a larger and longer study would be required to confirm these results. In a quote that would come to haunt Chasnoff for years afterward, he discussed the expense of caring for drug-addicted infants—roughly $28,000 for four to six weeks of intensive care treatment—saying, "We're being left saddled with infants and the mothers leave to continue their drug-abusing lives."

The media took the study and ran with the results, condemning cocaine and crack-using mothers. Two years after ABC's story about Jane, *NBC News* presented its audience with three women named Tracy, Erocelia, and Stephanie. Erocelia had given birth to a premature baby. Stephanie had surrendered her baby to the hospital and was heading to the crack house. NBC showed all three of these women smoking crack on camera.[9]

One 1989 headline screamed, "Crack Babies: The Worst Threat Is Mom Herself."[10] The media frenzy grew so intense that Chasnoff eventually started to confront this harsh rhetoric.[11] But the damage was already done. In the early '90s, states increased prosecution of drug-addicted pregnant women, and consequences for a positive drug test could range from jail time to losing child custody—punitive approaches that would not ameliorate the situation for the mother.

The women at the center of the storm were almost always women of color, even though the majority of pregnant addicts were white women. And because of these women's selfishness in using crack during pregnancy, they gave birth to crack-addicted babies, or so the story went. They were always considered a failure, not just as mothers and women but as symbols of their racial/ethnic groups. These women became the scapegoats for the larger issues of economic and social disenfranchisement in their communities. It was their fault that they were poor, it was crack's fault for addicting them, or it was some combination of the two. Yet, as Columbia University professor and neuroscientist Dr. Carl Hart put it, "Crack wasn't the real problem. The real problem was unemployment, lack of education, and lack of skills."[12] But instead of looking at the environments these women were living in and the reasons why they might have turned to crack, it was easier to vilify and punish them accordingly.

The media latched onto the images of the strung-out crack mom because they stirred up the primal feelings of the American public. Women are supposed to be caregivers. In Leslie Jamison's *The Recovering*, her stunning book on addiction and sobriety, she highlights the double standard between female drunks and their male counterparts: "When [women] were drunk, they were like animals or children: dumbstruck, helpless, ashamed. . . . If they weren't drinking like children, they were drinking instead of caring for their children. A woman escaping into drink was usually a woman failing to fulfill her duties to home and family."[13]

This judgment of women often begins before the baby is even born. In my case, my character as a mother was put in jeopardy by Juliet's father's accusations about my smoking. The thought process behind these prosecutions was the safety of the child—and of course, any parent who is truly in the throes of addiction and cannot care for a child does need help—but this policy has resulted in more adverse effects. Consistently, the intervention of law enforcement has had a negative effect on anything like recovery for the parent—if that is indeed the intent—or the emotional health of the child. But of course, drug use in pregnancy is just one part of the problem.

While writing this chapter in the fall of 2018, I saw a news alert pop up on my phone from *Time* magazine with the headline: "Pregnant Women Smoking Marijuana More." It's been almost ten years since Juliet's father's first ex parte and his allegations. In that time, American perceptions of marijuana use have become far more tolerant. As more states legalize marijuana and the nation edges closer to ending federal prohibition, that tolerance will grow. More people are realizing that the government's story about the dangers of cannabis isn't based on any real facts. It was these same false ideas that Juliet's father used to try to wrest custody of her in the courts, portraying me as someone who smoked pot throughout my pregnancy and as a generally neglectful woman.

While I was assembling my defense against Juliet's father's accusations, I was put in contact with Dr. Gil Martin, a pediatrician in Loma Linda. He agreed to testify as an expert on marijuana use in pregnancy and the effects on the newborn. In the hearing, he presented evidence that overwhelmingly showed no association between marijuana use and preterm birth. He explained to the judge that, even if Juliet's father's allegations had been true, smoking would not have harmed the fetus.

There is research going back to the '80s demonstrating the same conclusions. Researcher Melanie Dreher and her colleagues at the University of Massachusetts Nursing Education Department conducted a longitudinal study on the effects of a mother's cannabis use on infants and children in Jamaica. The pregnant Jamaican women in the study had smoked or otherwise ingested cannabis to ease nausea and fatigue, lessen the pains of labor, and speed up the birth process by facilitating uterine contractions. After the children were born, these women would wash the newborns with cannabis leaves. Sometimes they added cannabis to the baby's milk to soothe the baby or help them sleep. The Jamaican mothers would also use marijuana to cope with postpartum depression. Dreher matched thirty pot-smoking pregnant women by age and socioeconomic status with thirty pregnant nonusers. She found that "the ganja moms and their kids did not appear to be harmed by marijuana exposure in the womb; there were no physical abnormalities, no cognitive deficits, and no neonatal complications; nor were there any discernible disparities between the three-day-old nonexposed babies."[14]

Not only was there no noticeable difference between the exposed and unexposed babies, but time showed that the exposed babies enjoyed better health:

> Dreher was surprised to discover that after one month the babies of mothers who had used ganja throughout their pregnancy (whether nauseous or not) were actually healthier, more alert, and less fussy than one-month-old infants whose mothers did not take cannabis. Test results for one-month-old infants whose mothers also ingested ganja while breast-feeding were "even more striking," according to Dreher. Heavily exposed babies were more socially responsive and more autonomically stable than babies not exposed to cannabis through their mother's milk: "alertness was higher, motor and autonomic systems more robust, they were less irritable, less likely to demonstrate imbalance of tone, needed less examiner facilitation . . . than the neonates of non-using mothers.[15]

The unfortunate reality is that many parents lose their children due to their substance use problems. This ultimately does not help the children, because most of them end up homeless. So, what seems like the right answer might not be. Similarly, if you have a thriving crack trade in your neighborhood, protecting the community by sending all the crack dealers to prison might create far more damage. The issue is the socioeconomic situation that must be facilitating the abuse if it's so widespread.

12

SHARKS! SHARKS! SHARKS![1]

THE YEAR 2008 WAS LIFE-ALTERING for me. After my 2007 divorce, I focused on building my practice, and for the next year, I did well. By this point, I had started to earn some professional attention thanks to a profile in the *Los Angeles Times* and the "LA's Dopest Attorney" ads I had taken out across the city. Eventually, I moved into a small apartment in West Hollywood right next to the Trader Joe's.

A lot of things happened in 2008. The economic recession and the resultant crash of the housing market affected everything and everyone, including me and my small firm. I was still defending criminal clients who'd learned about me through either word of mouth or the billboards. In 2008, there were about eighty cities around California adopting moratoriums that either banned or limited cannabis clubs.[2] Eight counties and roughly thirty cities had established regulations to legitimize the clubs. Often, the federal, state, and local laws would conflict with or contradict each other. Cannabis club operators seeking legitimacy faced a legal labyrinth on the road to compliance. My medical marijuana clients were mostly people seeking to become legit and getting tripped up in the process.

Amid this internal battle in California over the cannabis clubs, Attorney General Jerry Brown released guidelines for the clubs in the summer of 2008, meant to protect patients and clubs from the federal government. The DEA was raiding marijuana dispensaries. San Francisco District Attorney Kamala Harris was overseeing 1,900 cannabis-related criminal convictions, substantially more than her predecessor. (Harris went on to actively fight a ballot measure for recreational cannabis in 2010, authoring an opposition argument in California's official ballot guide which claimed that legalization "seriously compromises the safety of our communities, roadways, and workplaces.") The guidelines that Brown issued in an eleven-page directive can be summed up as follows: state medical marijuana dispensaries were legal only if they operated as a collective or a cooperative, not if they were in business for profit. The goal, according to Brown and the law enforcement officers who backed this decision, was to weed out the for-profit medical marijuana dispensaries that were being operated by cartels as fronts for money-laundering purposes.[3] This distinction proved to be very difficult to police, as there were no bright-line rules explaining what amount of compensation would be deemed "profit," and the all-cash nature of the industry made it impossible to determine with any reliability who received how much money. Nevertheless, the guidelines were a game-changer for the people in medical marijuana who wanted to provide medicine to sick people.

Around the same time that my daughter, Juliet, was born, I took on a client named Joe Byron, who was a resident of Long Beach, California, and the owner of a popular local breakfast spot called Egg Heaven. Byron and his childhood friend, a man named Joe Grumbine, had been in business together since December 31, 2000. That was the year they created Mission Priority Lending, a mortgage brokerage company for the well-to-do in Long Beach's Belmont Shore neighborhood. When the housing market crashed in Southern California and the rest of the United States, their mortgage company crashed with it, forcing the two Joes to find a new business venture.

In the summer of 2008, right before Jerry Brown issued his guidelines for medical marijuana collectives in California, there were rumors that the Long Beach City Council was going to issue permits to the city's marijuana collectives. The permits would legitimize these collectives and protect them from both DEA raids and unpredictable local prosecutions, making them lower-risk investments. Over the next year, Byron and Grumbine would open two dispensaries in Long Beach and one in Garden Grove, a smaller city sixteen miles east of Long Beach.

Notably, Garden Grove is in Orange County, and Long Beach is in the southeastern tip of LA County. At the Joes' collective in Garden Grove, which they opened in March 2008, they got visits from the local cops, but they were simple routine checks, making sure the collective was compliant with the code and introducing a new member of the force to them. Byron and Grumbine even worked with the cops to show them how to tell the difference between a certified doctor's recommendation for medical marijuana and something mocked up on Photoshop. The Garden Grove collective, called Unit D, was a true collective. They distributed marijuana to patients with doctors' recommendations, and they gave out free food, clothing, and medicine to low-income patients. They became good friends with Charles Monson, director of the nonprofit group Wheels of Mercy. They even started installing wheelchair ramps for collective members who needed them.

Byron and Grumbine likely expected a similar reception in Long Beach. They went to all the city council meetings, they went to City Hall, and they kept up with the city's plans to draft an ordinance that would pave the way for dispensaries to get permits. At this time, most local governments were not giving out permits for cannabis collectives that would establish proof of legality, instead requiring operators to simply open up their shop and hope for the best. They rented two shops and opened for business.

At first, everything in Long Beach seemed fine. Byron and Grumbine got a call from the DA's office, just checking in. They were told this was a routine phone call for the DA's office to learn where all the dispensaries were so that, once the licenses went through, they would contact them again. Byron and Grumbine named their Long Beach locations Fourth and Elm Natural Health Collective and the 2200 Health Collective. The city later announced that the ordinance they were drafting would require each dispensary to grow its own marijuana. So, Byron and Grumbine rented a separate cultivation space and also started growing at their Fourth and

Elm location. For the next several months, the two Joes grew their marijuana and waited for the okay from the Long Beach City Council.

Then on December 17, 2009, Long Beach police officers in SWAT gear burst through the doors of Byron's cultivation warehouse with guns drawn. The police also raided Unit D in Garden Grove, where Grumbine was working, and Grumbine's home in neighboring Perris, where officers arrested his wife and nineteen-year-old daughter at gunpoint. In a coordinated raid, the cops also targeted the homes of Byron and Grumbine's seventeen employees. They were all arrested and sent to jail in Long Beach, where they endured body-cavity searches and were thrown in holding cells overnight. The next day, all of the employees were released without any charges filed.

Apparently, the police had been watching Byron and Grumbine's three dispensaries and the grow house for weeks, after a few undercover cops were able to purchase medical marijuana with their verified doctors' recommendations. They were tipped off when one of the employees accused Byron and Grumbine of stealing electricity to facilitate a grow operation. It seems the police believed that Byron and Grumbine were running a highly profitable operation. But they didn't file formal charges against anyone arrested in the raid. They did, however, seize about $35,000 in cash. The Joes swallowed that loss, shrugged, and got back to work after the holidays, continuing to look for news from City Hall.

Then Los Angeles District Attorney Steve Cooley declared war against LA's dispensaries. He repeatedly prosecuted medical marijuana dispensaries that engaged in over-the-counter sales, falsely claiming that such activity was inherently illegal and inconsistent with a collective of cannabis patients authorized under state law.

On December 8, 2010, Byron and Grumbine were arrested again. This time they were charged with eighteen felony counts of selling marijuana, plus other charges. They also charged Byron for failing to pay taxes on the marijuana sold at their dispensaries and for stealing electricity from SoCal Edison. This was when Joe Byron hired my law firm to represent him.

Not long before, on October 15, 2010, I had gotten a call from my dad asking me to join his law firm again, this time as a partner. I remember the exact date because I was dealing with payroll when he called. I hadn't worked with or for my dad since that disastrous attempt in 2003, which ended with me throwing a brick through his window. For some reason— maybe it was the stress I was feeling from being a new mom or from my ongoing custody battle with Juliet's father—I agreed.

Soon afterward I started preparing for the Byron case, which would be the longest jury trial of my career. It would take another year for the trial and pretrial to begin. By the time Byron and Grumbine appeared before a judge in 2011, the city of Long Beach had enacted a medical marijuana ordinance that expressly allowed the operation of dispensaries like theirs. The ordinance had its rules. For example, no dispensary could be within fifteen hundred feet of a high school or one thousand feet of a kindergarten, elementary, or middle school. No dispensary could operate within one thousand feet of another dispensary. Out of seventy applicants, only thirty-seven dispensaries could receive permits. Then another restriction was added: every dispensary was required to cultivate the marijuana it distributed on site.

To choose which collectives would be granted a license, Long Beach held a lottery, with seventy Ping-Pong balls representing the collectives applying for licenses from the city. The balls were supposed to be randomized in a machine that tumbled them like popcorn, but the machine didn't work, so the city officials dumped the balls in a bucket and inelegantly plucked them out by hand. Through these means, thirty-seven dispensaries were selected to receive permits.

After the final restrictions were added—including the rule that no club could operate within one thousand feet of a city park—the number dropped again from thirty-seven to twenty-three dispensaries that made the cut to get city permits. Two were operating at the addresses where Byron and Grumbine's dispensaries had been shut down. Byron and Grumbine were in a perfect position to benefit from the city's permits, but by this point, they were already facing felony charges.

In the middle of all this, my dad took off on one of his trips to India for a couple of weeks. When he left, he didn't give me any access to the bank accounts, so I had to go through his girlfriend's sister, who was also working there. I suspected that his girlfriend was stealing money, but I didn't have any proof. All I knew was that we had to make $50,000 a week just to maintain our staff of fifteen people. I worried about how we would make payroll, so I asked the sister if there was any way I could get a line of credit. She said there was no credit line, but a call to the bank said otherwise. I learned from the bank, however, that they would only speak to the signatory on the account, the girlfriend's sister. Beyond frustrated at this situation, I fired the girlfriend, her sister, and her niece, all of whom were working for my father's firm but didn't appear to do anything.

My dad returned from his trip to India to an uproar. His girlfriend was furious at him, which made him take it out on me. He tried to fire me, not understanding that partnership law does not allow for that. But, fed up with his office and the internecine politics therein, on Memorial Day 2011, I quit.

In the months that followed, my father would strip away my health insurance even though I had a young daughter. He tried to steal away the clients I attracted to my own firm. For the rest of the summer, my law partner, Raza, and I worked like hell to keep my father from putting our new firm out of business.

That winter, Byron's trial began in Long Beach. From the first day, I knew there was blood in the water. Our judge was Charles D. Sheldon. He had a full head of white hair, wire-rimmed glasses, and a Selleckian mustache. He hated us from the first day, and by us, I mean Raza, me, and Joe Grumbine's attorney, Christopher Glew. Judge Sheldon's first move was to bar any use of the term *medical marijuana* in our defense.

There was no reason for Judge Sheldon to bar us from saying "medical marijuana" in the defense of our clients other than for him to give an advantage to the prosecution, represented by Jodi Castano. It was a clear example of prejudice, but there wasn't much we could do about it. The trial had barely begun and it was already gaining notice. In the end, only a last-minute ruling from the California Court of Appeals on a writ application got Judge Sheldon to reverse his position and allow us the medical marijuana defense. Even then, when the time came for trial, Judge Sheldon urged the bailiff to erect temporary walls between the jury box and the audience. The purpose of this was to prevent the jury from seeing the sick patients—many of whom were members of Grumbine's nonprofit, The Human Solution International—in the audience. We could say the words medical marijuana, but we couldn't show who benefited from the plant.

Another cheap move from Sheldon was to wait until the last minute to tell the defense we could contact previously off-limits witnesses. When we asked for an additional week to restructure our cases, he refused, telling us the trial would start the next morning. I don't know about Glew's team, but ours had a rough night of preparing for the defense the next day. Eighteen felony counts are nothing to sneeze at, and I didn't want my client going to jail. It's a feeling I remembered having when I was sitting with my father in court long ago. It seemed wrong for nice people like the people my father defended, or Joe Byron, to go to prison. I only felt that more passionately now.

Joe Grumbine and Joe Byron were not bad dudes. They were not trying to make a quick buck off of sick patients. They were just unlucky. They had hedged the wrong bets. The purpose of their nonprofit organization was to provide medical marijuana to patients who needed it. It was these patients and their friends that assembled on the steps of the Long Beach courthouse with green ribbons and signs reading "Free Joe" and "No Jail For a Plant." Luckily, the judge in Byron's case was so clearly prejudiced that it attracted the attention of Nick Schou, an *OC Weekly* reporter and the author of the book *Kill the Messenger: How the CIA's Crack-Cocaine Controversy Destroyed Journalist Gary Webb*. Schou followed our case closely and filed daily coverage over the twenty-one-day trial. Having written about CIA cover-ups, Schou had no trouble spotting the corruption going on in Department K of the Long Beach courthouse. The trial, which was gaining more media attention by the day, made the front page of Schou's paper.[4]

Sometimes, as a criminal defense attorney, you get a judge who just doesn't like you. Rarely do you get a judge that is as hostile as this one was. Although I'd experienced unfriendly judges before, this was the first time it had happened in a higher-profile case. We, the defense, couldn't do anything right. I was chastised for showing up a few minutes late, for speaking too quickly. Any objection I made was instantly overruled, even if it had merit, even if another judge would have sustained many of them. I got the sense that Judge Sheldon disliked me most of all, out of everyone on the defense team. Typically, I like to stay on the judge's good side, but there was no chance at all of that happening here.

The very worst moment, however, was still to come. Eight days into the trial, my witness and I were standing in the courtroom chatting when the head district attorney, Sally Thomas, appeared to put her nails on the witness's shoulder in an effort to scoot by. I was already hypersensitive to the mood in the courtroom at this point. All of my senses and my awareness were ready to notice any further indication of bias on the part of the judge or the prosecution. Although DA Thomas was not representing the prosecution in this case, she had been observing the proceedings for the past week and a half. When DA Thomas grabbed my witness, I saw another threat, another example of intimidation. And I told anyone who would listen about it, feeling that if the judge wouldn't listen to me, then at least the other defense counsel and the media could hear what I had to say. It was Friday afternoon, the week had been long, and I was beyond frustrated at this point. I asked Raza to make a note of the DA's behavior on the record before court recessed for the weekend.

I've thought back to that day, and I don't know if I would make the same decision now that I made then. It seemed like a toothless protest at the time; I didn't expect anything to come of the note, but it was a chance for me to release some frustration. What happened next was my own mistake.

Monday morning, DA Thomas verbally ripped me to shreds, on the record. She recounted what she remembered of the events of that Friday afternoon: that she hadn't hit our witness, that she had merely tapped the woman on the shoulder to get her attention, that I was blowing the situation out of proportion:

> *It is beyond the pale in terms of unprofessional and unethical conduct on the part of counsel and unfounded accusations as it relates to me. And it is*

really unfortunate that counsel does not have the insight to be embarrassed and ashamed of her behavior.

But despite that, I am asking this court at this moment, because her—her rendition of the facts in open court, not on the record, has been so distorted—has so distorted the truth, it amounts to a lie, and now she has allowed it to be put on the record, which is completely inappropriate. It has gone far enough. Thankfully, my legal record speaks for itself.[5]

The DA asked the court to remove the record of her interaction with our witness. At this point I was crying. This was a room of my peers, and I was being scolded like a disobedient child. I couldn't imagine the situation getting any worse, so I asked for a brief recess, five minutes to compose myself. Judge Sheldon denied my request. The other defendant's attorney, Christopher Glew, also tried to get me a recess, but he denied him as well. So, the ladies and gentlemen of the jury filed into their seats, with a full view of me seated in the first chair, crying on the other side of the bar.

In December 2011, a jury found Byron and Grumbine guilty of illegally selling marijuana, tax evasion, and stealing electricity. It was clear to Glew and me that the jury could only have acquitted Byron and Grumbine through jury nullification. Luckily, Sheldon's conduct—which by now included screaming at the defense team and writing a complimentary letter to the prosecution before the trial was completed—allowed us to file for an appeal. In the moment, I was humiliated; but in the back of my mind, I also knew we had a case for a mistrial.

Throughout the course of the trial, I had become increasingly grateful for the attention that Nick Schou's *OC Weekly* coverage had brought to this case. His reporting was just what we needed to file a motion pursuant to section 170.1 of the Code of Civil Procedure, requesting to disqualify a judge, which would result in a mistrial. In order to qualify for the 170.1 motion, we needed to demonstrate that a "person aware of the facts might reasonably entertain a doubt that the judge would be able to be impartial."[6] Since the pretrial, Judge Sheldon had denied the defense time to prepare, showed clear bias in favor of the prosecution, and, after allowing the statement of DA Thomas, refused to let me take five minutes to wipe my tears before admitting the jury to the courtroom. In addition, Judge Sheldon admitted that he had sent a complimentary letter to the prosecutor before the case was completed, and the night before sentencing, he recused himself from the case. We cited all of this in our motion. And Nick Schou had reported on all of it for weeks. On April 13, 2012, our section 170.1 motion for a new trial was granted, a recusal for actual prejudice.[7] It was validation that we really were staring into the cold, black eyes of a prejudiced judge in Charles Sheldon. All of the charges were dropped against both of our clients.

The judge who granted the motion referenced the articles Nick Schou had written in *OC Weekly*. This judge also said, "This was a terrible trial. Terrible." Soon after we were granted the mistrial, Judge Sheldon retired. Now, from what I can tell, he lives a quiet existence. It seems our case is what did him in, although he claimed he had already been planning to retire.

Years after the trial of Byron and Grumbine, in the summer of 2016, there was a rash of shark attacks off the coast of Long Beach. Juliet was seven at the time, and I had given birth to my son Jaxin, then two years old, with my current husband, Jon. We liked to take family trips to the Aquarium of the Pacific, which sits serenely on the Long Beach shore, in sight of the Queen Mary. When the shark attacks happened, Jaxin became obsessed with sharks. To this day, I still cannot say the words "Long Beach" within Jaxin's earshot without hearing him shout, "Sharks! Sharks! Sharks!" like some kind of Pavlovian response.

When I was younger, my father would tell me the story of the Long Beach district attorney that had tried to frame him. In 1970, Bruce Margolin was one of the most successful self-made lawyers in Hollywood. He had graduated from law school in 1967, when the state of California made significant changes to the laws around search and seizure. Law enforcement had to read Miranda rights for the first time and had to have a warrant to search a subject's home or vehicle. The police were slow to learn about these changes, which meant that twenty-five-year-old Bruce knew more about the laws than the cops enforcing them. He quickly built a criminal practice—sustained by an endless stream of people who had been caught on marijuana possession, a felony—and found that he could get his clients off because of a warrant issue. The money was quick and easy. Bruce bought a house, he bought a car, he seemed unstoppable.

It wasn't long before he was gaining too much professional attention and attracting bitter enemies among area prosecutors, including a district attorney out of Long Beach. The Long Beach DA, motivated either by jealous spite (I think there are a lot of district attorneys who harbor some resentment over the freedom of the criminal defense attorney) or by a profitable alliance with a disgruntled ex-client or rival law firm, sent an undercover agent to Bruce's office for a consult. When Bruce welcomed the man into his office, the man offered him a bag of cocaine in exchange for legal counsel. This was before cocaine became as common as Coca-Cola in '80s-era offices; it was still rare, not nearly as common as pot. The agent offered his bag of cocaine to Bruce, sure that if Bruce took it, he'd have him on a felony charge. What neither the agent nor the Long Beach district attorney realized was that Bruce, although an avowed stoner and psychedelic disciple, was vehemently opposed to narcotics like cocaine. He demurred. The agent left the office without his evidence. It wasn't until months later that Bruce learned that the Long Beach DA had tried to set him up. Dismayed and worn out by this and other trying experiences, he closed his practice and went to India for a year.

The way my father told me this story, his encounter with the Long Beach DA was a vital part of his origin story. If he doesn't flee the country for India, he never meets Baba Ram Dass, who later introduces him to Tim Leary, who would become my father's most famous client. My father used the story to warn me about the sharks in the legal world, to tell me to never incriminate myself. He neglected to warn me about the sharks you cannot easily detect: the betrayal within your own family. Until 2008, I never understood how thin the line is between protector and predator.

PART 3
CLOSING ARGUMENTS

13

CANNABIS 2.0, "C" IS FOR CORRUPTION

WHILE THERE IS NO DOUBT that huge advances have been made in the last thirty years with regard to medical and recreational access to marijuana, as well as efforts to decriminalize marijuana and dismiss past convictions, the numbers of arrests and prosecutions are still disturbing. Echoing the experiences of the Prohibition era, local corruption has abounded in the pot industry. Just as multiple levels of government were implicated in bribery schemes in the 1920s, especially in the enforcement and interpretation arena (e.g., cops, mayors, customs, etc.), the current day has seen a proliferation of corruption in the pot sector.[1]

There are some interesting differences between the two eras, and some similarities. In both eras, local officials are investigated and prosecuted all over the country for bribery, tax evasion, and money laundering in connection with bribery schemes. The difference is that modern corruption involves city officials illicitly receiving money to favor cannabis development.[2] If not for the federal illegality of cannabis and California's overregulation of cannabis zoning, the level of corruption would not be as high as it is. That said, I don't want to minimize the current prevalence of bigger development bribery schemes, in which cannabis only plays a small part. In my four years in cannabis lobbying, I have found that the line between politics and criminality is often much thinner than it is in the Criminal Courts Building.

The answer to these endemic problems with corruption is twofold: deregulation, i.e., allowing the market to decide the number of all types of cannabis establishments, rather than relying on so-called merit competitions that lead to corruption; and legalization on the federal level. It would be ignorant to suggest these changes would completely eliminate corruption in development deals. But changing zoning so that as many people as possible can apply in as many places as possible, and making it a nondiscretionary and laissez-faire development system, can help mitigate corruption.

In one instance, our law firm helped a business apply for a cannabis retail license in the city of Solvang, California, where the city council had limited the zoning such that only two locations were eligible in the whole city. In addition, only one of those landlords was willing to rent to a cannabis licensee, so that property owner was set to determine who was going to exclusively dominate cannabis retail sales in the entire city.[3] By advocating for our client's interest to the city council and pointing out the extremely biased and uniquely ridiculous situation the city had created (even if an ostensibly sophisticated group of people had possibly done this on purpose), we were able to get the city to change their entire licensing regime. Even if all forces are against you, I have seen time and again that if you try, you can defeat what appears at first to be overwhelmingly formidable opposition.

In Los Angeles, the city established a "soft" cap on the number of cannabis storefront outlets in each neighborhood of one per ten thousand people. Any license above this number can be approved only if an applicant obtains a finding from the city council that the additional license would serve "public convenience or necessity"—an exceedingly vague standard that is ripe for corruption.[4] These restrictions have not only bred corruption but have also created an environment where thousands of illegal, unlicensed dispensaries operate throughout the city, not following any regulations or paying any local, state, or federal taxes. The only answer is to allow people to open without difficult zoning impediments.[5]

The only way to eliminate the illicit market is for cities to expedite city services so license holders can get up and running in three months rather than two and a half years. Additionally, if all illicit growers can get licensed without a problem and without having to shut down—that is, they get amnesty—the illegal market will be incentivized to quickly adjust. Last, we need to make sure any local, state, or federal tax is low enough to allow legal storefronts to compete with the illicit market, as the current cumulative tax rates are quite high and unduly burdensome in terms of having a cost-effective operation.[6]

Also, the testing regulations for cannabis are more demanding than those for agriculture, causing the cannabis edible market to stagnate and be less healthy than it otherwise could be, literally and figuratively.[7] The state assembly previously considered but failed to pass legislation that would allow for consumption lounges involving hot prepared foods. In one situation, MedMen, a multilocation dispensary company that was represented by the United Food and Commercial Workers (UFCW), was angry that the city of West Hollywood would not agree to grandfather in their medical license as a recreational one. So the UFCW on MedMen's behalf sabotaged West Hollywood's efforts to get the state to pass the consumption lounge legislation, which would have allowed the existing consumption license holders to have a legit operation that would not limit them to only serving prepared foods that had been tested first. One effort they used was submitting a proposal, the Close the Loopholes Initiative, asking the city to loosen their restrictive guidelines on operating consumption businesses and granting licenses to cannabis businesses in response to the city's restrictive ordinance on this topic.[8] This ordinance makes it difficult for consumption lounges to operate their business because the city is not allowing these businesses to sell anything but cannabis products. These businesses have argued that it has made it very difficult for them to operate because they planned to use the sale of food and drinks to keep their businesses profitable.[9] The city's restrictive laws require complicated and extensive testing but still prevent on-site consumption.[10] Without the state changing or passing some sort of legislation, there won't be any sort of change.

At the time of writing this book, dozens of states have decriminalized, partially legalized, or legalized the consumption of cannabis by adults, and many more states have begun the legalization process. Burbles of gestures to legalize or decriminalize cannabis have even occurred at the federal level, an indicator that some mitigation of the arcane, racist, classist, and draconian national cannabis laws and perspective will occur at some time in the next ten years.[11]

That's a good thing, right? After all, licensed dispensaries are correlated with a reduction in crime.[12] That is why I'm writing this book, after all. So why don't we activists just sit back, put our feet up, and congratulate ourselves on a job well done while we watch the process unfold on CNN? Well, because as we've discussed throughout this book, the laws and attitudes that got us here have become entrenched in our culture, our conduct, and our legal system. Over the past fifty years those Prohibition-style laws and punishments have fostered the shaping and subsequent hardening of legal and societal attitudes toward drugs, their consumers, their sellers, and their farmers and manufacturers. And those attitudes have had real-world consequences for everyone, not just drug takers and makers.

The economic consequences are staggering. The War on Drugs has cost the United States an estimated amount of over $1 trillion.[13] Now imagine how much national, state, and local economic output was never realized by not pointing those same tax dollars toward areas that lead to increased GDP output, such as infrastructure, affordable access to higher education, and more affordable health care. For example, the Los Angeles County Sheriff's Department was recently granted $5 million to crack down on cannabis operations.[14] The negative economic outcomes from the drug war at home and abroad are even greater than wasted tax-dollar spending, because we must also consider that each victim of the drug war experienced loss of economic activity through death, incarceration, and stigmatization, and those effects would cascade to family and friends who would have to spend time, energy, and money filling the gaps left by their loved ones.

There are also significant consequences for the identity of our country. We live in a society that purports to value freedom, but we are not free to alter our consciousness because there are laws that restrict what we can do with our time and our own bodies. Yet there are many who argue that drug laws only add an asterisk to the notion of American freedom for drug users and drug sellers, two groups so stigmatized in this country that they are in effect second-class citizens. The effect of that point of view is a snake eating its own tail: drug laws only affect druggies and pushers, so who cares if their freedom is infringed? They are only in this situation because they say yes to drugs. In fact, let's create even tougher drug laws because those people are such a drain on our society. But as we've discussed in these pages, the origin story of drug laws and the American drug war is racist, classist, and ageist, and in real-world applications, those laws have been historically enforced to the massive detriment of people of color, the poor, young adults, and any other group or subgroup that the powers that be see fit to marginalize.

All this means that the journey from drug prohibition to legalization is bound to be fraught with problems that are created or informed by the institutionalized racism, classism, and ageism that have been reinforced and hardened for three generations. This is evident in the California cannabis legalization story. California, considered by many to be progressive, is experiencing a messy transition.

Ultimately, marijuana should not be regulated as it is now. It is ridiculous. In California, Proposition 64 allows for local control, which was brought about in order to get it to pass, so I'm not angry about or opposed to that strategy as a way to get things rolling. But now that provision should be changed so that it is clear that anywhere in the state zoned for agriculture should allow both "mixed light" (indoor/outdoor light) cultivation and outdoor cultivation of marijuana. And any industrial areas in any city or state should allow indoor cultivation, manufacturing, distribution, and testing. Furthermore, any commercial area should allow a dispensary or delivery service, period. This would eliminate a lot of issues.

Of course, marijuana should be descheduled federally, but this would not change the situation above, as descheduling would allow the states to control policy. Perhaps a federal descheduling bill needs to include a section covering the areas listed above. (This would be different from alcohol, where there are still dry counties, but I don't think alcohol prohibition turned into a race war, since it was only around for a few years.) The federal legislation needs to have constitutional floors regarding due process and the states' licensing procedures. Also, any federal legislation must somehow preclude merit-based competitions, which are steeped in corruption. In addition, Congress should pass a preamble to the First Amendment that explicitly acknowledges the the right to use marijuana as a fundamental right (and of course I think the amendment should go further to recognize the inalienable right to alter our consciousness).

On the other hand, a federal statute may work because it could come under the commerce clause of the US Constitution, like the federal minimum wage.[15] For example, when the federal minimum wage was challenged in court, the minimum wage was upheld under the commerce clause.[16] In another case, the US Supreme Court found in *Gonzales v. Raich*, 545 U.S. 1 (2005), that because of interstate commerce, marijuana could be regulated based on the federal interest of excluding any goods produced under substandard labor conditions. Here the federal interest would have to be articulated, but ironically the case decided that the feds have an interstate commerce interest in state-produced and state-distributed products.

A good example of the legal developments resulting from these court decisions came up in the case we handled for our client Noah Kleinman, a thirty-nine-year-old who had been convicted of six felony counts related to marijuana distribution and was sentenced to seventeen years in federal prison. At this point, state laws were changing in favor of allowing medical marijuana, but the federal laws were not budging. Raza and I took on this case after Kleinman got rid of his other lawyer. We were trying everything we could to get him probation, since he was a father of two and was given a sentence that was unreasonably high.

A few years before Kleinman's case, the Supreme Court made its ruling in *Gonzales v. Raich,* holding that the federal government can criminalize those who produce and use homegrown cannabis despite California state law allowing for cannabis to be used medicinally at the time. Then at around the time of Kleinman's case, on December 14, 2014, the

Rohrabacher-Farr amendment was passed into federal law as part of an omnibus spending bill. This law said that the federal government may not interfere with states implementing medical cannabis laws.[17] Then in *United States v. McIntosh,* the court interpreted this statute to mean that someone with a case that involves strict compliance with state medical marijuana guidelines has an affirmative defense against the federal government.[18] We tried to use this argument in Kleinman's favor for his appeal, but the court held that because Kleinman was allegedly using his business for both non-medical and medical purposes, the amendment would not apply, and he could be sentenced to the federal minimum.[19]

The judge hearing Kleinman's case, Otis D. Wright II, almost sent Raza and me to jail because Raza tried to play to the jurors' sympathies by calling Kleinman a "regular family man." As a *Los Angeles Times* article stated: "As Lawrence finished his opening, he took a risk. Kleinman 'may have been involved with dispensaries, just like you see all over L.A.,' he said. 'Convicting him would be like convicting any patient at one of those dispensaries.'"[20] The prosecutor handling the case, Julie Shemitz, stood up and immediately objected. During the break, Wright stood up and told Raza there would now be a jury nullification instruction to the jurors, telling them that they would be violating their oath if they did not follow the law and instead let their emotions hold sway over their rationales about this case.

Unfortunately, despite our best efforts, Noah Kleinman was sentenced to the original seventeen years and seven months in federal prison.[21] However, after six years, Kleinman benefited from a presidential commutation of his sentence by Donald Trump (even though I am not a supporter of former President Trump). Trump granted executive clemency to 237 people, and while many were his friends and other VIPs, a large number of those pardoned were nonviolent drug offenders.[22] Moves like these point the way toward a new beginning for criminal justice and clemency reform.

These additional points make Kleinman's case noteworthy:

Earlier on the same day that President Trump commuted Kleinman's sentence, the US Department of Justice filed a lengthy motion opposing

Noah's separate pending motion for a compassionate release, which was to be heard by his trial court judge. Despite Mr. Kleinman's tragic family circumstances, exemplary behavior in prison, serious and chronic health conditions, and nonviolent record, federal prosecutors argued in filings right before President Trump commuted his sentence that Mr. Kleinman should stay locked up because he was a "danger to society" given his "irresponsible social habits," that he couldn't be trusted to avoid killing people by spreading his COVID-19 infection, and that he shouldn't be released until he could prove how he would pay for his own healthcare upon release. Given federal prosecutors' ruthless determination to keep Mr. Kleinman imprisoned, Trump's decision to commute his sentence came as a gratifying surprise.[23]

The Aleph Institute was integral in securing Kleinman's release. From the institute's website:

The Aleph Institute is a 501(c)(3) certified nonprofit Jewish organization dedicated to assisting and caring for the well-being of members of specific populations that are isolated from the regular community: US military personnel, prisoners, and people institutionalized or at risk of incarceration due to mental illness or addictions. Aleph addresses their religious, educational, and spiritual needs, advocates and lobbies for their civil and religious rights, and provides support to their families at home left to fend for themselves. The Aleph Institute is committed to criminal justice reform and recidivism reduction through preventive-education and faith-based rehabilitation programs, reentry assistance, alternative sentencing guidance and counsel, and policy research and recommendations.[24]

The pardon process, like the criminal justice system, is broken and in need of reform. There is actually something to be learned from the Trump administration concerning this. We tried to get Kleinman pardoned under the Obama administration but ultimately were denied. This is because the system is flawed in that it typically only takes pardon recommendations from judicial institutions, rather than from organizations such as Aleph, which President Trump heard out. A *PBS NewsHour* article explains the presidential pardon process in more detail:

> *Someone who has been convicted of a federal crime and wants to be pardoned makes a request for a pardon to the Justice Department's Office of the Pardon Attorney, which assists the president in exercising his pardon power. Department rules tell pardon seekers to wait at least five years after their conviction or their release from prison, whichever is later, before filing a pardon application. It's then up to the pardon office to make a recommendation about whether a pardon is warranted. The office looks at such factors as how the person has acted following their conviction, the seriousness of the offense and the extent to which the person has accepted responsibility for their crime. Prosecutors in the office that handled the case are asked to weigh in. The pardon office's report and recommendation gets forwarded to the deputy attorney general, who adds his or her recommendation. That information is then forwarded to the White House for a decision.* [25]

Perhaps on Donald Trump's last day he did one thing right, and that was to shine a light on and grant clemency to a large number of nonviolent drug offenders. This broken system needs to be revamped, and Joe Biden can pick up in this one area where Donald Trump left off. Biden has an opportunity to create a fair and just clemency system. He has an opportunity to reach out to outside organizations like the Aleph Institute and work with these groups in helping to reintegrate former inmates back into society and to take recommendations for who might be worthy of release. The collateral damage of a federal conviction runs deep: "There are approximately 45,000 collateral consequences of a felony conviction imposed by federal, state, and local governments, ranging from the right to vote to access to housing." [26] Society is not kind to former prisoners, and employment and other opportunities may be closed to them; but executive clemency eliminates that damage. For Noah Kleinman, the Department of Justice was about to deny his motion for compassionate release earlier on the same day that President Trump commuted his sentence.

According to nonprofit news organization The Appeal, "at its core, reforming the system must at the very least involve removing the Office of Pardon Attorney from the DOJ and removing the DOJ's ostensible veto power over the process. The establishment of a bipartisan board to advise the president and make recommendations would not only improve the efficiency of the process, it would also bolster the public's confidence in it. And by doing so, the new process would offer the president more opportunities to grant mercy and forgiveness to those who are worthy of it."[27]

14

A NEW TARGET: DOCTORS[1]

BEFORE OCTOBER 10, 2013, Michael Malenkov's only run-in with the law was a couple of speeding tickets. But that morning, a voice shouted, "Fairfield Police, open up!"

At the time, Michael was a baby-faced man in his early twenties, tall and slender. He lived in a two-story home at the end of a cookie-cutter cul-de-sac in Fairfield, just east of Napa's vineyards. When the police arrived, the only other person around was his roommate, Alex. They'd only lived in that house for two months and had not yet saved enough money to furnish the place. All they owned was a desk for work and two beds; the rest of the house was empty.

The evidence later showed that Michael likely believed the police must have been at his door to warn them about something happening in the neighborhood, maybe a fire. Their development was tucked into the same arid hills that produced wine grapes, and wildfires have always been common in California, a tinderbox 770 miles long.

Michael went to the front door. The second after he cracked it open, he caught a glimpse of a group of large men in bulletproof vests and machine guns standing behind a couple of officers in the stiff, black uniforms of the Fairfield police department. The men rushed in.

One of the SWAT guys punched Michael in the face, giving him a black eye and knocking him to the ground. The SWAT guy also shoved a knee into his back and started barking, spit flying, "Where's Malenkov?!" With his face smashed against the wood floor, Michael struggled to tell the man that he was, in fact, the Malenkov they were looking for.

While he was on the ground, the rest of the SWAT team poured into the home. They tore out light fixtures and cut holes in the ceiling. They marched upstairs and found his roommate, dragging him downstairs. They searched kitchen drawers and cabinets, trashing the home as thoroughly as they could without having any furniture to flip over. Eventually, Michael realized the SWAT team was looking for drugs. But he didn't use drugs. Neither he nor his roommate even smoked weed. The strongest substance they used was coffee.

Someone pulled Michael off his front hallway floor and sat him on his living room floor next to Alex. Both men were placed in handcuffs—another first for Michael. He watched as the SWAT team started seizing what little they could find: laptops, paperwork, batteries, extension cords, right down to the bank cards and $3,952 in cash on the desk.

A female SWAT officer started shouting questions at Michael. He had been living in the United States for four years since emigrating from his native Ukraine, so his English wasn't bad, but he likely had a difficult time understanding what she was saying: *Are you a spy? Why do you have spy sunglasses?*[2] *Where is your vehicle? What do you mean you don't own a car? Where's all the furniture? How much is your rent? How do you afford that?* Finally, the relevant questions: *Do you know Dr. Brown?* And, *Do you work with him?*

"Yes," Michael answered, likely realizing this raid had something to do with the medical marijuana evaluation clinic he worked for. "I know Dr. Brown. We do marketing for him."

The officer said, "That's it?"

Anyone in Michael's shoes would have been confused. What was their crime? It was not illegal to provide marketing services for doctor's clinics, which is essentially what medical marijuana evaluation clinics are. The doctors at these clinics were licensed physicians seeing patients and writing recommendations for medical marijuana cards, which used to be a requirement for anyone who wanted to legally buy weed in California. (Today, a few years into legalized recreational marijuana, this rule feels like something out of the Stone Age.)

The services Michael and his partners provided as marketers for the medical clinic were no different from what other marketers did for other doctor's clinics. Anyone in Michael's position could have reasonably believed that he or she was doing honest work. So why was Michael in handcuffs?

After nearly four hours of questioning and watching the SWAT team tear their house apart while they sat in handcuffs, Michael and his roommate Alex were finally released. The SWAT team exited, taking everything they'd found.

When the home was empty and they could finally hear the sound of the trucks and cop cars pulling away, Michael and his roommate probably looked at each other with the same question on their lips: *What the fuck?*

While Michael's home was being raided, simultaneous raids were happening at three other locations: Dr. Brown's home in Oakland, his clinic in downtown San Jose, and a home in Bel-Air where Michael used to reside. The man responsible for these raids—and the beginning of Michael's legal woes—was an investigator with the Medical Board of California named Ralph Hughes.

Hughes has a ruddy complexion, a receding gray hairline, a thick beer belly, and the smug confidence that seems endemic to government employees. On the day of the raids, Hughes was at the Bel-Air home where he believed Michael was living. He hung back, allowing the SWAT team to break down the door and start searching all seven thousand square feet of the mansion. He found the bewildered homeowner, a man named Cornelius, and shouted, "Where's Michael?"

A perplexed Cornelius told Hughes that Michael used to rent a room in his house but had moved out a few months earlier. He gave Hughes the only documentation he had left of Michael, a photocopy of his driver's license. The SWAT officers didn't find Michael, or the large cannabis grow they suspected was the cause of the home's high electric bills.[3] After trashing the home, kicking over furniture, and tearing holes through the walls and ceilings, they left.

At the raid of the San Jose clinic, the SWAT officers seized roughly $6,000 in cash, along with the clinic's computers and hard drives. From Brown's home they took the $20,000 cash he had saved, and they scared the doctor and his wife.

But no arrests were made that day. Not one of the four raids yielded any proof of wrongdoing, such as an illegal cannabis grow, hundreds of thousands of dollars in cash, or drug paraphernalia. What they seized instead was standard electronic equipment and the amount of cash appropriate to running a medical marijuana clinic, by law a cash-only business.

After the raid, nothing happened. No charges were filed; no case opened. Still, Dr. Brown decided to close the clinic after only seven months of operation. Because he was the owner of the clinic, it was Brown's decision. Brown hoped that would be the end of their run-ins with law enforcement. Michael probably also hoped the raid was a freak event that would not amount to anything. But they were not to be so lucky. The October 10 raid was just the first in a series of raids, the beginning of a cat-and-mouse game between Michael, the medical board, and the Santa Clara County district attorney's office.

Raids on medical marijuana clinics and dispensaries are nothing new. Ever since California passed Proposition 215 in 1996, legalizing medical marijuana, there have been problems for everyone associated with the plant.

The first raid of a marijuana dispensary actually happened a few months before the passage of Proposition 215. Dennis Peron, a Vietnam vet, legendary weed dealer, and gay man living in San Francisco at the height of the AIDS epidemic, saw how marijuana eased the suffering of AIDS patients when his own partner, Jonathan West, was diagnosed with the virus. Peron found that smoking pot helped his lover regain his appetite and cope with his nausea. When West died from AIDS complications in 1990, he was in far less pain than he otherwise would have been because of the relief he found through medical marijuana. Peron made it his mission to advocate for the legalization of medical marijuana.[4] In 1991, he gathered signatures to put Proposition P, which would allow the medical use of marijuana within San Francisco's city limits, on the ballot. The measure passed by a 4-to-1 margin.

Following the success of Proposition P, Peron opened the San Francisco Cannabis Buyers Club. The club provided marijuana to AIDS patients, cancer patients, and anyone else with serious or life-threatening illnesses. Peron also became one of the authors of Proposition 215 and a driving force behind the Yes on 215 campaign.

A few months before Prop 215 passed, California state law enforcement raided Peron's Cannabis Buyers Club. They seized sixty pounds of marijuana and $750,000 in cash, and they swiftly shut down the club. They indicted Peron on drug charges across the bay in Alameda County and accused him of using the club as a front to sell marijuana. Peron pled "morally not guilty."[5] He accused California Attorney General Dan Lungren of staging the raid to derail the efforts of the medical marijuana movement.

Peron, as it would turn out, was right. Lungren, along with other likeminded politicians, led the opposition against Prop 215. Lungren even wrote the "No" argument in the voter's guide. The day after Prop 215 passed, Lungren told reporters for the *Los Angeles Times* and the *San Francisco Chronicle* that he would use "every legal avenue to fight [the new law]."[6] He also issued a memo to every DA, sheriff, and police chief in California to call them all to an emergency conference in Sacramento on December 3. The memo also recommended that law enforcement continue to use their normal methods to determine probable cause while Lungren consulted with federal officials about how best to reconcile his obligation to uphold Prop 215 with federal law.

Peron wasn't the only person facing constant harassment from law enforcement. Dr. Tod Mikuriya started studying the therapeutic potential of pot in the 1960s, first as the director of the New Jersey Neuropsychiatric Institute Drug Addiction Treatment Center, then as director of the National Institute of Mental Health (NIMH) marijuana research program.[7]

He left NIMH after only four months. He felt the agency was looking for research that highlighted the negative effects of marijuana, ignoring all the evidence to the contrary. In the fall of 1967, he moved to Berkeley to become involved with California's medical marijuana movement. Almost thirty years later, he became one of the authors of Prop 215, or the Compassionate Use Act.

Even after the Compassionate Use Act passed, Dr. Mikuriya was one of only a handful of doctors willing to write medical marijuana recommendations. The legality of medical marijuana did not protect doctors from prosecution. The whole medical marijuana system elicited nothing but scorn from federal authorities. The White House drug czar, Barry McCaffrey, called Dr. Mikuriya's medical marijuana practice a "Cheech and Chong show" at a 1996 press conference.[8] McCaffrey scrutinized Dr. Mikuriya's list of over 250 ailments that marijuana could help relieve— including stuttering, insomnia, PMS, vomiting, poor appetite, and writer's cramp—and decided they were absurd.[9]

Even though the language of the Compassionate Use Act explicitly protected medical marijuana doctors from prosecution, pot was, and remains, a federally controlled substance.[10] The passage of Prop 215 created a conflict between state and federal law, causing ire both within McCaffrey's office and the office of Attorney General Dan Lungren. McCaffrey rightly believed that medical marijuana in one state would lead to similar programs in other states.[11] The day after Prop 215 passed, Lungren, a former Republican congressman, told the Los Angeles Times "we're going to have an unprecedented mess."[12]

Lungren's role as California's attorney general meant he was sworn to uphold the state's laws, even if they conflicted with federal law. Instead, Lungren swore to cooperate with federal officials to help them enforce federal law. For the rest of the year, California prosecutors and law enforcement officials met with the feds to figure out how to cut off this medical marijuana threat at the knees. It was McCaffrey who decided the best way to do this without interfering with state's rights was to go after the doctors.[13] The thinking was that if there were no doctors willing to write medical marijuana recommendations, there was no way for patients to get the plant.

Fifteen "pot docs" wrote most of California's medical marijuana recommendations, including Dr. Mikuriya. The Medical Board of California investigated eleven of them, but they specifically targeted Dr. Mikuriya, who included the language in Prop 215 that allowed patients to use cannabis for "any other illness for which marijuana provides relief."[14] In 2000 the board accused Dr. Mikuriya of unprofessional conduct and incompetence for recommending marijuana to sixteen patients without completing proper physical exams. Their "evidence" against Dr. Mikuriya was accumulating, but they needed more.

Then in January 2003, a narcotics agent named Steve Gossett visited Dr. Mikuriya's practice undercover. He complained about insomnia and a sore shoulder, and after a twenty-minute examination, Dr. Mikuriya wrote him a recommendation for cannabis. Gossett took this recommendation to the medical board and confessed that he had lied about his symptoms. This made a seventeenth complaint against Dr. Mikuriya.

At Dr. Mikuriya's six-day disciplinary hearing that September, Gossett was the first witness for the prosecution. Even though Gossett said on the stand that he had lied about his symptoms, the judge determined that Dr. Mikuriya had committed "gross acts of negligence" in not properly examining his patients.[15] In March of 2004, the board put him on professional probation for five years and slapped him with a $75,000 fine.[16] Dr. Mikuriya was able to appeal the ruling and continue his practice under the supervision of a state-appointed monitor.[17]

From 1996 to his death in 2007, Dr. Mikuriya wrote recommendations for an estimated nine thousand patients.[18] In 2000 he founded the California Cannabis Research Medical Group (later called the Society of Cannabis Clinicians), which was a way for physicians to not only learn about the plant's medical uses but also to collectively brainstorm how best to deal with the authorities.[19] The list of conditions that could be treated with cannabis is still known among the veterans of the medical marijuana movement as "Dr. Tod's List."[20]

As the stigma surrounding medical marijuana lessened, thanks to activists like Peron and Dr. Mikuriya, more doctors began writing recommendations and opening evaluation clinics, often recognizable by a green cross over the door. Marketers and office managers like Michael became ancillary, but necessary, parts of the medical marijuana machine. They helped doctors manage the administrative tasks of these clinics so the doctors' focus could remain on their patients. But, as Michael would discover, even marketers weren't safe from the attentions of the Medical Board of California.

On April 13, 2013, six months before the raids that gave Michael his black eye, the board received a complaint from a Dr. Syal, stating that the owner of a clinic named THC Doctor (or 420 MD) was not a doctor. Dr. Syal was referring to Michael.

This was a serious accusation. California Business and Professions Code §2052(a) states that only licensed physicians can legally own and operate medical marijuana clinics. Breaking that rule will earn you a charge of unlawful practice of medicine, a felony.

The board assigned Investigator Hughes to look into the complaint. He sent a few undercover investigators to THC Doctor to acquire their own medical marijuana recommendations. It's common practice for undercover officers to visit medical marijuana evaluation clinics to see if the doctors are providing thorough examinations or if they are simply churning out as many recommendations as possible.

Dr. Brown spent his customary thirty minutes examining Hughes's undercover investigators—which is certainly longer than any other medical marijuana evaluation I have ever heard of (or, indeed, any doctor's visit of any kind). The investigators took their recommendations back to Hughes, who inspected the certificates and documents and checked them with the city of San Jose. His search led him to conclude that Brown was indeed the owner of THC Doctor, not Michael.

Hughes took this finding back to Dr. Syal, who confessed he had received the tip from *his* office's marketer and manager, Nadia.[21] Hughes followed up with Nadia, whom he remembered from raiding her business two years before. In that raid, Hughes seized almost $200,000 in cash, jewelry, and designer handbags. He had started to build a case against her alleging that she owned the chain of evaluation clinics she managed—sound familiar?—when, suddenly, the case was dismissed. There was never an explanation why.

Nadia told Hughes that she believed she'd seen an ad for THC Doctor offering a cash rebate, which she thought was illegal. Furthermore, she heard rumors about Michael being involved with organized crime and the Ukrainian mafia.[22] She advised Hughes to keep digging into Michael's business, and he obeyed.

On July 23, 2013, Hughes and another medical board investigator named Victor Sandoval walked into THC Doctor and spoke to Diana, the receptionist working the front desk that day. They asked her who signed her checks and if she got regular lunch breaks.[23] She later told a reporter that the investigators were so dogged, "I couldn't get up even for water."[24]

Then Hughes and Sandoval spoke to Dr. Brown in a separate room. They asked him how he'd met Michael, how their business relationship worked, and what his salary was. Brown cooperated and told them about having posted on Craigslist seeking a job. After over thirty-five years as an OB/GYN, he was looking to shift his career. Michael saw Brown's post and offered him a deal. Brown would open a medical marijuana clinic; Michael and his partners would provide marketing services for the clinic and manage its daily operations. Brown would be free to write medical marijuana recommendations. His salary was $24,000 a month.

The investigators left for a couple of hours, returning at around 3:00 p.m. Diana called Dr. Brown to come from the back office, where he was seeing a patient. This time Hughes and Sandoval asked Brown about the corporate structure of 420 MD. They held up a picture of Michael and asked Brown if he knew him. Brown said he did and confirmed it was a picture of Michael. After two rounds of questioning in one day, Brown asked the investigators, "Should I be concerned?"[25]

The answer, unfortunately, was "yes." After that visit to the clinic, Hughes requested search warrants for the four locations that were later raided on October 10, 2013. He crafted a narrative that Michael was not only the real owner of THC Doctor but that he was also part of organized crime and using the clinic as a way to launder money for contacts in Ukraine. He based that latter claim on a "stack" of shipping receipts seized in the raid on the Fairfield home. This so-called "stack" of receipts was actually about five blank receipts Michael used to ship items like new iPhones to his friends and family back in Ukraine. Michael, nothing if not efficient, preferred to fill these forms out at home.

But when that first raid didn't turn up any concrete evidence of wrongdoing or a mafia connection, Hughes let the case go. A few months later, in March 2014, Hughes received another "anonymous" tip that Michael was opening more clinics. He began looking into Michael again.

Since Brown closed the clinic after the first raid, Michael had tried to make money by doing marketing for Charles Nordlinger, a doctor who already owned a clinic. Dr. Nordlinger was a tall, stooped man in his mid-seventies. For years, he had written medical marijuana recommendations for other clinics, including one of Nadia's, before he set up his own shop. He agreed to pay Michael to upgrade his clinic's advertising and help open up a few more clinics under the name 420 MD.

On October 23, 2014, Hughes showed up at Nordlinger's home in a suburb south of San Francisco. It was so early in the morning that the doctor was still wearing his bathrobe when he opened the door, yet he obliged Hughes with a forty-minute interview. During that interview Hughes tried to get Nordlinger to say that Michael was the owner of the clinics. At first Nordlinger denied it, saying he was the owner. But around the thirty-minute mark, Hughes started to turn up the pressure on Nordlinger.

HUGHES: You're the medical director.

NORDLINGER: Yeah.

HUGHES: But you're not the owner.

NORDLINGER: Okay, if you say so. (laughs) If you say that!

HUGHES: (laughs) I'm not saying so. But I mean, are you, you understand. Let me, let me make sure you understand. If you actually owned these four clinics—

NORDLINGER: Yeah.

HUGHES: Do you understand that you're responsible for all the taxes?

NORDLINGER: Yeah.

HUGHES: That could be millions. Do you understand that?

NORDLINGER: Yes.

HUGHES: You sure? Think about it. Not just the $5,000 that you get, but if the accounting is not handled correctly, you're on the hook for the taxes for the whole shebang, for all four of these clinics. Do you understand that?

NORDLINGER: No, I didn't know that.

HUGHES: Think about it.[26]

When listening to the recording of this interview, it's clear that Hughes has found a way to get to Nordlinger. His further mentions of the IRS and the Franchise Tax Board spook the doctor until, finally, Nordlinger says what Hughes wants to hear.

HUGHES: You don't own these clinics!

NORDLINGER: Okay.

HUGHES: Nor do you want to own these clinics!

NORDLINGER: No.

HUGHES: Now do you understand?

NORDLINGER: Yeah.

HUGHES: Okay, so [Michael] owns these clinics. Correct?

NORDLINGER: I guess so. I guess he owns them. I know I don't want to be on the hook for millions of dollars.

That same month, the Santa Clara District Attorney's office charged Michael with the unlawful practice of medicine and aiding and abetting the unlawful practice of medicine. That's when Michael hired me.

Traditionally, the Medical Board of California focused on the doctors writing recommendations, like Dr. Mikuriya. Michael's case was one of the first of its kind, marking a shift that rippled throughout the medical marijuana industry. The medical board was no longer just going after medical marijuana doctors. They were investigating the corporate structures of these clinics, including the management companies.

A few months before Michael's first raid in 2013, the Second District Court of Appeals came to a decision on *People v. Superior Court of Los Angeles County*, otherwise known as the Cardillo case. The big question of the Cardillo case was whether a person without a medical license could be criminally charged with practicing medicine without a license if they owned a corporation that operated a medical marijuana clinic.

The medical board was investigating Sean Cardillo and his business partner Michael Cettei, neither of whom were doctors, for allegedly owning a couple of medical marijuana evaluation clinics in Venice, California. Cardillo and Cettei maintained that they formed a company named Kush Dr., leased office space, and provided management services for the doctors who wrote recommendations. They were not the owners of these clinics. None of the doctors in the case ever testified that they felt they were employees of Kush Dr. Over three years, from the start of the medical board investigation in January 2010 to the decision on July 31, 2013, Cardillo and Cettei insisted they conducted business legally and were merely leasing the offices to doctors.

But the court ruled against them. It found that a nonphysician owner of a corporation operating a medical marijuana clinic could be charged with practicing medicine without a license, and it charged both Cardillo and Cettei with that crime.[27] When the case went before a jury, Cardillo and Cettei won. But the prosecutors took it to the California Court of Appeals, which remanded the decision, slapping the charges back on the two men.[28] Investigator Hughes mentioned the outcome of the Cardillo case in his initial police report; in 2013, it was the only case law on the subject of management companies and medical marijuana evaluation clinics.

Michael's arraignment hearing took place on December 3, 2014. Bail was set at the absurdly high amount of $400,000.[29] This was fifty times the normal bail amount for a charge violating California's Business and Professions Code. He was arrested in the courtroom and kept in jail for two weeks. Then the judge released him from police custody but gave him an ankle monitor. None of the other defendants received a monitor, but since Michael is Ukrainian, the court believed he posed a flight risk. He wore that monitor for two years.

From 2014 to 2019, the cases piled on. Just before Christmas in 2015, the People filed a first amended complaint to add seven more felony charges to the charges from 2014. A few months later, the People filed a second amended complaint that repeated the same charges and sprinkled in some charges of tax evasion. Then, less than a month later, in March 2016, the People filed a *third* amended complaint.

Then we thought we had caught a break. The California Court of Appeals, Second Appellate District published a decision on *Epic Medical Management, LLC v. Paquette,* a case involving a physician and a management company. Dr. Justin Paquette had entered into a contract with Epic Medical Management, wherein Epic would manage the nonmedical aspects of running a doctor's office—like finding and maintaining the office space, providing marketing services, purchasing equipment, and hiring nurses and other nonphysician personnel—and for these services Paquette would pay Epic a percentage of the revenue he earned. After three and a half years of this arrangement, Paquette terminated his agreement with Epic. The arbitration that followed found that Paquette had breached the contract by not paying part of the management fees he owed to Epic. Paquette moved to vacate this decision. His argument was that if he had paid the fees he owed, he would have violated the antireferral prohibitions in the California Business and Professions Code, since Epic Medical Management referred a small number of patients to Paquette.

When a trial court denied Dr. Paquette's motion to vacate, he took it up with the court of appeals. The Second Appellate District court upheld the trial court's decision. Furthermore, the court ruled that this type of agreement between a doctor and a management company did not violate the law.[30]

The decision in *Epic Medical Management, LLC v. Paquette,* which was published in 2016, bolstered our defense for Michael—and frankly, we needed it. The DA's office was like a dog with a bone, determined to trap Michael in an endless legal battle. I've seen a few judges look at the size of a case file and kick it over to the next judge, not wanting to bother with such a complicated matter. At the height of his troubles, Michael faced seventy felony charges, including unlawful practice of medicine, conspiracy to commit unlawful practice of medicine, tax fraud, money laundering, unlawfully structuring transactions, falsifying documents, and using fraudulent identification/license. By my own estimation, over the course of five-plus years on this case, my firm filed fifteen motions and appeared in court at least fifty times. Michael's Sixth Amendment right to a speedy trial has been violated time and again.

The misconduct by the DA's office has affected me, too. In late 2015 the former DA on the case, Victor Chen, filed a recording request form and got access to the calls Michael made to me from jail in 2014. The only way I learned about the existence of these recordings was by stumbling across an internal office memo buried in the People's discovery from Chen to Hughes stating that the sheriff's department had recorded attorney-client communications. Furthermore, that memo stated that Chen and the DA's office intended to use these recordings to investigate me for potential felony charges. He planned to use my calls with Michael so he could turn me into a witness against my own client. Later, I learned that the DA's office also had recordings of the jail calls between Michael and me after his 2016 arrest.

The DA's office used those improperly obtained recordings to try to recuse me and my firm from the case and to threaten to file criminal charges against me. I had to hire my own attorney to protect myself against these allegations. We took the matter of the recordings to the judge on July 30, 2019, and asked that all the charges be dismissed. The judge ordered the DA's office to delete their recordings but did not determine that the DA's office had violated Michael's constitutional rights.

There is no oversight of the DA's office. Complaints against specific prosecutors can be made directly to the DA's office, but I never trusted the office to take any action. It is a system where a determined prosecutor can file case after case, trapping defendants like Michael in the quicksand of the courtroom for years.

My team and I decided our best option was to try to take Michael's case to the California Court of Appeals. We had to write a writ of mandamus, considered an extraordinary measure by many defense attorneys because you are asking the court of appeals to overturn the decisions of the trial court. We filed a writ to dismiss all the charges against Michael on October 1, 2019, almost six years after the first raid. We outlined all the details of the case: the prosecutorial misconduct; the illegal recordings of attorney-client phone calls; the yawning space where evidence should have backed up the DA's allegations. But the court of appeals denied our writ.

In February 2020, I was able to get our firm off of Michael's case. I asked that the same attorney I had hired to represent me—Zenia Gilg, a great lawyer who ironically had represented Stephanie Landa before I did—become appointed as Michael's new lawyer, and the court accepted it.[31]

As of this writing, Michael still faces seventy-five felony charges, but the case has been continued indefinitely because of the state-ordered quarantine in response to the COVID-19 pandemic.

In 1996, the same year that Prop 215 passed in California, the pharmaceutical company Purdue Pharma released its newest opiate, OxyContin. Like its Purdue predecessor MS Contin, OxyContin had a time-release formula that allowed it to provide pain relief for several consecutive hours. The difference was that MS Contin released morphine, and OxyContin released oxycodone, which would prove to be highly addictive.

When MS Contin hit the market in 1984, most physicians were wary about overprescribing opiates. Purdue Pharma made sure they never called MS Contin a "risk-free" painkiller, but still there were some cases of MS Contin abuse popping up.

Things were different by the '90s. Suddenly, the focus in medicine was not on the dangers of prescribing opiates—which have been known to be addictive since the late 1800s—but on alleviating pain. Doctors started to call pain the "fifth vital sign." The rules around prescribing opiates started to relax just around the time that OxyContin became available.

The addictive potential of other opioids like Vicodin, Lorcet, Lortab, and Percocet was widely known. Those prescriptions were restricted to small doses and were mixed with acetaminophen, or Tylenol, to prevent addicted patients from liquefying the pills and shooting up for a quicker hit.[32] OxyContin, which contained large 40 mg or 80 mg doses of oxycodone, had no such limitations.

OxyContin also benefited from the most sophisticated pharmaceutical marketing team in American history. In 1997, the FDA relaxed its rules on pharmaceutical ads so drug companies could broadcast the medical benefits of their drugs on television without rolling out a detailed list of eyebrow-raising side effects.[33] That policy change led to an almost 400 percent increase in spending on advertising from drug manufacturers within a few years.[34]

Purdue sent sales reps to the doctors who were already prescribing large amounts of Percocet and Vicodin to hawk OxyContin for its long-lasting effects and higher potency. They downplayed the risk of addiction, if the subject ever came up at all. They rewarded the physicians who prescribed large amounts of the drugs with more wining and dining and OxyContin-branded swag. The reps brought flowers and spa coupons to charm the receptionists at these doctor's offices. They paid for expensive dinners at fancy restaurants where the doctors could dig into a free filet mignon while listening to another pharmaceutical pitch.

By 2000, the pharmaceutical industry was spending $4.04 billion on direct marketing to doctors.[35] And the investment paid off. In the mid-1990s, cancer doctors were writing the most prescriptions for long-acting opioids. At the dawn of the new millennium, at the same time that the Medical Board of California was going after medical marijuana doctors like Dr. Mikuriya, family doctors were writing tens of thousands of Oxy-Contin prescriptions across the country, from Alaska to Appalachia.

Compared to the rest of the country, California has not been hit as hard by the opioid epidemic.[36] This is despite the fact that California is home to the infamous Tijuana/San Diego smuggling corridor, which is how some cartels smuggle drugs into the United States from Mexico. One of the reasons why California has mostly been spared, despite the proximity of opioid painkillers like Vicodin and OxyContin as well as heroin, is the same medical marijuana that has been such a target for prosecutors and the medical board.

There have been several studies showing that states with legalized medical or recreational marijuana have lower rates of opiate addiction. A 2017 study from the University of California San Diego showed that hospitalization rates for opioid dependence and abuse dropped an average of 23 percent in states that legalized medical marijuana. The same study showed that hospitalization rates for opioid overdoses dropped by 13 percent.[37]

Dr. March Bachhuber, a professor at the Albert Einstein College of Medicine and Montefiore Medical Center in New York City, published a 2014 study showing that deaths from opioid overdoses fell by 25 percent in states that had legalized medical marijuana.[38] Bachhuber told Reuters that many of his patients were using medical marijuana to help them quit opioids and wean themselves off prescription painkillers.

These findings were prefigured in a *60 Minutes* broadcast on medical marijuana from 2007, which showed a man speaking to correspondent Morley Safer about how he used marijuana to manage his anxiety and ease his neck and back pain. "It seems to be the only thing that works that is not an opiate derivative," he told Safer.[39]

If it seems like a coincidence that the pressure on medical marijuana doctors happened at around the same time as the beginning of the opioid crisis, consider this: the same pharmaceutical companies that funded the research defending the safety of prescribing opioids like OxyContin also bankrolled antimarijuana propaganda as more and more states voted to legalize the plant.

In 2016, *The Guardian* reported that pharmaceutical company Insys Therapeutics, which manufactures the fentanyl-derived prescription painkiller Subsys, contributed $500,000 to Arizona's antimarijuana legalization drive.[40] That year, Arizonans would vote on Proposition 205, which would legalize recreational marijuana for adults over the age of twenty-one. With their half-a-million-dollar contribution, Insys became the single largest donor to the campaign against Proposition 205,[41] bank-rolling television ads that warned against the dangers that Arizona's children would face if pot were legalized. Even with these efforts at smearing adult-use marijuana, Proposition 205 only failed by a narrow margin: 51.3 percent of Arizonans voted no.[42]

At the same time that Insys was funding Arizona's antipot efforts, the company was in the development stages of a synthetic substitute for THC called Syndros.[43] The new drug was released on July 31, 2017, one day before Prop 205 failed.[44]

This is part of a new trend of Big Pharma moving into medical marijuana.[45] Teva, one of the largest pharmaceutical companies in the world, signed a deal with medical cannabis company Canndoc to distribute their products to hospitals and pharmacies in Israel. In Canada—which became the second nation in the world to legalize recreational marijuana in 2018—seven of the top ten cannabis patent holders are major pharmaceutical companies.[46] In the United States the majority of cannabis patents are held by companies like AbbVie, Sanofi, and Merck. For perspective, AbbVie holds fifty-nine US cannabis patents; the US Department of Health and Human Services only holds thirteen.[47]

Still, the pattern of pharmaceutical companies backing antimarijuana causes continues on a national level. Purdue Pharma and Abbott Laboratories, which manufactures the painkiller Vicodin, are two of the biggest contributors to the Community Anti-Drug Coalition of America, one of the nation's largest antidrug organizations.[48]

In 2007, the same year the segment on medical marijuana aired on *60 Minutes,* Judge James Jones in Abingdon, Virginia, sentenced three Purdue executives to three years of probation and four hundred hours of community service each for their role in addicting the community's young people to OxyContin.[49] Investigators started raiding "pill mills" where doctors churned out hundreds of prescriptions for opiates without discrimination. There were reports of sweeping raids across the country, dragnets meant to round up every doctor who overprescribed opiates.

Meanwhile, in my world as an attorney and legalization advocate, I found myself having to educate people who believed legal marijuana would lead to more cannabis-related hospitalizations. The opposite was true. The rate of addiction among patients who are prescribed opioids for chronic pain is about 21 to 29 percent.[50] Contrary to popular belief, marijuana does have a potential for addiction, but the proportion of addicts is much smaller: only 9 to 10 percent of pot users will become addicted.[51]

In fact, California's medical marijuana program saved the state from the worst of the opiate epidemic, which claimed almost forty-seven thousand American lives in 2018 alone.[52] When you include deaths from heroin overdoses, that number grows to sixty-four thousand dead in one year because of opioids, more than any other cause of death.[53] Meanwhile, there is no recorded case of anyone ever dying from a marijuana overdose.

There are still medical marijuana doctors in California, even with legal recreational weed. People still seek physicians' recommendations for a number of reasons: to avoid the steep taxes on medical marijuana products; to be able to grow their own plants; and to have access to higher-potency products, which is especially important for cancer patients and chronic pain sufferers.

While many state medical boards continue to revoke the licenses of medical marijuana doctors, the Medical Board of California is now targeting doctors for writing opioid prescriptions. In a July 2017 meeting, the board announced[54] it would be investigating doctors who prescribed opioids to patients who died from an overdose, even if that overdose happened months or years after the prescriptions were written. The "Death Certificate Project" led to about 450 doctors and over seventy nurses and physician assistants being threatened with disciplinary action.[55] The doctors who received these letters from the medical board—peppered with troubling terms like "complaints," "allegations," "overprescribing," and "toxic levels"[56]—called the Death Certificate Project a witch hunt.

Many doctors reacted to the letters by changing the way they approached pain, shying away from prescribing opioids even to the patients who needed them, or referring pain patients to other specialists.[57] This scrutiny has made it harder for people who are suffering from pain to get opioids. Ironically, or perhaps predictably, this has caused more pain patients to turn to medical marijuana for relief.[58]

Every decade has been characterized by a big, bad drug crisis. The 1990s had heroin, the 2000s had meth, now we have opioids. Every time we go through a cycle of crime and punishment, we look for a scapegoat, whether it's the doctors, the drug dealers, or the pharmaceutical companies.

But America's drug overdose problem is bigger than any one drug. According to a 2018 study in *Science,* there has been "exponential growth" in overdose deaths since 1979.[59] Data from the Centers for Disease Control and Prevention showed a recent increase in overdose deaths from psychostimulants like meth and cocaine and synthetic opioids like fentanyl.[60] A 2020 study published in *JAMA* showed that alcohol-caused deaths increased by 78 percent among American men from 2000 to 2016 and more than doubled for American women in that same time period.[61]

These data points paint a larger and more troubling portrait of the United States in the twenty-first century. For three years in a row, from 2015 to 2017, Americans' life expectancy dropped.[62] The causes of these earlier deaths are "deaths of despair," like drug overdoses, suicides, and alcohol-related diseases.

These deaths of despair do not just indicate a crisis around drug abuse. As long as people still experience pain, whether physical or psychological, they will seek relief in any form that is available to them. It is the job of health care professionals to help responsibly ease that pain while doing the least possible harm. Most doctors do not enter that profession expecting to become targets for medical board investigators. They want to help people get well, make a living, and do honest work.

I would argue that Michael had similar goals when he first partnered with Dr. Brown and Dr. Nordlinger to open medical marijuana clinics. There is risk involved in any business venture, of course, but when your business involves a controlled substance, the odds of prosecution skyrocket. What started with a dream has ended in a Kafkaesque legal nightmare. Between the almost unchecked power of the DA's office and the political agenda of the medical board, people like Michael and the medical marijuana doctors can be trapped in the court system for years. And as more states legalize medical marijuana, while the United States maintains its federal prohibition of the plant more people will find themselves in Michael's position.

The system needs to change to reflect reality. The Medical Board of California still considers management companies like Michael's to be in violation of the law. In the eyes of the medical board, only physicians can advertise their practices.[63] This standard is not only absurd; it also fails to recognize that most physicians do not have the skill set to market their own services. Hiring management companies like Michael's to place advertising and handle day-to-day administrative tasks ought to be legal.

Finally, the medical board needs to be more than an agency that licenses and punishes physicians. There should also be a more robust system protecting doctors, whether they recommend marijuana or prescribe opioids for pain. Since there is little oversight over prosecutors and the district attorney's office, there should be a professional physician watchdog within the medical board.

As this agency operates now, physicians not only have to worry about the best way to treat their patients, but they also have to be aware of political consequences. After the medical board began its Death Certificate Project, many doctors found that they were not prescribing opioids even for patients suffering from legitimate and chronic pain.[64]

Overzealous prosecutors and medical board investigators like Ralph Hughes are not just hurting marketers and doctors. The patients are affected, too.

15

GEORGE, DAVID, AND GEORGE[1]

TWO COMPANIES HAVE FIGURED OUT how to manufacture pharmaceutical-grade opiates cheaply and secure a massive supply of precursors so they can sell them to everyone, including the group among which they have been most popular historically: rural and suburban whites.[2]

Johnson & Johnson engineered a superpoppy with unnaturally high amounts of thebaine, an alkaloid opiate classified as a Schedule II controlled substance, and refined the supply chain so they could make the pharmaceutical opiates oxycodone and hydrocodone cheaply and in plentiful supply. Purdue released OxyContin, which contains oxycodone, and engaged in an aggressive national marketing campaign to convince doctors that time-release opiates can be prescribed for treating all manner of pain.

The way for this campaign was paved by the apparent perception among some health care professionals that the dangers of addiction to medication were overstated. For instance, in 1974 researchers evaluated Vietnam veterans who had become addicted to substances during their tour of duty and who had no prior history of addiction. The researchers concluded that "most addicted Vietnam soldiers either gave up their narcotic use voluntarily shortly before their departure or did not revert to use after brief forced detoxification subsequent to their discovery as users at departure."[3]

A 1980 letter to the editor of the *New England Journal of Medicine*, written by two staffers of a drug surveillance program at Boston University Medical Center, made a similar point:

> *Recently, we examined our current files to determine the incidence of narcotic addiction in 39,946 hospitalized medical patients who were monitored consecutively. Although there were 11,882 patients who received at least one narcotic preparation, there were only four cases of reasonably well documented addiction in patients who had no history of addiction. The addiction was considered major in only one instance. The drugs implicated were meperidine in two patients, Percodan in one, and hydromorphone in one. We conclude that despite widespread use of narcotic drugs in hospitals, the development of addiction is rare in medical patients with no history of addiction.*[4]

Sam Quinones, author of *Dreamland,* offers the following observation of the impact of the *New England Journal of Medicine* letter: "That shorthand, in turn, lent prestige to the tiny thing and the claim attributed to it: that less than 1 percent of patients treated with narcotics developed addictions to them."[5]

As pain medication became more widespread and powerful new painkillers were developed, the idea was that pain medicine would come as a complement to physical rehabilitation; but ultimately the treatment was stripped down to just a pill. To get the pill covered by insurance was far easier than obtaining coverage for other recommended services that were more obviously costly.[6]

While many doctors had to be persuaded to prescribe massive amounts of opiates, other doctors saw the opportunity to make a killing in churning prescriptions, especially in suburban and rural white America, a community unused to opiate addiction and the subsequent fallout from massive usage of opiates.

At precisely the same time, black tar heroin from Mexico, already available in most major cities, became widely accessible to suburban and rural America, especially to white and Latino populations through the efforts of decentralized operators. Those operators recognized the opportunity created by OxyContin, and they marketed black tar to

Oxy users as a cheaper, more powerful alternative. According to the National Institute on Drug Abuse, "people often assume prescription pain relievers are safer than illicit drugs because they are medically prescribed; however, when these drugs are taken for reasons or in ways or amounts not intended by a doctor, or taken by someone other than the person for whom they are prescribed, they can result in severe adverse health effects including substance use disorder, overdose, and death, especially when combined with other drugs or alcohol. Research now suggests that misuse of these medications may actually open the door to heroin use."[7]

Users jumping from pills to black tar not only increased the number of heroin users in the country but also the number of opiate users overall. In addition, some white middle-class people learned about heroin through OxyContin, and many skipped trying the pills first and went right to heroin.

While the FDA was making it easier to market powerful pharmaceuticals and the DEA was approving ever-increasing amounts of opiate production, the Department of Justice and the State Department escalated the drug war by dropping the hammer on Mexico, especially through interdiction and eradication of opiate cultivation and production. When the Mexican government balked at these measures, the federal government halted the export of US pharmaceutical opiates to Mexico, especially those needed for patients in postsurgery recovery or suffering from intractable cancer pain. This move forced Mexico to begin massive eradication efforts, which led to substantially increased violence and turmoil, which, of course, affected supply and thus price.

Concurrently, US law enforcement and prosecutors perfected a legal strategy called parallel construction, which they used to take down heroin dealers. The first step of parallel construction is for the police to obtain illegal wiretaps by hiding behind a Hobbs motion, "a motion that is filed to force the prosecution to disclose the identity of a material confidential informant. It essentially challenges the validity of a sealed search warrant. Usually the police agency conducting the search warrant wants to keep all or any part of search warrant affidavit from being revealed so as to protect an informant's identity."[8]

Judges often rubber-stamp these requests for a wiretap warrant. Once police get their first warrant, they use it to go to other judges to get more warrants and ultimately a big state case. Often those first warrants were shaky, if not downright unconstitutional. For instance, police would sometimes use Cellebrite—a technology to grab information between a cell phone and an access point—to gain their initial information illegally, and then they would cite this ill-gotten information as having come from a confidential informant. This technique led to substantial turnover in street-level dealers and put pressure on supply, driving up prices and making black tar more difficult to obtain.

It is difficult, if not impossible, to talk about the drug war and its casualties without talking about race and how racism has been used as a rationale for laws seeking to control minority populations. The entire basis for drug wars in this country going back to the nineteenth century has racist roots. George Floyd's case indicates how attitudes toward drug users, and particularly African American drug users, are still tightly tied to racist perspectives so prevalent as to make them the norm. This was certainly the case when Billie Holiday sang "Strange Fruit," written by Abel Meeropol, who penned the song under the name Lewis Allan:

> *Southern trees bearing a strange fruit*
> *Blood on the leaves and blood on the root*
> *Black bodies swinging in the Southern breeze*
> *Strange fruit hanging from the poplar trees*

In the supposed age of freedom for Black Americans, they were still being strung up and hung for no other sin than the color of their skin. Today's Black American experience is not so different. A *New York Times* article about "Strange Fruit" that includes an interview with one of Abel Meeropol's adopted sons, Michael—a retired professor of economics, radio host, and son of convicted spies Julius and Ethel Rosenberg—brings up that very point:

And in 2021, as the nation continues to reckon with a series of killings of unarmed Black people by the police—often captured in gruesome footage of Black men being shot or, in the case of George Floyd, knelt on by white officers—"Strange Fruit" has maintained its place in the national conversation about racism. The song "is going to be relevant until cops start getting convicted for murdering Black people," Michael told CBS This Morning before Derek Chauvin, a former Minneapolis police officer, was convicted of murdering Mr. Floyd. "When that happens, maybe then 'Strange Fruit' will be a relic of a barbaric past," he said. "But until then, it's a mirror on a barbaric present."[9]

In a radio commentary, Michael stated: "We have to make mass incarceration, vigilante 'justice' and police lynchings equally unacceptable today. And police lynchings will only cease when the very culture of policing changes. The blue wall of silence must come down. District attorneys and attorneys general must start investigating killer cops. Grand juries must start indicting them. Finally, juries must stop immediately crediting the five magic words ('I feared for my life') and begin convicting police officers of murder."[10]

One of Billie Holiday's poisons of choice, alcohol, had been decreed legal by constitutional amendment, but that didn't prevent her from being targeted by the newly formed Federal Bureau of Narcotics. Her other poison of choice was heroin. As a Black woman who could not only sing but also had a voice, Billie Holiday was demonized. She had power in that voice—and Harry Anslinger, head of the FBN, was after her. When Anslinger came across another heroin user—Judy Garland, "America's sweetheart"—he treated her very differently. As Johann Hari observes in *Chasing the Scream:*

One day, Harry Anslinger was told that there were also white women, just as famous as Billie, who had drug problems—but he responded to them rather differently. He called Judy Garland, another heroin addict, in to see him. They had a friendly chat, in which he advised her to take longer vacations between pictures, and he wrote to her studio, assuring them she didn't have a drug problem at all. When he discovered that a Washington

society hostess he knew—"a beautiful, gracious lady," he noted—had an
illegal drug addiction, he explained he couldn't possibly arrest her because
"it would destroy . . . the unblemished reputation of one of the nation's most
honored families." He helped her to wean herself off her addiction slowly,
without the law becoming involved.[11]

George Floyd, an opiate user, was positive for COVID-19 when he died. But he, unlike many others, didn't die of COVID-19, suicide, or an overdose. He had lost his job at a Salvation Army and was taking care of his kid, recovering from COVID, doing a little bit of drugs, and going to the fucking market—and by the way, no one I know except my mom, my kid's tutor, and my best friend go to the market totally sober. That a fentanyl overdose was raised as defense reminds me of how little we've moved forward since Billie Holiday was targeted, bullied, and ultimately arrested on her deathbed by the Federal Bureau of Narcotics for singing about lynching.

For George's murder, the only crime that was committed was that the cops were not wearing masks and they committed battery against George, who had asked the police to please get into the police vehicle for only a few seconds so he wouldn't have a panic attack. But fentanyl? You have got to be kidding me. To say that an opiate could cause violence is straight from the racist handbook of the drug war. The signs of fentanyl overdose are being unable to talk though being awake; a limp body; shallow or slow breathing; pale, ashen, or clammy skin; and loss of consciousness.[12]

Discovered in the 1960s and used in surgery since then, its use expanded in the 1990s because of the development and widespread use of the fentanyl patch. Also, fentanyl analogues have been developed and are considered novel psychoactive substances. According to the Drug Policy Alliance, fentanyl and fentanyl analogues have both been hitting the streets.[13]

Fentanyl is so deadly because it is fifty times stronger than heroin, so a minuscule amount can cause an overdose. According to a study done by Ohio Harm Reduction,[14] for a nontolerant opioid user, 500 to 1,000 micrograms "will put you at death's door." One microgram is a millionth of a gram, so 1,000 micrograms is 1/1,000 (0.001) of 1 gram. A raisin, for example, weighs about a gram. So a fatal dose of fentanyl for a nonuser is equivalent to dividing a raisin into a thousand equal pieces and eating one of those pieces, which has the mass of one grain of sand. A nonfatal amount, on the other hand, is 25 micrograms, with 50 being considered a modest risk, and 150 significant.

Prior to writing this book, I never knew the difference between a fatal and a nonfatal dose of fentanyl. Neither did my husband, Jon, who is one of five siblings; his brother David was the youngest. In high school, David played the trumpet and would make his way to Long Beach on the weekends to play with a few octogenarians. Sometimes he lived in Santa Monica with his dad, and sometimes with his mom. I knew the situation with the dad was fucked up. No one in his family admitted that this was his reality, even in private. Jon's mom had David a few years after she and Jon's dad got divorced—and four children later, when she couldn't take care of the first four. The dad was a major alcoholic, from what I understood, but I didn't know the true extent; I just knew that when David was young, his dad had threatened to kidnap him. Also, the dad's boyfriend was kind of the dad's stepdad too, but no one was sure whether the guy might just be a john for David's dad.

I wasn't one to judge or get involved more than necessary in someone's life more than they wanted. I thought David was basically okay; in fact, I thought he had a bright future ahead of him. After finishing Santa Monica High School, he went on to get an associate's position in San Luis Obispo. A few years later, David was dead. I didn't even know that he was doing fentanyl until he died of an overdose on it. The family said David had overdosed a few years before on Xanax and caused some kind of crazy injury to his leg by collapsing on it. That said, when the family told me they were going to send him to rehab, I told them not to. I said that if they did so, he would die. Any rehab modality relies on a zero-sum mentality, and abstinence in my experience has led to a lot of death. Those who are using drugs to the point where it is negatively affecting their daily lives are using it to treat trauma, and they would otherwise kill themselves.

The substance use disorder treatment industry is full of fraud and abuse. According to the Center for Health Journalism at the University of

Southern California, "the opioid epidemic has given rise to an illicit gold rush as patient brokers and treatment centers exploit desperate addicts, funneling them to shoddy treatment centers and fraudulent 'sober' homes at a profit of thousands per head. The profiteering, unfolding in communities across the country, has bilked insurers out of millions and created a shady subculture that takes advantage of a vulnerable population."[15] Depriving someone of access to that resource in an artificial setting often leads to overdose in the days, months, or years after going to rehab.

In David's case, he left rehab, spent a couple of weeks at his mom's, then returned to his home. His girlfriend found him unresponsive the next morning. David seized upon his first night alone to make all the pain go away. The stigma and shame that addicted people feel every time they "use," and the idea of "throwing away time and years" because they've been using drugs, are not healthy and lead to the extreme shame that often results in death.[16]

According to a 2018 *Health Affairs* article, the increase in unethical addiction treatment providers in response to the opioid epidemic is "fraud's newest hot spot." The authors write: "Substance use disorder is a chronic, often relapsing, disease that can be treated with the same effectiveness as other diseases, such as asthma or diabetes. However, long-standing stigma and the misconception that addiction is a moral failing, instead of a disease, has resulted in punitive responses for those in need, rather than medical treatment."[17]

More than a hundred years after the first federal legislation on drugs, we are in the midst of the most lethal drug purity crisis our country has seen. This crisis is in part a result of the War on Drugs. Eradication of Afghan poppy fields that were producing heroin increased the pressure on cartels to find synthetic drugs that have a smaller production footprint. Very minuscule amounts of fentanyl produced in labs in China and Mexico earn dealers the same money, if not more, as large amounts of heroin would, and they don't need to be grown. Due to easy production, compelling economics, and powerful highs, synthetic drugs are proliferating and are much more likely to cause overdose deaths than drugs in the past. We could meaningfully reduce the number of overdoses in this

country if we passed legislation that would allow for easy and safe pharmaceutical access to the most potent and abused drugs, like fentanyl.[18]

Under this proposal, those who willingly choose to use fentanyl would
have access to carefully measured, nonlethal doses, along with information regarding all of its dangers. And if we provide controlled access to
heroin and other drugs that are often secretly cut with synthetics like
fentanyl, we could cut down on the number of people who tragically die
every year after accidentally ingesting a lethal drug cocktail they weren't
expecting.

When the man I now call St. George entered the race for Los Angeles
County district attorney, I felt chills. I still do, just writing about it. District Attorney George Gascón has drawn a lot of attention for his progressive new policies that are a sharp break from what most of us are used to
hearing from traditional law-and-order lock-'em-up prosecutors. On his
first day on the job, Gascón announced that his office will, among other
things: end cash bail, allowing people who are presumed to be innocent
until proven guilty to be freed while awaiting trial; never seek the death
penalty in any prosecution; stop filing all sentencing enhancements,
including under the "three strikes" sentencing law; allow resentencing of
thousands of people currently in prison based on retroactive application
of these sentencing policies; and prioritize release of people convicted of
nonviolent crimes, those with demonstrated records of rehabilitation or
who are otherwise deemed to be at low risk for recidivism, senior citizens,
people at increased risk for COVID-19, and people sentenced to adult
prison terms as children. Gascón also announced he will reopen use-of-
force investigations involving killings by police dating back to 2012. He
has also described being arrested as "traumatic and dehumanizing," and
he says "our rush to incarcerate generations of kids of color" has torn apart
"the social fabric of our communities. . . . The status quo hasn't made us
safer."[19]

Like Gascón, Governor Gavin Newsom of California wants to make
our cities more safe. "I'm just sick and tired of this 'either/or' debate,

which I think is rather lazy and unfortunate," he has said. "And as long as I'm here, I'm going to try to drive to improve public safety, and a lot of these reforms have actually enhanced public safety."[20]

Perhaps most notably, Gascón has issued a new list of "do not prosecute" offenses—laws that his office will simply not enforce. Except in special circumstances, LA will no longer file or prosecute criminal cases against anyone suspected of trespassing, disturbing the peace, being a minor in possession of alcohol, driving without a license, driving with a suspended license, making criminal threats, drug and paraphernalia possession, being under the influence of a controlled substance, public intoxication, loitering to commit prostitution, or resisting arrest. This policy is essentially the opposite of Mayor Rudy Giuliani's "zero-tolerance" policing policy in New York City, where he ramped up enforcement of relatively minor, victimless crimes, which resulted in young people of color being disproportionately targeted by police, along with increased complaints of police misconduct and abuse of force.

Gascón's policies are designed to revolutionize the roles of police and prosecutors in our society, ending our culture of mass incarceration for victimless crimes. They go well beyond what self-proclaimed "progressive prosecutors" like Vice President Kamala Harris have advocated in the past when they've had the power to change the system. Gascón's directives will free up the police and prosecutors to focus their time and efforts on investigating and prosecuting serious and violent crimes, while allowing other social services and community groups to address quality-of-life issues arising from drug addiction, family dysfunction, and homelessness.

I have been very encouraged by Gascón's bold reimagining of how our criminal justice system can best serve society. In order to make this transformation effective and complete, however, Gascón should consider adding another category of offenses to his "do not prosecute" list: *sales* of controlled substances. People who become addicted to illicit drugs and who are not independently wealthy typically end up selling drugs to other people in consensual transactions to support their habit. Branding such people as felons who should be imprisoned does not help the drug addicts improve their lot in life, nor does it protect any "victims." Studies show that people who are locked up are more likely to engage in criminal behavior in the future, not less likely, due to their exposure to the criminal system, especially if their incarceration occurs when they are young and most impressionable. Their felony conviction will make it difficult or impossible to find legitimate future employment in the legal market. And their sustained exposure to people convicted of all types of crimes while in custody is likely to cause them to emulate this new peer group.

It is unclear whether there are any benefits at all from locking up drug dealers. Anyone seeking drugs will simply buy them elsewhere in the marketplace. And the profit margins available in the illicit market ensure there will always be a steady stream of new sellers to replace anyone who gets caught and becomes imprisoned. Thus, the drug war becomes a game of whack-a-mole, with new sellers popping up every time an old one goes away, and the people going away becoming even more hardened criminals fully committed to a life of crime.

Prosecutors have always had the power and duty to decide which types of cases to pursue and which ones to decline. It is commonly accepted that one of the most important duties of a prosecutor is the exercise of "prosecutorial discretion"—deciding which potential criminal violations to turn into criminal cases, and which ones to let go. Prosecutors have a duty to do justice, not to maximize convictions. Only a small fraction of criminal violations end up being prosecuted, due both to limited resources of police and prosecutors, and to public policy choices about which types of defendants deserve to be prosecuted and which prosecutions will improve the general welfare.

Prosecutors are free to use their discretion to refuse to prosecute victimless "crimes," such as consensual sex, gambling, and narcotics offenses. Prosecutors seeking to do justice could conclude that such prosecutions only harm society by destroying the lives of those prosecuted and their families, imposing substantial expenses on taxpayers who must pay for prosecuting and incarcerating the nonviolent defendants, and providing no countervailing benefit to the public.

Prosecutorial discretion is what allowed President Obama's Deferred Action for Childhood Arrivals (DACA) policy, preventing the deportation of hundreds of thousands of undocumented immigrants who arrived in the United States as children. Although DACA beneficiaries have technically violated federal criminal immigration laws, the president, as head of the executive branch, is allowed to set the priorities and policies for prosecutions and to carve out certain classes of offenses that will not be prosecuted. Prosecutorial discretion, however, can also be used for nefarious purposes, including targeting political enemies or racial or religious groups.

Hopefully, Gascón's thoughtful approach to prosecutorial discretion will usher in a new era across the country, where everyone in the criminal justice system will think about how to use the system to do good, improve lives, and focus on protecting innocent people from being victimized by predators. For decades, the War on Drugs has brainwashed many police officers and prosecutors into dehumanizing drug addicts and focusing their efforts on the futile task of rooting out consensual sales or products for which there is a high demand. Law enforcement and prosecution tend to attract people inclined to follow the leader and adhere to strict loyalty to a party line without debate. Thus, electing bold visionaries like George Gascón with the courage to set the right tone at the top is the only way to achieve true progress in the criminal system.

AFTERWORD

JUST BECAUSE YOU DON'T HAVE great trauma in your life, or you think you have a great life and a lot to be appreciative of and are doing good things, that doesn't mean you won't use or abuse drugs. The point of this book is that if you do, 1) it's actually not your fault, as everyone passes down trauma; 2) it's how you deal with it that counts; and 3) using drugs as one means to escape or ease your suffering doesn't make you bad, a failure, an immoral mess, or anything other than an animal trying to cope.

Knowing this and accepting drug use for what it is seem to be the keys to not abusing it. Indigenous cultures all over the world do not shun drug use. They respect and ceremonialize it, and until the introduction of alcohol and trauma, that in and of itself did not create additional trauma that led to abuse. The oppression of Indigenous cultures by Europeans—the rejection of native sexualities, religious practices, and drug use—is what has led to problems. Erasing stigmatization through decriminalization and legalization is the first step in healing the trauma. We need to recognize drugs as "just dope" and as one of the many ways in which one can manifest an addiction.

But we must be vigilant when reforming drug laws to ensure that we do not create environmental injustice or continue oppression under the name of regulation.

By the way, I could write an entire book on my colleagues and myself and the antics, drama, and heartache of running an office—the finances, personalities, wives, husbands—but that will be the next one . . .

ACKNOWLEDGMENTS

I WOULD LIKE TO THANK my husband, Jon; my mom, my dad, Jeffrey, and Marin, my sister. Plus, my friends who stayed with me, inspired me, and helped me along the way: my grandmother Guta, a woman who convinced a Nazi not to rape her, who kept my school papers, ranging from my D.A.R.E. speech to my high school creative writing contest entry "The Butcher and the Prostitute"; my great-grandmother Sara and Grandpa Henry; Jana Rausch, Kim Goldman, Sergio Camacho, Arif Kabir, professor and great lawyer Peter Barton Hutt, Marty Glick, and all my teachers—Mrs. Kiekle, Ms. Fleishman, Zanka, Opal Stevens, Ms. Boraz, Mrs. Reese, Professor Charles Cameron, and Richard Pious; Vanessa, my son's gifted teacher; Gabby, Minal, Nicole, Gupika, and Jason; Terrence Mumford aka Mr. T; and the one who put it all together, neuropsychologist Dr. Stephanie Meyer. My office peeps who helped along the way, present and former. To Desirée Castro, who came in at a critical point to help me finish this book. Max Sinsheimer, my agent, without whom this book would not be, and the editing staff at North Atlantic, Keith Donnell, Janelle Ludowise, and Brent Winter, without whom you would not be reading this. And of course, my kids, who are very, very sweet to me, encourage me, and are perfect playmates for me.

NOTES

1. When the Birds Chirp

1 For those unfamiliar with the topography of Los Angeles, this might be confusing. The homes on the edges of the canyon are deep within the mountains, sitting high above the flats of Beverly Hills.

2. What about Addicts?

1 www.cdc.gov/genomics/disease/epigenetics.htm

2 Ewen Callaway, "Fearful Memories Passed Down to Mouse Descendants," *Scientific American,* December 1, 2013, www.scientificamerican.com/article /fearful-memories-passed-down/.

3 Dennis Waweru, "Study Finds Video Games To Cause Heart Problems In Children," Gadgets Africa, September 20, 2019, https://gadgets-africa.com /2019/09/20/study-finds-video-games-to-cause-heart-problems-in-children/.

4 Anna Lembke, *Dopamine Nation* (New York: Penguin Random House, 2021), 16.

5 Alex Lockie, "Top Nixon Adviser Reveals the Racist Reason He Started the 'War on Drugs' Decades Ago," *Insider,* July 31, 2019, https://www .businessinsider.com/nixon-adviser-ehrlichman-anti-left-anti-black-war-on -drugs-2019-7; Dan Baum, "Legalize It All," *Harper's Magazine,* April 2016, https://archive.harpers.org/2016/04/pdf/HarpersMagazine-2016-04 -0085915.pdf.

6 https://journalofethics.ama-assn.org/article/how-structural-violence -prohibition-and-stigma-have-paralyzed-north-american-responses-opioid /2020-08

7 David Herzberg, *White Market Drugs* (Chicago: University of Chicago Press, 2020), 7, 13.

8 Herzberg, *White Market,* 55.

9 Jack Herer, *The Emperor Wears No Clothes: Hemp and the Marijuana Conspiracy*, 14th ed. (Las Vegas: Herer Media and Publishing, 1998).

10 James A. Inciardi, *The Drug Legalization Debate* (Thousand Oaks, CA: Sage Publications, 1996), 63.

11 Lance Dodes, *The Heart of Addiction* (New York: HarperCollins, 2002), 69.

12 Dodes, *Heart,* 73.

13 Dodes, *Heart,* 70.

14 Dodes, *Heart,* 71.

15 Nils Bejerot, *Addiction and Society* (Springfield, IL: Thomas, 1970), 202.

16 Andrew Weil and Winifred Rosen, *Chocolate to Morphine: Understanding Mind-Active Drugs* (Boston: Houghton Mifflin, 1983), 168.

17 *Reefer Madness,* directed by Louis J. Gasnier (1936; Dover, DE: Motion Picture Ventures), https://archive.org/details/reefer_madness1938.

18 Johann Hari, *Chasing the Scream* (New York: Bloomsbury, 2015), 14.

19 "Discussion, Playboy Panel: The Drug Revolution," *Playboy,* February 1970, 53–74, 200–201.

20 Hari, *Chasing,* 373.

21 *What to Know about Drug Addiction* (Washington, DC: Public Health Service, 1951).

22 Carl Hart, *High Price* (New York: HarperCollins, 2014).

3. It's My Party

1 Facts about Guta's life in this chapter are taken from: Jane Ulman, "Survivor: Guta Peck," *Jewish Journal,* March 18, 2015, https://jewishjournal.com/culture/lifestyle/164927/.

2 Daniel Kazez, "A Jewish History of Lodz, Poland," Łódź KehilaLinks, March 26, 1999, https://kehilalinks.jewishgen.org/lodz/history.htm.

3 Facts about the German occupation of Łódź in this chapter are taken from: Alan Adelson and Robert Lapides, eds., *Łódź Ghetto: Inside a Community under Siege* (New York: Viking Penguin, 1989).

4 Hannah Cleaver, "German Ruling Says Dresden Was a Holocaust," *Telegraph,* April 12, 2005, www.telegraph.co.uk/news/worldnews/europe/germany/1487678/German-ruling-says-Dresden-was-a-holocaust.html.

5 Ulman, "Survivor."

6 www.ptsd.va.gov/professional/treat/essentials/history_ptsd.asp

7 www.ptsd.va.gov/index.asp; www.npr.org/sections/health-shots/2017/12/16/569961321/reverberations-of-war-complicate-vietnam-veterans-end-of-life-care

8 Krista Tippett, "Rachel Yehuda: How Trauma and Resilience Cross Generations," July 30, 2015, in *On Being with Krista Tippett,* podcast, 52:10, https://onbeing.org/programs/rachel-yehuda-how-trauma-and-resilience-cross-generations-nov2017/

9 Helen Thomson, "Study of Holocaust Survivors Finds Trauma Passed on to Children's Genes," *The Guardian,* August 21, 2015, www.theguardian.com /science/2015/aug/21/study-of-holocaust-survivors-finds-trauma-passed -on-to-childrens-genes.

10 Rachel Yehuda et al., "Influences of Maternal and Paternal PTSD on Epigenetic Regulation of the Glucocorticoid Receptor Gene in Holocaust Survivor Offspring," *American Journal of Psychiatry* 171, no. 8 (2014): 872–80, www.ncbi.nlm.nih.gov/pubmed/24832930.

11 Maia Szalavitz, *Unbroken Brain* (New York: Picador, 2016), 66–67.

12 Bessel van der Kolk, *The Body Keeps the Score* (New York: Penguin Books, 2015), 39–43.

13 Szalavitz, *Unbroken,* 66–67.

14 Gabor Maté, *In the Realm of Hungry Ghosts: Close Encounters with Addiction* (Toronto, ON: Knopf Canada, 2008), 198–200.

15 Maté, *Hungry Ghosts,* 198–200.

16 J. D. Higley and M. Linnoila, "Low Central Nervous System Serotonergic Activity Is Traitlike and Correlates with Impulsive Behavior," *Annals of the New York Academy of Science* 836 (December 29, 1997): 39; see also A. S. Clarke et al., "Rearing Experience and Biogenic Amine Activity in Infant Rhesus Monkeys," *Biological Psychiatry* 40, no. 5 (September 1, 1996): 338–52; see also J. D. Higley et al., "Nonhuman Primate Model of Alcohol Abuse: Effects of Early Experience, Personality, and Stress on Alcohol Consumption," *Proceedings of the National Academy of Sciences* 88 (August 1991): 7261–65.

17 The company is Numinus Health, stock symbol TRUFF. Julie Creswell, "There Is a Lot of Fungus Among Us," *New York Times,* April 24, 2021, www .nytimes.com/2021/04/24/business/there-is-a-lot-of-fungus-among-us.html. The article documents the rise of psychedelics as a near panacea to a myriad of illnesses, from cluster headaches to anxiety. Psychedelics are even proving effective in treating something as nebulous, yet prevalent—and highly descriptive of the experience of any moderately conscious person—as "existential angst," in the words of J. R. Rahn (founder of MindMed, a company devoted to studies of psychedelic compounds, www.mindmed.co). J. R. Rahn, "LSD, ADHD, and Decriminalization," interview by Mark Alexander, *Psychedelics Today,* March 2, 2021, https://psychedelicstoday.com/2021/03/02 /pt233-jr-rahn-of-minmed-lsd-adhd-and-decriminalization/.

18 While researching this chapter, I learned that Dr. Goodman was arrested in 2018 for possessing child pornography. It seems that he had good reason for being invested in researching behavioral addictions. This crime does not affect

Dr. Maté's story or the value of his book *Hungry Ghosts,* which was first published in 2008. For more on Dr. Goodman's arrest, see www.startribune.com /st-paul-psychiatrist-charged-with-possessing-child-pornography/474866033/.

19 Maté, *Hungry Ghosts,* 240–42.

20 Mark Wolynn, *It Didn't Start with You: How Inherited Family Trauma Shapes Who We Are and How to End the Cycle* (New York: Penguin Books, 2017), 25.

4. Jumping Mouse

1 https://qz.com/1163140/us-nuclear-tests-killed-american-civilians-on-a -scale-comparable-to-hiroshima-and-nagasaki/

2 http://childhoodtraumarecovery.com/2013/10/13/arrested-psychological -development-and-age-regression/

3 My dad told this story during a 2017 interview with Zach Leary: https:// itsallhappeningshow.libsyn.com/episode-109-with-bruce-margolin.

4 http://law.jrank.org/pages/1105/Exclusionary-Rule-Origins-development -rule.html

5 http://nymag.com/daily/intelligencer/2013/11/strange-saga-of-jfk-and-dr -feelgood.html

6 Don Lattin, *Harvard Psychedelic Club* (New York: HarperCollins, 2011), 135.

7 Lattin, *Harvard,* 37.

8 Lattin, *Harvard,* 53–54.

9 Lattin, *Harvard.*

10 Martin A. Lee, *Smoke Signals* (New York: Scribner, 2012), 80.

11 Lee, *Smoke,* 114.

12 Nicole Charky, "The Real Reason LSD and Opium Are Illegal," *ATTN:,* August 18, 2015, www.attn.com/stories/2831/why-are-psychedelics-drugs-illegal.

13 Zach Leary, "Episode 109 with Bruce Margolin," December 16, 2017, in *It's All Happening,* podcast, 1:10:32, https://itsallhappeningshow.libsyn.com /episode-109-with-bruce-margolin.

14 Bill Minutaglio and Steven L. Davis, *The Most Dangerous Man in America: Timothy Leary, Richard Nixon and the Hunt for the Fugitive King of LSD* (New York: Twelve, 2018), 338–39.

5. Latigo Canyon

1 Bill Minutaglio and Steven L. Davis, *The Most Dangerous Man in America: Timothy Leary, Richard Nixon and the Hunt for the Fugitive King of LSD* (New York: Twelve, 2018), 338–39.

2 Zach Leary, "Episode 109 with Bruce Margolin," December 16, 2017, in *It's All Happening,* podcast, 1:10:32, https://itsallhappeningshow.libsyn.com /episode-109-with-bruce-margolin.

3 Leary, *It's All Happening.*

6. A Brief Hope, Quickly Extinguished

1 Joan Didion, *The White Album* (New York: Simon and Schuster, 1979).

2 http://latimesblogs.latimes.com/thedailymirror/2009/08/ritual-killings -terrorize-la--1.html

3 Maria L. La Ganga and Erik Himmelsbach-Weinstein, "Charles Manson's Murderous Imprint on L.A. Endures as Other Killers Have Come and Gone," *Los Angeles Times,* July 28, 2019, www.latimes.com/california/story/2019 -07-27/charles-manson-family-murders-50-years-later.

4 Don Lattin, *The Harvard Psychedelic Club* (New York: HarperCollins, 2011), 141.

7. Paranoia and Policy

1 Larry Sloman, *Reefer Madness: The History of Marijuana in America* (New York: St. Martin's Griffin, 1998), 60–63.

2 Sloman, *Reefer Madness,* 61–62.

3 Laura Smith, "This Axe Murderer Helped Make Weed Illegal," July 21, 2017, https://timeline.com/this-axe-murderer-helped-make-weed-illegal -5696b480b16c; Jennifer McKaig, "Improving Mental Health Care with Data," May 14, 2019, https://towardsdatascience.com/improving-mental -health-care-with-data-84489f69d8c9.

4 Ajay Chaudry et al., *Poverty in the United States: 50-Year Trends and Safety Net Impacts,* (March 2016), https://aspe.hhs.gov/sites/default/files/private /pdf/154286/50YearTrends.pdf.

5 *Encyclopaedia Britannica Online,* s.v. "Economic Opportunity Act," accessed December 20, 2021, www.britannica.com/topic/Economic-Opportunity-Act.

6 www.dea.gov/drug-information/csa

7 John Robert Greene, "Gerald Ford: Domestic Affairs," https://millercenter .org/president/ford/domestic-affairs.

8 "Carter Asks Congress to Decriminalize Marijuana Possession," *New York Times,* March 15, 1977, www.nytimes.com/1977/03/15/archives/carter -asks-congress-to-decriminalize-marijuana-possession-cocaine.html.

9 Claire D. Clarke, "Peter Bourne's Drug Policy and the Perils of a Public Health Ethic, 1976–1978," *American Journal of Public Health* 105, no. 2 (February 2015): 283–92, www.ncbi.nlm.nih.gov/pmc/articles/PMC4318314/.

10 www.pbs.org/wgbh/pages/frontline/shows/drugs/interviews/bourne.html

11 U.S. Department of Justice/Office of the Inspector General. *The CIA-Contra-Crack Cocaine Controversy: A Review of the Justice Department's Investigations and Prosecutions,* by Michael R. Bromwich (December, 1997), https://oig.justice.gov/sites/default/files/archive/special/9712/ch02p1.htm. See also Gary Webb, "Dark Alliance" series, *San Jose Mercury News*, August, 1996. Archived by *Narco News,* June 23, 2005, https://www.narconews.com/darkalliance/drugs/start.html.

12 Stanford Law School, "Three Strikes Basics," https://law.stanford.edu/three-strikes-project/three-strikes-basics/.

13 John Hockenberry, "Retro Report: The Making of 'Three Strikes' Laws," December 2, 2013, in *The Takeaway,* podcast, 5:34, www.wnycstudios.org/podcasts/takeaway/segments/retro-report-looks-back-legacy-three-strikes.

14 https://ballotpedia.org/California_Proposition_184,_Three_Strikes_Sentencing_Initiative_(1994)

15 Lisa Stolzenberg and Stewart J. D'Alessio, "'Three Strikes and You're Out': The Impact of California's New Mandatory Sentencing Law on Serious Crime Rates," *Crime and Delinquency* 43, no. 4 (1997): 457–69.

16 Brent Staples, "California Horror Stories and the 3-Strikes Law," *New York Times,* November 24, 2012, www.nytimes.com/2012/11/25/opinion/sunday/california-horror-stories-and-the-3-strikes-law.html.

17 Stanford Law School, "Three Strikes."

8. This Is Your Brain on Drugs

1 Allison Margolin, "On the Right to Get High" (third-year thesis, Harvard Law School, 2002), 36, https://dash.harvard.edu/handle/1/8889470.

2 Partnership for a Drug-Free America (PDFA), "This Is Your Brain on Drugs," 1987, www.youtube.com/watch?v=3FtNm9CgA6U.

3 The D.A.R.E. program created and implemented a middle school curriculum in 1984 and a high school curriculum in 1989 (see https://dare.org/history/).

4 www.usmagazine.com/celebrity-news/news/corey-haim-sad-lifelong-struggle-to-stay-sober-2010103/

5 www.washingtonpost.com/archive/lifestyle/1992/04/30/patti-davis-says-mother-popped-pills/abc9ac5a-7838-41a3-a587-9f6dc32030c6/?utm_term=.e6b2e21f5c49

6 https://apnews.com/article/08278f9726f2e7c5be633d24392a255e

7 https://deserthopetreatment.com/addiction-guide/administration-methods/

9. No One Needs to Die at the Viper Room

1 Judith Michaelson, "Chronicle of a Death Unfolds: Media: Tabloid and Straight News Merged in the Reporting of River Phoenix's Collapse and the Questions Surrounding Its Circumstances," *Los Angeles Times,* November 4, 1993, https://www.latimes.com/archives/la-xpm-1993-11-04-ca-53161-story.html.

2 Rich Connell and Carla Hall, "Drug Overdose Killed Phoenix, Coroner Says," *Los Angeles Times,* November 13, 1993, https://www.latimes.com/archives/la-xpm-1993-11-13-mn-56484-story.html.

3 John Glatt, *Lost in Hollywood: The Fast Times and Short Life of River Phoenix* (New York: St. Martin's Press, 1996), 266.

4 Connell and Hall, "Drug Overdose."

5 Connell and Hall, "Drug Overdose."

6 Tad Friend, "River, with Love and Anger," *Esquire,* March 1994, archived at www.aleka.org/phoenix/zines/phoenix7.html.

7 Friend, "River."

8 Friend, "River."

9 Friend, "River."

10 Friend, "River."

11 Gayle Guthman, "The Phoenix Children, River and Rain, Are Natural Musicians," *St. Petersburg Times,* May 19, 1979.

12 Guthman, "Phoenix Children."

13 Gavin Edwards, *Last Night at The Viper Room: River Phoenix and the Hollywood He Left Behind* (New York: Dey Street Books, 2014), 14.

14 Glatt, *Lost,* 16.

15 Glatt, *Lost,* 17.

16 Glatt, *Lost,* 18–19.

17 Glatt, *Lost,* 19.

18 Glatt, *Lost,* 18–19.

19 In one of Berg's epistles from on high, written the same year the Bottoms joined the cult, he "described himself as a 'toilet' to catch the 'damned hippies' and other waste products of society. We flush them, channel them, filter them, cleanse them, distill them and cause them to be recycled so that they actually vanish into thin air, they evaporate." Glatt, *Lost,* 16.

20 Edwards, *Last Night,* 19.

21 Michael Angeli, "Young Man River," *Movieline,* September 1991, archived at http://aleka.org/phoenix/zines/phoeni50.html.

22 Angeli, "Young Man."

23 Grace Catalano, *River Phoenix: Hero & Heartthrob* (London: Starfire Publishing, 1988).

24 Edwards, *Last Night,* 21.

25 Edwards, *Last Night,* 21.

26 Joe Dolce, "River's Edge," *Details,* November 1991, archived at www.aleka.org/phoenix/zines/scans/details_91_nov_d.jpg.

27 Edwards, *Last Night,* 23.

28 Edwards, *Last Night,* 16.

29 V. J. Felitti et al., "Relationship of Childhood Abuse and Household Dysfunction to Many of the Leading Causes of Death in Adults: The Adverse Childhood Experiences (ACE) Study," *American Journal of Preventive Medicine* 14, no. 4 (May 1998): 245–58, www.ncbi.nlm.nih.gov/pubmed/9635069.

30 Edwards, *Last Night,* 23–24.

31 Glatt, *Lost,* 263–64.

32 Edwards, *Last Night,* 59.

33 Edwards, *Last Night,* 57.

34 Glatt, *Lost,* 58.

35 Glatt, *Lost,* 59.

36 Glatt, *Lost,* 65.

37 Edwards, *Last Night,* 115.

38 Edwards, *Last Night,* 105–6.

39 Glatt, *Lost,* 108.

40 Friend, "River."

41 Friend, "River."

42 Edwards, *Last Night,* 54.

43 Edwards, *Last Night,* 135.

44 Friend, "River."

45 Barry C. Lawrence, *In Search of River Phoenix: The Truth behind the Myth* (Ware, UK: Wordsworth Publishing, 2004).

46 Friend, "River."

47 Joseph B. Treaster, "With Supply and Purity Up, Heroin Use Expands," *New York Times,* August 1, 1993, www.nytimes.com/1993/08/01/nyregion/with-supply-and-purity-up-heroin-use-expands.html.

48 Edwards, *Last Night,* 123.

49 Edwards, *Last Night,* 116.

50 Glatt, *Lost,* 205.

51 Edwards, *Last Night,* 149.

52 Edwards, *Last Night,* 157–60.

53 Edwards, *Last Night,* 164.

54 Edwards, *Last Night,* 168.

55 Friend, "River."

56 Roger Ebert, "The Thing Called Love" (review), *Chicago Sun-Times,* January 21, 1994, www.rogerebert.com/reviews/the-thing-called-love-1994.

57 Edwards, *Last Night,* 198.

58 Chris Snyder, *Hunting with Barracudas: My Life in Hollywood with the Legendary Iris Burton* (New York: Skyhorse Publishing, 2009).

59 Edwards, *Last Night,* 204.

60 Salley Rayl, "A Drug Expert Discusses the Hollywood Fad That Makes Some Stars High and Others Dead," *People,* March 29, 1982, https://people.com /archive/a-drug-expert-discusses-the-hollywood-fad-that-makes-some -stars-high-and-others-dead-vol-17-no-12/.

61 Rayl, "Drug Expert."

62 M. Gossop et al., "Cocaine: Patterns of Use, Route of Administration, and Severity of Dependence," *British Journal of Psychiatry* 164, no. 5 (May 1994): 660–64, www.ncbi.nlm.nih.gov/pubmed/7921717.

63 Bailey Rahn, "Ingest or Inhale? 5 Differences between Cannabis Edibles and Flowers," *Leafly,* July 17, 2014, www.leafly.com/news/cannabis-101 /differences-between-marijuana-edibles-and-flower.

64 Lorig Kachadourian et al., "Alcohol Expectancies, Alcohol Use, and Hostility as Longitudinal Predictors of Alcohol-Related Aggression," *Psychology of Addictive Behaviors* 26, no. 3 (September 2012): 414–22, www.ncbi.nlm.nih .gov/pmc/articles/PMC4030542/.

65 Maia Szalavitz, "How What You Believe Affects What You're Like When You're High," *Vice,* August 4, 2015, www.vice.com/en_us/article/xd7g8a /how-what-you-believe-affects-your-high.

66 See www.narcan.com, which describes the drug Narcan, currently available.

67 Lawrence, *In Search.*

68 Every US state has some form of a "Good Samaritan law," meant to protect citizens from potential lawsuits after helping someone in an emergency situation, including an overdose. You can find California's Good Samaritan law in California Health and Safety Code 1799.102, https://law.onecle.com /california/health/1799.102.html.

69 https://undark.org/2021/04/29/forgotten-history-supervised-injection/

70 https://journalofethics.ama-assn.org/article/how-structural-violence -prohibition-and-stigma-have-paralyzed-north-american-responses-opioid /2020-08

71 Friend, "River."

10. Flying through the Weeds of the Aughts

1 www.foundsf.org/index.php?title=Chinatown%27s_Opium_Dens

2 www.thesun.co.uk/news/3902373/inside-americas-19th-century-opium-dens-which-spread-across-the-country-creating-thousands-of-dope-addicts/

3 Henrik Ibsen, *A Doll's House* (New York: Global Classics, 1879), 98.

4 www.cognitiveliberty.org/on-cognitive-liberty-boire/

5 Richard Glen Boire, "Brief in Defense of Cognitive Liberty," application for leave to file amicus curiae brief in *United States of America v. Dr. Charles Thomas Sell, D.D.S.,* appeal from the United States District court for the Eastern District of Missouri, Crim. No. 01-1862, p. 6.

6 Mark Tyndall and Zoë Dodd, "How Structural Violence, Prohibition, and Stigma Have Paralyzed North American Responses to Opioid Overdose," *AMA Journal of Ethics* 22, no. 8 (2020): E723–28, https://journalofethics.ama-assn.org/article/how-structural-violence-prohibition-and-stigma-have-paralyzed-north-american-responses-opioid/2020-08.

7 Donna Harati, "Inside Insite: How a Localized Social Movement Led the Way for North America's First Legal Supervised Injection Site" (Harvard Law School, Irving Oberman Memorial Student Writing Prize: Law and Social Change, June 2015), https://dash.harvard.edu/bitstream/handle/1/16386592/InSite%20Paper.pdf?sequence=1&isAllowed=y.

8 California's mandatory minimums for drug offenses did not end until October 5, 2021, when Governor Gavin Newsom signed Senate Bill 73. Until then, California state law "bar[red] probation or suspended sentences for first-time offenders convicted of certain drug offenses including selling or possessing for sale more than a half-ounce (14 grams) of heroin or the hallucinogenic drug commonly known as PCP or angel dust. It also bar[red] probation for repeat offenders convicted of crimes including possessing or agreeing to sell or transport opiates or cannabis or forging prescriptions." See https://apnews.com/article/gavin-newsom-scott-wiener-san-francisco-california-legislature-4d07934b97f4f212f13c48f725374cd5.

9 https://leginfo.legislature.ca.gov/faces/codes_displaySection.xhtml?lawCode=PEN&sectionNum=1210.1

10 Mikki and Chris are the authors of *Shattered Lives,* a mandatory minimum drug law reform book/manifesto published in 1998; see www.amazon.com/Shattered-Lives-Portraits-Americas-Drug/dp/0963975439. As described on Amazon, "This is the first book to use photos and personal case stories to show the human cost of the US Drug War. . . . This approach highlights the dignity,

warmth and humanity of its subjects, contrasted to the stark statistics and harsh penalties of the Drug War. It is perfect to open up the eyes of even the hardest-hearted drug warrior, showing how the children and families of the prisoners are also hurt, how circumstantial hearsay evidence is used to construct cases against low-level or even innocent defendants, how family homes and property are seized with no evidence whatsoever, innocent people killed by law enforcement, and policies used for cultural and racial suppression. One of the most powerful books ever written on the unintended consequences of the drug war, this is a book that can change people's minds, and it also offers hope as it discusses policy alternatives to help drug addicts, control drug use and promote tolerance."

11 https://drugpolicy.org/staff/ethan-nadelmann-founder

12 www.lamayor.org/mayor-garcetti-appoints-cat-packer-first-executive -director-la-department-cannabis-regulation

13 https://maps.org/research/mdma/ptsd/phase3/timeline/6994-mdma -phase-3-trials-fda-and-dea-to-host-breakthrough-therapy-meetings

14 Hutt argued the case of *Powell v. Texas.*

15 Allison Margolin, "On the Right to Get High" (third-year thesis, Harvard Law School, 2002), 36, https://dash.harvard.edu/bitstream/handle/1/8889470 /Margolin.html?sequence=2&isAllowed=y.

16 Margolin, "On the Right."

17 United States v. Landa, 281 F. Supp. 2d 1139 (N.D. Cal. 2003).

18 United States v. Landa, 223 Fed. Appx. 604 (9th Cir. 2007), Court Opinion.

11. Juliet

1 Shelby Hartman, "Parents Who Use Medicinal Marijuana Face Scrutiny by Child Protective Services," *LA Weekly,* January 13, 2017, www.laweekly .com/news/parents-who-use-medicinal-marijuana-face-scrutiny-by-child -protective-services-7815971.

2 https://www.ocregister.com/2016/12/15/marijuana-is-legal-in-california -but-prop-64-wont-help-you-in-a-custody-battle/

3 Hartman, "Parents."

4 See also this study from the National Institutes of Health (www.ncbi.nlm.nih .gov/books/NBK64904/) and this study on alcohol abuse as a risk factor for child safety (https://pubs.niaaa.nih.gov/publications/arh25-1/52-57.htm).

5 www.pewresearch.org/fact-tank/2018/10/08/americans-support-marijuana -legalization/ft_18-01-05_marijuana_line_update/

6 www.washingtonpost.com/local/even-where-its-legal-for-parents-to
-smoke-pot-what-about-the-kids/2015/06/06/dd4549c8-f977-11e4-9030
-b4732caefe81_story.html

7 Drew Humphries, *Crack Mothers: Pregnancy, Drugs, and the Media* (Columbus: Ohio State University Press, 1999), 29–30.

8 www.washingtonpost.com/archive/politics/1986/05/22/mothers-drug
-abuse-spurs-infant-addiction-panel-told/527472fb-30ef-4aab-ba64
-39ed8a5ee543/?noredirect=on&utm_term=.583d5812a096

9 Humphries, *Crack,* 19–20.

10 Douglas J. Besharov, "Crack Babies: The Worst Threat Is the Mom Herself," *Washington Post,* August 6, 1989, www.washingtonpost.com/archive
/opinions/1989/08/06/crack-babies-the-worst-threat-is-mom-herself
/d984f0b2-7598-4dc1-9846-3418df3a5895/?utm_term=.793d7a4f5eb8.

11 Humphries, *Crack,* 62. See also: Ira Chasnoff, "Missing Pieces of the Puzzle," *Neurotoxicology and Teratology* 15 (1993): 287–88.

12 www.nytimes.com/2014/06/29/magazine/carl-hart-crack-wasnt-the-real
-problem.html

13 Leslie Jamison, *The Recovering* (New York: Little, Brown and Company, 2018), 30–32.

14 Martin A. Lee, *Smoke Signals* (New York: Scribner, 2012), 146–48.

15 Lee, *Smoke,* 146–48.

12. Sharks! Sharks! Sharks!

1 Any information in this chapter pertaining to former clients comes from records obtained from the district attorney's office, such as police reports, records of preliminary hearings, and records of grand jury proceedings. Please note that the material in this chapter includes some added dramatization for creative flair. However, privileged attorney-client conversations were not used in the writing of this book.

2 Jesse McKinley, "Marijuana Hotbed Retreats on Medicinal Use," *New York Times,* June 9, 2008, www.nytimes.com/2008/06/09/us/09pot.html

3 Eric Baily, "State Issues Guide to Legal Pot Use," *Los Angeles Times,* August 26, 2008, www.latimes.com/archives/la-xpm-2008-aug-26-me-medpot26
-story.html

4 Nick Schou, "Joe Byron and Joe Grumbine Are Buds," June 9, 2011, *OC Weekly,* www.ocweekly.com/joe-byron-and-joe-grumbine-are-buds
-6417635/.

5 Court Reporter's Transcript, DA Sally Thomas on record addressing the court. *The People of the State of California vs. Joseph Byron and Joe Grumbine* (2011), 7–15.

6 http://leginfo.legislature.ca.gov/faces/codes_displaySection.xhtml?section Num=170.1.&lawCode=CCP

7 www.presstelegram.com/2012/04/13/motion-granted-for-new-trial-in-long -beach-medical-marijuana-case/

13. Cannabis 2.0, "C" Is for Corruption

1 www.politico.com/news/2020/12/27/marijuana-legalization-corruption -450529

2 www.justice.gov/usao-cdca/pr/former-mayor-cudahy-sentenced-federal -prison-taking-bribes-medical-marijuana. See also: www.law360.com/cannabis /articles/1377045/corruption-trial-puts-mass-pot-regime-under-microscope; www.latimes.com/california/story/2020-07-01/la-cannabis-marijuana -licensing-rules; https://wjla.com/news/nation-world/cannabis-corruption -how-state-and-local-leaders-are-profiting-off-the-burgeoning-industry; www.lohud.com/story/news/investigations/2019/04/05/recreational -marijuana-anti-pot-lobbying-pharma/3362646002/; www.leafly.com/news /politics/indicted-ukrainians-nevada-cannabis-licenses.

3 William D'Urso, "Dispensary Applicants in Solvang Have One Building to Choose From," *Santa Maria Sun,* October 14, 2019, www.santamariasun .com/news/18938/dispensary-applicants-in-solvang-have-one-building -to-choose-from/.

4 Los Angeles Municipal Code §104.06.1(b).

5 https://abc7.com/marijuana-dispensary-la-county-legal-pot-dispensaries -weedmaps-near-me/5603143/

6 www.fool.com/investing/2020/02/04/taxes-are-growing-problem-for-the -cannabis-industr.aspx

7 https://ehp.niehs.nih.gov/doi/full/10.1289/EHP5265

8 https://weho.granicus.com/MetaViewer.php?view_id=22&clip_id=3523 &meta_id=188906

9 https://beverlypress.com/2020/03/changes-for-cannabis-in-west-hollywood/

10 City of West Hollywood ordinance no. 17-1016.

11 www.politico.com/news/2021/06/27/republicans-weed-496390; www .law360.com/cannabis/articles/1429725/warren-booker-urge-ag-garland -to-decriminalize-cannabis

12 www.sciencedirect.com/science/article/abs/pii/S016604621830293X#!

13 www.americanprogress.org/issues/criminal-justice/reports/2018/06/27
/452819/ending-war-drugs-numbers/

14 www.dailynews.com/2021/10/05/la-county-sheriffs-department-gets-5
-million-to-shut-down-illegal-grow-operations-dispensaries/

15 J. R. Lawrence, personal conversation, August 31, 2021.

16 United States v. Darby, 312 U.S. 100 (1940).

17 http://nofba.org/wp-content/uploads/Rohrabacher-Farr-Amendment.pdf

18 https://cdn.ca9.uscourts.gov/datastore/opinions/2016/08/16/15-10117.pdf

19 https://cdn.ca9.uscourts.gov/datastore/opinions/2017/06/16/14-50585.pdf

20 www.latimes.com/local/great-reads/la-me-c1-pot-prosecutor-story.html

21 www.latimes.com/local/crime/la-me-marijuana-sentence-20141221-story.html

22 https://www.pewresearch.org/fact-tank/2021/01/22/trump-used
-his-clemency-power-sparingly-despite-a-raft-of-late-pardons-and
-commutations/

23 www.margolinlawrence.com/justice-delayed-but-not-defeated-for-former
-m-l-federal-client-noah-kleinman/

24 https://aleph-institute.org/wp/

25 www.pbs.org/newshour/politics/presidents-pardon-power-works

26 www.nacdl.org/getattachment/4a1f16cd-ec82-44f1-a093-798ee1cd7ba3
/collateral-damage-america-s-failure-to-forgive-or-forget-in-the-war
-on-crime-a-roadmap-to-restore-rights-and-status-after-arrest-or
-conviction.pdf

27 https://theappeal.org/the-lab/research/how-joe-biden-can-fix-the-broken
-clemency-process/

14. A New Target: Doctors

1 Any information in this chapter pertaining to former clients comes from records obtained from the district attorney's office, such as police reports, records of preliminary hearings, and records of grand jury proceedings. Please note that the material in this chapter includes some added dramatization for creative flair. However, privileged attorney-client conversations were not used in the writing of this book. In addition, Michael Malenkov's current attorney, Zenia Gilg, states: "Because the Santa Clara County district attorney has repeatedly, but unsuccessfully, tried to make me a witness in Michael's case, I have made certain that none of the information described in this chapter is based on conversations I had with Michael while I was his

attorney, and therefore, I am in no way infringing on our attorney-client privilege. Indeed, my contributions to this chapter are based on my own interpretation of the injustices Michael has been subjected to for nearly a decade."

2 Michael had ordered a pair of "spy" sunglasses online as a joke. The SWAT officers found the box.

3 Actually, the "high" electric bill was about average for a house that size, about seven thousand square feet.

4 Mark Evans, "Force Behind Proposition 215 Says His Push Began as 'Legacy of Love'," *Los Angeles Times,* December 1, 1996, https://www.latimes.com/archives/la-xpm-1996-12-01-mn-4581-story.html.

5 Evans, "Force."

6 Patrick McCartney, "California and U.S. Officials Conspired to Block Prop 215," *O'Shaughnessy's,* Autumn 2004, www.beyondthc.com/wp-content/uploads/2015/09/McCartney-2004.pdf.

7 Martin A. Lee, *Smoke Signals: A Social History of Marijuana—Medical, Recreational, and Scientific* (New York: Scribner, 2012), 124.

8 "Tod H. Mikuriya, 73; Psychiatrist Who Championed Legal Medical Marijuana," *Los Angeles Times,* September 16, 2014, www.latimes.com/local/la-me-potdocs6-story.html.

9 Margalit Fox, "Tod H. Mikuriya, 73, Dies; Backed Medical Marijuana," *New York Times,* May 29, 2007, www.nytimes.com/2007/05/29/health/29mikuriya.html.

10 From the text of the Compassionate Use Act of 1996: "Notwithstanding any other provision of law, no physician in this state shall be punished, or denied any right or privilege, for having recommended marijuana to a patient for medical purposes." See https://leginfo.legislature.ca.gov/faces/codes_displaySection.xhtml?sectionNum=11362.5.&lawCode=HSC.

11 In fact, that same year voters in Arizona voted 65 percent in favor of Proposition 200, which allows doctors to prescribe marijuana, as well as heroin, cocaine, and any other Schedule I drug.

12 Lee, *Smoke Signals,* 248.

13 Lee, *Smoke Signals,* 252.

14 Eric Bailey, "Taking a Leaf from 'Pot Docs,'" *Los Angeles Times,* November 6, 2004, https://www.latimes.com/archives/la-xpm-2004-nov-06-me-potdocs6-story.html. See also: Lee, *Smoke Signals,* 239–40.

15 Lee, *Smoke Signals,* 310–14.

16 Bailey, "Taking a Leaf."

17 Fox, "Tod H. Mikuriya."

18 "Tod H. Mikuriya," *Los Angeles Times.*

19 Lee, *Smoke Signals,* 312.

20 "Dr. Tod's List—Chronic Conditions Treated with Cannabis," American Alliance for Medical Cannabis, updated September 10, 2004, www .letfreedomgrow.com/cmu/DrTodHMikuriya_list.htm.

21 Her name has also been changed for her and my safety.

22 In fact, there is reason to believe that Russian money did fund many medical marijuana clinics and dispensaries throughout the 2000s. In October 2019, the *Sacramento Bee* reported that a few Russian businessmen who had invested in Sacramento's cannabis industry were indicted as part of a federal campaign finance probe. See: Dale Kasler and Theresa Clift, "Sacramento Cannabis Industry Drawn into Scandal: What We Know about Its Links to Russia," *Sacramento Bee,* October 22, 2019, www.sacbee.com/article236340178.html. Russian and Ukrainian investors have put money in cannabis businesses across the state of California. However, there is no evidence suggesting that Michael has ever been a leader of organized crime.

23 Jennifer Wadsworth, "Prosecutors Claim 420 Clinics Worked with Organized Crime," *San Jose Inside,* March 4, 2015, www.sanjoseinside.com/2015/03/04 /prosecutors-claim-420-clinics-worked-with-organized-crime/.

24 Wadsworth, "Prosecutors."

25 Wadsworth, "Prosecutors."

26 This is a direct excerpt from the interview Hughes conducted with Dr. Nordlinger.

27 For more on *People v. Superior Court of Los Angeles County,* see https:// caselaw.findlaw.com/ca-court-of-appeal/1640764.html.

28 "Operation of Medical Marijuana Clinics Is Practice of Medicine," My LicenseAttorney.com, July 9, 2014, https://mylicenseattorney.com/2014/07 /operation-of-medical-marijuana-clinics-is-practice-of-medicine/.

29 Wadsworth, "Prosecutors."

30 Paul A. Gomez, "Recent California Court Decision Provides Useful Guidance for Management Services Organizations (MSOs)," *National Law Review,* June 14, 2016, www.natlawreview.com/article/recent-california -court-decision-provides-useful-guidance-management-services.

31 Under California case law, a court may appoint a lawyer who has already appeared on a case if the client has become indigent.

Notes

32 Sam Quinones, *Dreamland: The True Tale of America's Opiate Epidemic* (New York: Bloomsbury Publishing, 2015), 124–27.

33 Gary Humphreys, "Direct-to-Consumer Advertising Under Fire," *Bulletin of the World Health Organization* 87, no. 8 (August 2009): 576–77, www.who .int/bulletin/volumes/87/8/09-040809.pdf.

34 In 1995, drug manufacturers spent $360 million on advertising. In 1998, that number swelled to $1.3 billion. Beth Macy, *Dopesick: Dealers, Doctors, and the Drug Company That Addicted America* (Boston: Little, Brown, 2018), 31.

35 Macy, *Dopesick,* 32.

36 "California Opioid Summary," National Institute on Drug Abuse, March 2019, www.drugabuse.gov/drugs-abuse/opioids/opioid-summaries-by -state/california-opioid-summary.

37 Ronnie Cohen, "Would Legalizing Medical Marijuana Help Curb the Opioid Epidemic?" Reuters, March 27, 2017, www.reuters.com/article/us-health -addiction-medical-marijuana-idUSKBN16Y2HV.

38 Cohen, "Would Legalizing."

39 *60 Minutes,* "The Debate on California's Pot Shops," hosted by Morley Safer, aired September 23, 2007, on CBS, www.cbsnews.com/news/the-debate -on-californias-pot-shops/.

40 Alfonso Serrano, "Inside Big Pharma's Fight to Block Recreational Marijuana," *The Guardian,* October 22, 2016, www.theguardian.com/sustainable -business/2016/oct/22/recreational-marijuana-legalization-big-business.

41 Ray Stern, "Arizona Drug Firm Insys Makes Synthetic Pot Compound, Spends Big to Defeat Legal Pot," *Phoenix New Times,* September 8, 2016, www.phoenixnewtimes.com/news/arizona-drug-firm-insys-makes -synthetic-pot-compound-spends-big-to-defeat-legal-pot-8628614.

42 "Arizona Proposition 205—Legalize Marijuana—Results: Rejected," *New York Times,* August 1, 2017, www.nytimes.com/elections/2016/results /arizona-ballot-measure-205-legalize-marijuana.

43 "Insys Announces Availability of SYNDROS, the First and Only FDA-Approved Liquid Dronabinol, by Prescription," *Global Newswire,* July 31, 2017, www.globenewswire.com/news-release/2017/07/31/1064808/0/en/Insys -Announces-Availability-of-SYNDROS-the-First-and-Only-FDA-Approved -Liquid-Dronabinol-by-Prescription.html. Also reported here: Stern, "Arizona Drug Firm."

44 "Insys Announces."

45 Javier Hasse, "Exclusive: One of the Largest Pharma Companies in the World Has Made a Big Move in Cannabis," *Forbes,* September 12, 2019,

www.forbes.com/sites/javierhasse/2019/09/12/big-pharma-teva-cannabis
/#5ce682e151f7.

46 Katie Jones, "The Big Pharma Takeover of Medical Cannabis," *Visual Capitalist,* August 12, 2019, www.visualcapitalist.com/the-big-pharma-takeover
-of-medical-cannabis/.

47 Jones, "Big Pharma." It may surprise some people to learn that the Department of Health and Human Services holds any medical patents at all, but the National Institutes of Health employs thousands of PhD-level scientists specifically to invent new technologies or make discoveries in health. After review, the NIH determines if it will apply for a patent. Even if the research or technology involves a controlled substance like cannabis, the NIH may file for patents and then advertise the patents as available for licensing to both private and public research entities. Alicia Wallace, "Patent No. 6,630,507: Why the U.S. Government Holds a Patent on Cannabis Plant Compounds," *Denver Post,* August 28, 2016, www.denverpost.com/2016
/08/28/what-is-marijuana-patent-6630507/.

48 Lee Fang, "The Real Reason Pot Is Still Illegal," *The Nation,* July 2, 2014,
https://www.thenation.com/article/archive/anti-pot-lobbys-big-bankroll/.

49 Barry Meier, "3 Executives Spared Prison in OxyContin Case," *New York Times,*
July 21, 2007, www.nytimes.com/2007/07/21/business/21pharma.html.

50 "Opioid Overdose Crisis," National Institute on Drug Abuse, last updated January 2019, www.drugabuse.gov/drugs-abuse/opioids/opioid-overdose
-crisis.

51 "Is Marijuana Addictive?" National Institute on Drug Abuse, July 2020,
www.drugabuse.gov/publications/research-reports/marijuana/marijuana
-addictive.

52 "Overdose Death Rates," National Institute on Drug Abuse, March 2020,
www.drugabuse.gov/related-topics/trends-statistics/overdose-death
-rates.

53 Jesse Hyde with reporting from Daphne Chen, "The Untold Story of How Utah Doctors and Big Pharma Helped Drive the National Opioid Epidemic,"
Deseret News, October 26, 2017, https://www.deseret.com/2017/10/26
/20635281/the-untold-story-of-how-utah-doctors-and-big-pharma-helped
-drive-the-national-opioid-epidemic.

54 "Death Certificate Project Described by MBC Enforcement Committee,"
excerpt from the meeting minutes of the Medical Board of California,
July 27, 2017, www.documentcloud.org/documents/4792519-Enforcement
-Committee-Minutes-Quotes-Fellmeth.html#document/p6/a450374.

55 Cheryl Clark, "Doctors Call California's Probe of Opioid Deaths a 'Witch Hunt,'" *Los Angeles Times,* January 28, 2019, www.latimes.com/science /sciencenow/la-sci-sn-opioid-prescription-crackdown-20190117-story.html.

56 April Dembosky, "California Doctors Alarmed as State Links Their Opioid Prescriptions to Deaths," *NPR,* January 23, 2019, www.npr.org/sections /health-shots/2019/01/23/687376371/california-doctors-alarmed-as-state -links-their-opioid-prescriptions-to-deaths.

57 Cheryl Clark, "'Death Certificate Project' Terrifies California Doctors," *Med-Page Today,* August 30, 2018, www.medpagetoday.com/painmanagement /painmanagement/74856.

58 Max Filby, "Chronic Pain Sufferer Switches to Marijuana as Opioid Pre-scriptions Get Harder to Come By," *Columbus Dispatch,* December 16, 2019, https://www.dispatch.com/story/lifestyle/health-fitness/2019/12/16 /chronic-pain-sufferer-switches-to/1982741007/.

59 Hawre Jalal et al., "Changing Dynamics of the Drug Overdose Epidemic in the United States from 1979 through 2016," *Science,* September 21, 2018, https://www.science.org/doi/epdf/10.1126/science.aau1184.

60 F. B. Ahmad et al., "Provisional Drug Overdose Death Counts," National Center for Health Statistics, 2021, www.cdc.gov/nchs/nvss/vsrr/drug -overdose-data.htm.

61 S. Spillane et al., "Trends in Alcohol-Induced Deaths in the United States, 2000–2016," *JAMA Network Open* 3, no. 2 (2020): e1921451, https:// jamanetwork.com/journals/jamanetworkopen/fullarticle/2761545.

62 Melissa Healy, "Suicides and Overdoses among Factors Fueling Drop in U.S. Life Expectancy," *Los Angeles Times,* November 26, 2019, www.latimes.com /science/story/2019-11-26/life-expectancy-decline-deaths-of-despair.

63 *Guide to the Laws Governing the Practice of Medicine by Physicians and Sur-geons,* 7th ed. (Sacramento: Medical Board of California, 2013), 25–26.

64 Dembosky, "California Doctors."

15. George, David, and George

1 Any information in this chapter pertaining to former clients comes from records obtained from the district attorney's office, such as police reports, records of preliminary hearings, and records of grand jury proceedings. Please note that the material in this chapter includes some added dramatization for creative flair. However, privileged attorney-client conversations were not used in the writing of this book.

2 See in general: David Herzberg, *White Market Drugs* (Chicago: University of Chicago Press, 2020).

3 Lee N. Robins, Darlene H. Davis, and David N. Nurco, "How Permanent Was Vietnam Drug Addiction?" *American Journal of Public Health* 64, suppl. 12 (1974): 38–43.

4 Jane Porter and Hershel Jick, "Addiction Rare in Patients Treated with Narcotics," *New England Journal of Medicine* 302 (1980): 123.

5 Sam Quinones, *Dreamland: The True Tale of America's Opiate Epidemic* (New York: Bloomsbury Publishing, 2015), 170–71.

6 Quinones, *Dreamland.*

7 NIDA, "How is Heroin Linked to Prescription Drug Misuse?," *National Institute on Drug Abuse*, July 16, 2021, www.drugabuse.gov/publications /research-reports/heroin/how-heroin-linked-to-prescription-drug-misuse.

8 https://definitions.uslegal.com/h/hobbs-motion/

9 Bryan Pietsch, "Behind 'Strange Fruit,' Billie Holiday's Anti-Lynching Anthem," *New York Times,* April 25, 2021, www.nytimes.com/2021/04/25 /arts/music/strange-fruit-united-states-v-billie-holiday.html.

10 Michael Meeropol, "Why the Anti-Lynching Song 'Strange Fruit' Remains Relevant Today," WAMC Northeast Public Radio, July 3, 2020, www.wamc .org/commentary-opinion/2020-07-03/michael-meeropol-why-the-anti -lynching-song-strange-fruit-remains-relevant-today.

11 Johann Hari, *Chasing the Scream* (New York: Bloomsbury, 2015), 37.

12 https://drugpolicy.org/blog/facts-not-fear-truth-about-fentanyl

13 https://drugpolicy.org/drug-facts/what-are-fentanyl-analogues

14 www.harmreductionohio.org/how-much-fentanyl-will-kill-you-2/

15 https://centerforhealthjournalism.org/content/profiteers-tragedy -making-money-americas-opioid-addicts

16 www.psychologytoday.com/us/blog/addiction-in-society/201307/rehab -cause-death; https://sanfrancisco.cbslocal.com/2018/11/08/unethical -drug-rehab-body-brokering-leads-to-tragic-death/

17 Anuradha Rao-Patel, Michael Adelberg, Samantha Arsenault, and Andrew Kessler, "Fraud's Newest Hot Spot: The Opioid Epidemic and the Corresponding Rise of Unethical Addiction Treatment Providers," *Health Affairs,* April 26, 2018, www.healthaffairs.org/do/10.1377/forefront.20180423 .449595/full/.

18 https://drugpolicy.org/blog/facts-not-fear-truth-about-fentanyl

19 Emily Bazelon and Jennifer Medina, "He's Remaking Criminal Justice in L.A. But How Far Is Too Far?" *New York Times Magazine,* November 17, 2021, www.nytimes.com/2021/11/17/magazine/george-gascon-los-angeles.html.

20 Lara Korte, "What Gavin Newsom Says He'll Do About 'Organized Retail Mobs,' Guns and Drugs," *Sacramento Bee,* December 17, 2021, www .sacbee.com/news/politics-government/capitol-alert/article256682992 .html#storylink=cpy.

INDEX

Society of Cannabis Clinicians, 181
Solgot, Suzanne, 103, 119
Soros, George, 130
speedball
    John Belushi, 102, 121
    River Phoenix, 102, 120
St. George. *See* Gascón, George
Stand by Me, 101–113, 118, 124
Stanton, Elizabeth Cady, 28
Steve. *See* Kern, Steve
stigmatization from criminalization, 124
"Strange Fruit", 200–201
stress, 52
    adverse childhood experiences
        (ACEs), 55–56, 63
    impact on dopamine, 54–55
Stutthof concentration camp, 46–47
substance use disorder, 27
Subsys, 191
suffragists, 28
Supreme Court
    Mapp v. Ohio, 65
    Miranda v. Arizona, 65
    United States v. Booker, 134
swearing-in ceremony, California Bar,
    7–9, 15
Syndros, 192
synthetic drugs, 204
Szalavitz, Maia, 53–54
Szalavitz, Miklos, 54

T

Tampa Times, 82
Tarlow, Barry, 63
Tate, Sharon, 75
Tate–LaBianca murders, 59, 60,
    75–77, 80
Teens for Christ, 105
temperance movement, 28–29
THC, 121
THC Doctor (420 MD) clinic, 177, 178,
    182–184. *See also* Malenkov, Michael
The Recovering (Jamison), 147
theses
    Harvard Law, 129, 131
    Columbia University, 11, 93–94

The Thing Called Love, 104, 119
Thomas, Sally, 158, 159
Thorazine, 83
Three Strikes Reform Act, 87
three-strikes law, 86–87
Time, 148
Timmins, Bob, 118
trauma
    addiction, 19
    adverse childhood experiences
        (ACEs), 55–56, 63
    cortisol, 52
    Holocaust survivors, 52–57
    intergenerational trauma, 52–57
    posttraumatic stress disorder
        (PTSD), 51–52
treatment, 130
    fraud and abuse in industry, 203–204
    unethical addiction treatment
        providers, 204
Trump, Donald, presidential pardons/
    commutation of Noah Kleinman
    sentence, 171–173
Twenty-First Amendment, 29
Tyndall, Mark, 129

U

Uebelhoer, Friedrich, 43–44
*Unbroken Brain: A Revolutionary New
    Way of Understanding Addiction*
    (Szalavitz), 33, 54
United States v. Booker, 133–134
United States v. McIntosh, 171
US Department of Agriculture (USDA),
    domestic hemp production, 24
US Department of Health and Human
    Services cannabis patents, 192
US Drug Enforcement Agency (DEA)
    destruction of Monticello
        poppies, 24
    raiding of marijuana dispensaries,
        152
US Federal Bureau of Narcotics (FBN),
    34–36, 81–83, 201–202
US Public Health Service, 39
US Sentencing Commission, 133

ABOUT THE AUTHOR

PHOTO CREDIT: HEIDI GIBBS

ALLISON MARGOLIN lives in Los Angeles, her hometown, with her husband, Jon, a famed cannabis grower and amazing person, and her two kids, Juliet and Jaxin. She also lives with a variety of nonhuman animals—she is the proud caretaker of dogs, cats, a hamster, a lizard, and a chameleon—and she highly values her time with them. She practices law throughout the state and enjoys reading about the legends of Mount Shasta (where she also has a home/office), looking for Sasquatch, driving down Pico Boulevard, studying UFOlogy, running her online digital magazine *Dark Matters* (https://darkmattersmag.com) devoted to all those subjects, and civil rights. Allison also loves to study and trade psychedelic stocks. As her perspective has slowly started to take root with more and more people in the Establishment, she has begun to collaborate with Democratic candidates for state and federal office. She is honored to be a graduate of Columbia University, where she earned a BA in political science and a certificate in creative writing. She graduated from Harvard Law School in 2002.

About North Atlantic Books

North Atlantic Books (NAB) is a 501(c)(3) nonprofit publisher committed to a bold exploration of the relationships between mind, body, spirit, culture, and nature. Founded in 1974, NAB aims to nurture a holistic view of the arts, sciences, humanities, and healing. To make a donation or to learn more about our books, authors, events, and newsletter, please visit www.northatlanticbooks.com.